Against Amnesia

Penn Studies in Contemporary American Fiction

Emory Elliott, Series Editor

A complete list of books in the series
is available from the publisher.

Against Amnesia

Contemporary Women Writers and the Crises of Historical Memory

Nancy J. Peterson

PENN

University of Pennsylvania Press

Philadelphia

Copyright © 2001 University of Pennsylvania Press
All rights reserved
Printed in the United States of America on acid-free paper

10 9 8 7 6 5 4 3 2 1

Published by
University of Pennsylvania Press
Philadelphia, Pennsylvania 19104-4011

Library of Congress Cataloging-in-Publication Data
Peterson, Nancy J.
    Against amnesia : contemporary women writers and the crises of historical
memory / Nancy J. Peterson.
        p. cm. — (Penn studies in contemporary American fiction)
    Includes bibliographical references (p.   ) and index.
    ISBN 0-8122-3594-0 (cloth: alk. paper)
    1. American literature — Minority authors — History and criticism.
2. Literature and history — United States — History — 20th century.   3. Women
and literature — United States — History — 20th century.   4. American
literature — Women authors — History and criticism.   5. American literature —
20th century — History and criticism.   6. Klepfisz, Irena, 1941–   — Criticism
and interpretation.   7. Erdrich, Louise — Criticism and interpretation.
8. Morrison, Toni — Criticism and interpretation.   9. Kogawa, Joy — Criticism
and interpretation.   10. Ethnic groups in literature.   11. Minorities in
literature.   12. Memory in literature.   I. Title.   II. Series.
PS153.M56 P48 2001
810.9′920693 — dc21   00-047944

PS153
.M56
.P48
2001

For Willem, Samuel, and Louise

Contents

Chapter One
History as Wound

"History is what hurts." Fredric Jameson makes this declaration in *The Political Unconscious: Narrative as a Socially Symbolic Act* to save history from deconstruction.[1] Acknowledging that under the tenets of poststructuralist theory history is only a text, a narrative construction of the past that has little or no relation to what really happened, Jameson rejects such thoroughgoing deconstruction by insisting that even though History is an absent cause, the effects of history can be registered and reckoned with. "History is what hurts" because the painful effects of past events continue to pressure the present moment. Jameson's attempt to negotiate the claims of historical reference with the implications of poststructuralist theory acts as a key moment in contemporary cultural criticism, a moment that resonates among numerous theorists, historians, literature scholars, and cultural critics who have followed in his wake to grapple with this same urgent issue. "History is what hurts" also speaks to the profound engagement with history that can be found in many works by contemporary women writers of color, writers who, for many reasons and often reaching far beyond Jameson's impetus to save history from deconstruction, have approached history as a wound. "History is what hurts" for these writers and their texts because the history they remember is painful, because minority histories have never come into full cultural consciousness, because mainstream American history is so relentlessly optimistic and teleological that it has become painfully difficult to articulate counterhistories that do not share these values, and because postmodern culture works against the sustained engagement with memory and commitment to complexity that is crucial for these histories.

A case in point is Maxine Hong Kingston's *China Men*, a companion volume to the stories of her female relatives presented in *The Woman Warrior*.[2] Published in 1980, *China Men* tells the stories of Kingston's male relatives who were significantly involved in the making of America yet were "driven out" physically and denied an American identity. One of Kingston's purposes in *China Men* is to claim America for Chinese Americans by telling the stories of the men who worked on Hawaiian sugar cane plantations, who built the transcontinental railroad, who contributed the work that built America as a nation in many other ways. Kingston at the same time calls attention to their erasure from history, a point made most vividly in her discussion of the transcontinental railroad. When it is completed, the white officials utter self-aggrandizing statements such as " 'only Americans could have done it,' " thus denying the labor of the Chinese workers that made the railroad possible (145). And as soon as the last spike is driven into the ground, the Chinese men are dismissed, so that the narrator's (Kingston's own) grandfather, Ah Goong, and his fellow workers do not appear in any of the photographs taken and distributed to mark this great accomplishment of nation-building. They are made invisible in the official records and in popular versions of American history. Facing history as a wound that has not recorded the accomplishments of her people, Kingston turns to literature to shape a narrative that can correct the historical record.

China Men also presents other wounds of history. While it is true that typical historical or official accounts erase the presence of Chinese men in America, it is also true that the historical record is marked by gaps because the men themselves have remained silent — not only to Anglo-American officials but to their own families. History as wound is so painful in certain respects that they will not or cannot tell the stories of their lives. The daughter-narrator of *China Men*, for instance, never knows for sure where and how her father entered the United States: he may have immigrated legally or illegally, through Angel Island or through Ellis Island, as a stowaway on a ship, or with proper or false documents. Neither does the daughter know her father's birth year or very much at all about his life in China. The disjunction between the father born and raised in China, who was trained as a scholar and teacher, and the American father who works at menial labor in a laundry is so great, so traumatic, that the father becomes unable to articulate the story of his own life.

Reckoning with this silence involves the narrator-daughter in two kinds of strategies. First, she unfolds the historical conditions that helped to create the silence. While most of *China Men* is devoted to telling the stories of the men, the narrative flow is oddly interrupted midway through with a chapter entitled "The Laws," which at first glance seems out of place. This chapter chronologically describes U.S. exclusion acts and other policies concerning Chinese Americans, acts that severed families and created disjunctive identities—a Chinese self and an American self that never find a point of coherence. "The Laws" is also unusual because of its narrative voice, a voice that is reportorial in perspective and tone, and which thus seems strikingly incongruent with the characteristic lyricism used throughout the rest of the text. Why would Kingston allow such a presumably clumsy narrative moment? She in fact addresses this question in a 1980 interview:

The mainstream culture doesn't know the history of Chinese-Americans, which has been written and written well. That ignorance makes a tension for me, and in the new book [*China Men*] I just couldn't take it anymore. So all of a sudden, right in the middle of the stories, plunk—there is an eight-page section of pure history. It starts with the Gold Rush and then goes right through the various exclusion acts, year by year. There are no characters in it. It really affects the shape of the book, and it might look quite clumsy. But on the other hand, maybe it will affect the shape of the novel in the future. Now maybe another Chinese-American writer won't have to write that history.[3]

Wanting to write the stories of her male relatives in *China Men*, Kingston is forced to narrate the history that will make their lives intelligible. Although Kingston expresses hope that the writers who come after her will not have to face similar instances of historical amnesia, she is not the only contemporary writer to face this situation. Rather, she is part of a group of contemporary women writers, especially women writers of color, who in attempting to narrate the lives, experiences, and events of their people have found themselves taking on the role of historian alongside that of writer.

One goal of this book is to call attention to this double burden— to write both literature and history—for women writers of color and to make visible its pervasiveness. Another goal is to analyze how the writers grapple with this burden, how they write history and literature at the same time, and how they negotiate the very different claims of these disciplines or genres. Kingston's *China Men* is exemplary in this respect since literature, or the strategies of fiction more broadly, becomes necessary for her to narrate the missing personal histories. To imagine the stories she has not been told, the narrator-daughter of *China Men* learns to read gestures and silences, and thus she begins to understand the seething anger and despair that her father embodies. She also comes to a postmodern realization that "clarity was a matter of preference and culture" (294) as she fashions the convoluted and ambiguous narratives through which the stories of her male relatives must be told. Literature, in the hands of writers like Kingston, becomes a crucial means of narrating these wounded and lost histories.

*   *   *

In America we have only the present tense.
—Adrienne Rich, "The Burning of Paper Instead of Children"
(1968)

Adrienne Rich's lament for the vacuous historical understandings circulating in contemporary American culture identifies yet another exigency that writers like Kingston must face. Rich's observation above refers to a cultural crisis concerning American history and American memory, a crisis we might call American amnesia. Such national, collective repression has also troubled Toni Morrison and is an important impulse behind the creation of Morrison's historical novels. "We live in a land where the past is always erased and America is the innocent future in which immigrants can come and start over, where the slate is clean," Morrison commented to interviewer Paul Gilroy. "The past is absent or it's romanticized. This culture doesn't encourage dwelling on, let alone coming to terms with, the truth about the past. That memory is much more in danger now than it was thirty years ago."[4]

To find evidence in support of Morrison's critical perspective we might look no further than the fierce contentions that rocked the National Air and Space Museum in 1994 when it was developing an exhibition featuring the Enola Gay and analyzing the atomic bombing of Hiroshima and Nagasaki. Designed originally to commemorate the courage of the crew that flew the bomber as well as to question the necessity for dropping the bomb, the exhibit was to include the fuselage of the Enola Gay, photographs of the crew, information about the danger of their mission, photographs of the destruction, and artifacts related to civilian casualties. Cultural conservatives and veterans groups, however, besieged the Smithsonian's Board of Regents and various government officials, criticizing the exhibit for portraying Americans as aggressors and racists and for downplaying the Japanese militarism that led to the war. In the face of this vehement public opposition, on January 30, 1995, the Smithsonian announced that the exhibit would be dramatically scaled back to include only the Enola Gay, information about its crew, and a commemorative plaque.[5]

This is only one example of the contentious "history wars" and cultural debates that have occupied the United States in recent decades.[6] Collective historical memory in America has always been more attracted to the mythic (the heroic stories of Paul Revere's ride and of George Washington and the cherry tree, for example) than to the realistic. But since the mid-1960s — through such vehicles as the civil rights and women's liberation movements, Vietnam, and Watergate — heroic narratives of America have been increasingly called into question. These events have created fissures in dominant national narratives, and these fissures have made possible the articulation of various counterhistories by those previously relegated to the margins of American culture. The establishment of Black History Month (February) and National Women's History Month (March) are only two instances of efforts to correct the historical record and to influence collective memory in America.[7]

There are, however, clear limits to what *official* histories and counterhistories can tell, and so to investigate the aporias of American history one must also turn to *unofficial* histories. This book does so by carefully examining the historicist dimensions of literature written by Louise Erdrich, Toni Morrison, Irena Klepfisz, and Joy Kogawa. Such texts attempt to intervene in official versions of American history and identity by bringing to consciousness counterhistories that trouble the conventional narrative. But it is also significant that literature is an unofficial, unauthorized site for writing history. As unofficial histories, literary texts can address issues and events that are marginalized or ignored by the rules of safe politics and clear evidence that underlie official historical accounts.

In identifying literature as a significant historical and cultural intervention, *Against Amnesia* takes its lead, and its title, from Adrienne Rich, who has observed in various remarkable essays and lectures over the years the significance of feminist literature and multicultural literature in transforming received ideas of America and American culture. In a 1983 essay titled "Resisting Amnesia: History and Personal Life," Rich urges feminists "to become *consciously* historical," to strive "for memory and connectedness against amnesia and nostalgia."[8] Such historicism is important to Rich, first of all, for identifying a pernicious problem in the feminist movement, what she calls "the whiteness of white feminism." It is also important, however, because of the problem of historical memory in contemporary America, where capitalism in the interest of net profit packages history as entertainment or spectacle and where the pressure to assimilate — to forget one's personal and ethnic history in order to become fully "American" — remains immense. Rich identifies literature by women of color that calls attention to what has been previously undocumented or forgotten as one vital means of resisting amnesia. She cites in particular the efforts of African American women writers to function as historians, "creating a new kind of historical fiction, writing novels which are quite consciously intended as resources in Black women's history."[9]

In her 1993 book on poetry as an important cultural and national resource, *What Is Found There: Notebooks on Poetry and Politics*, Rich widens her scope, citing "a multicultural literature of discontinuity, migration, and difference" as essential for providing a much needed corrective to official American history.[10] "The poetry of this continent has become increasingly a poetry written by the displaced," Rich writes, "by American Indians moving between the cities and the reservations, by African-Americans, Caribbean-Americans, by the children of the internment camps for Japanese-Americans in World War II, by the children of Angel Island and the Chinese Revolution, by Mexican-Americans and Chicanos with roots on both sides of the border, by political exiles from Latin America." This poetry performs significant cultural work by illuminating what Rich describes as the tragic paradox of America: "the extraordinary cruelty, greed, and willful obliteration on which the land of the free was founded." An American history that ignores such knowledge is little better than "a national fantasy," Rich suggests.[11]

Contemporary literature by marginalized women writers not only seeks to document what has been occluded in feel-good American history, it also turns to literature as a genre because "what really happened" is often so excruciatingly painful that to articulate these events as American history would be to invite utter disbelief. As I argue in the chapters that follow, historical tragedies like the loss of land and sovereignty for Native Americans, or the terrors of the Middle Passage and slavery for African Americans, are so difficult to comprehend or to imagine that they may stun readers into incredulity. When Morrison, for instance, alludes to "Sixty Million / and more" in her epigraph to *Beloved*, she opens up an incommensurable, gaping wound — and indeed the author has been asked on more than a few occasions to explain her accounting. To even begin to tell these kinds of stories, then, requires the capacity to exceed normative narrative expectations. And so, of necessity, wounded histories are written as literature, or fiction, and not as history, for only literature in our culture is allowed the narrative flexibility and the willing suspension of disbelief that are crucial to the telling of these histories.

This is precisely the point Shoshana Felman and Dori Laub reach in their influential collaborative effort, *Testimony: Crises of Witnessing in Literature, Psychoanalysis, and History*. Felman and Laub turn to literature and film, as well as to the testimony of survivors, to investigate the challenges the Holocaust poses to witnessing, language, and narrative. They argue in the foreword to their book that history as a discipline and a genre is inadequate for understanding the Holocaust, that to address "the consequent, ongoing, as yet unresolved *crisis of history*," one must turn to literature, for "literature becomes a witness, and perhaps the only witness, to the crisis within history which precisely cannot be articulated, witnessed in the given categories of history itself."[12] *Against Amnesia* follows Felman and Laub's important breakthrough by turning to literature to read tragic and traumatic moments of American history — Native American genocide and dispossession; slavery, migration, and displacement for African Americans; the Holocaust; and the internment of people of Japanese ancestry during World War II. Such wounds and traumas threaten to exceed clean lines of articulation and comprehension, and so, as Felman and Laub demonstrate in their reading of Holocaust texts, literature, not history, becomes the only adequate witness to these historical events.[13]

Postmodern Histories

At the very moment, however, when writers such as Kingston, Erdrich, Morrison, Klepfisz, and Kogawa are narrating the wounded
histories of their people, the writing of history has come to significant theoretical impasses. It seems epistemologically naïve today to
believe in the existence of a past to which a historian or novelist has
unmediated access. Radicalized in the poststructuralist movement,
language and linguistics have not only led to skepticism concerning
access to the past but also instigated a debate about whether historical narratives can be regarded as objective representations or are
(merely) subjective constructions of a researcher's and a culture's
ideologies. Extending the theories of Saussure, Lacan, and Althus-
ser, prominent French poststructuralists have asserted the textuality of history—that there is no direct access to the past, only
recourse to texts about the past. Roland Barthes's deconstruction
of the ontological status of historical "facts" is one such instance:
"It turns out that the only feature which distinguishes historical
discourse from other kinds is a paradox: the 'fact' can only exist
linguistically, as a term in a discourse, yet we behave as if it were a
simple reproduction of something on another plane of existence
altogether, some extra-structural 'reality.' "[14]

Similarly deconstructing the linkage of written history and past
events, Jacques Derrida demonstrates in *Of Grammatology* the degree to which historicity depends on writing. His often cited pro-
nouncement that "there is nothing beyond the text" has been read
by some commentators as indicating a radical ontological and epistemological skepticism that makes history pure fiction, with no referential link to events of the past.[15] The influence of French poststructuralism on historiography in America can best be seen in the
work of Hayden White, whose groundbreaking *Metahistory: The Historical Imagination in Nineteenth-Century Europe* demonstrates the
degree to which history writing avails itself of literary, hence fictional, plots and modes.[16] *Metahistory*, along with White's subsequent books and essays, destabilized the working assumptions of
historians who saw their discipline as a science, who saw themselves
as successfully struggling to eliminate bias and subjectivity from
their writing.

The deconstruction of historiography along these lines is both
troubling and necessary. If we are resigned to saying that all knowl-

edge of the past is contingent and uncertain, then how can one argue against those who deny the Holocaust ever happened or those who assert that the internment of Japanese Americans during World War II was for their own protection? Do counterhistories matter much if history is purely fictional? And how can claims for justice be vigorously pressed without a firm sense of "what really happened"? For these reasons, those who have been marginalized in official historical accounts might tend to endorse an idea of history as a science, as an objective and empirically based discipline. But increasingly in the twentieth century, we have had to face certain tragedies, events, and traumas that exceed articulation, let alone scrupulous historical explanation.[17] And we have become more aware of the limits of documentation and archives for repairing historical memory, for those who have been considered less than fully "American" have also been marginalized in the records. In such cases, turning to written evidence or using conventional historical methods is not entirely helpful or effective in reconstructing history. The writers examined at length in this study — Erdrich, Morrison, Klepfisz, and Kogawa — record historical knowledge that has not become part of America's collective memory in their literary texts. At the same time, however, they interrogate whether correcting the record in itself is an adequate strategy to address this problem. Because they are writing literature and not history, they can employ what I term a postmodern poetics of absence and silence to emphasize the limits of recovery efforts. What has gone unrecorded in the documents and archives that sustain official history must remain undocumented no matter how much good will an individual historian might have, as Walter Benjamin points out when he writes, "There is no document of civilization which is not at the same time a document of barbarism."[18] The conventions of history do not allow imaginative speculation to restore the record, and so literary texts are essential, if not to restore the record through speculation, to mark the spaces, gaps, aporias that cannot be filled.

   In calling attention to the limits of documentation and archival knowledge, these texts would seem to fall under the rubric Linda Hutcheon uses for the postmodern novel — *historiographic metafiction*.[19] Through this coinage, Hutcheon identifies the obsession with history found in many postmodern novels and the deconstruction of truth claims postmodern novels bring into play. While Hutcheon is careful to note that asserting the textuality of history is not the same as asserting ontological skepticism about the past, she sees the primary function of these novels as deconstructive; that is, she pays more attention to the ways in which postmodern texts question the assumptions of historiography rather than examining their interest in producing counterhistories. The texts considered in *Against Amnesia* insist upon their own history-effects, however, and to acknowledge this quality, it is more accurate to describe these literary texts as *postmodern histories*, rather than as historiographic metafiction.

Even though Hutcheon's analysis of historiographic metafiction may be limited for understanding the double burden of writing history and literature that marginalized women writers face, her move to call attention to women writers as postmodernists is unquestionably significant. Literary scholars and postmodern theorists today continue to describe postmodern fiction as a game that men, usually white men, play. This position is present in most of the book-length studies of contemporary/postmodern historical fiction. For instance, David Cowart's *History and the Contemporary Novel* and David W. Price's *History Made, History Imagined* analyze fifteen historical novels between them, but only three are by women writers.[20] Other studies of postmodern historical fiction focus exclusively on the first wave of postmodern experimentalism, examining novels such as E. L. Doctorow's *The Book of Daniel* (1971) and *Ragtime* (1975), Norman Mailer's *The Armies of the Night* (1968), John Barth's *The Sot-Weed Factor* (1967), Thomas Pynchon's *Gravity's Rainbow* (1973), Robert Coover's *The Public Burning* (1977), and Ishmael Reed's *Mumbo Jumbo* (1972). These novels, though often based on scrupulous historical research, emphasize more than anything else the fictionality of history. Stacey Olster, in fact, aptly coins the term *subjective historicism* to describe the postmodern playfulness with history found in most of these works.[21] Similarly, Elisabeth Wesseling, in *Writing History as a Prophet*, is drawn to the utopian, alternative histories made available in postmodern novels through parody and what she terms "uchronian fantasies."[22] In contrast to first-wave postmodern texts and their exuberant historical fantasizing, the literature by contemporary minority women writers examined in this book claims some sort of referential linkage to what really happened and avoids the kind of paranoia surrounding history that can be found in many of the novels named above. Furthermore, by offering rigorously contextualized readings of women's historical fiction and poetry in the chapters that follow, *Against Amnesia* refuses to collapse history entirely under literature, but instead insists that these texts significantly maintain a productive tension between their status as literature and their status as history, even while they acknowledge the ways in which postmodernism compromises any easy claims to historical representation and referentiality.[23]

By focusing on postmodern histories written solely by women writers of color, *Against Amnesia* not only insists that their texts be read as part of postmodernism, but also argues for reconceptualizing postmodernism so that the narratives and issues of concern to women and minority writers are no longer seen as eccentric but as fundamental to the postmodern condition. Postmodernism has been rejected as a useful framework by many feminist and ethnic studies scholars precisely because of this impasse. David Palumbo-Liu, a noted Asian American studies scholar, for instance, has argued that the current trendiness of postcolonial and postmodern theory has produced decontextualized, dehistoricized misreadings of ethnic American literature. In particular, he cautions ethnic studies scholars against embracing postmodern theory if it means that "the very material histories that have shaped ethnicity in importantly different ways" become elided.[24] Rafael Pérez-Torres, a Chicano studies scholar, has noted similar problems that arise from an uncritical linking of postmodernism and multiculturalism, but he maintains that the two bodies of knowledge have much to offer each other. "A multicultural postmodernism," Pérez-Torres insists, "foregrounds the localism of context, the specificity of devalued knowledges and histories repressed by the hegemonic 'political unconscious,' and the potential for the local to achieve some significant and lasting social change."[25] By introducing the term *postmodern histories* to describe the work of Erdrich, Morrison, Klepfisz, and Kogawa, I wish to emphasize the possibility of working toward a theory of postmodernism that problematizes, but does not deny, historical reference. As Lois Parkinson Zamora argues in her comparative study of United States and Latin American fiction, *The Usable Past*, the literature of marginalized racial and ethnic writers "does not reflect 'the disappearance of a sense of history,' " as some theorists of postmodernism contend, but instead uses the tension between history and literature, between "historical truth and narrative truth" as "a primary source of their narrative energy."[26]

There are, of course, many critics of postmodernism who are skeptical that any profound historical understanding can be achieved in a high tech, fast food culture. In *Postmodernism, or, the Cultural Logic of Late Capitalism,* Jameson identifies "a crisis in historicity" as one of the predominant characteristics of postmodernism and famously laments the status of history in postmodern American culture: "we are condemned to seek History by way of our own pop images and simulacra of that history, which itself remains forever out of reach." For Jameson, the exemplary novelist of this crisis is E. L. Doctorow, and Jameson praises *Ragtime* in particular as a postmodern historical novel, which shows that the "historical novel can no longer set out to represent the historical past; it can only 'represent' our ideas and stereotypes about that past."[27] Retreating from his attempt to save History from deconstruction in *The Political Unconscious,* Jameson turns the crisis of referentiality and of historicity into one of the hallmark characteristics of postmodernism.[28]

Recognizing a crisis in referentiality, however, does not necessarily mean that all referential claims of history must be relinquished. On this point, Benjamin offers a helpful distinction: "To articulate the past historically does not mean to recognize it 'the way it really was' (Ranke). It means to seize hold of a memory as it flashes up at a moment of danger."[29] The moment of danger Benjamin speaks of here draws history into the present, makes available memories of the past — imperfect and subjective, perhaps, but nonetheless memories — that offer historical insight. This is the situation writers such as Erdrich, Morrison, Klepfisz, and Kogawa find themselves in; they live and work at a cultural moment when minority histories are not known in their complexity and so they strive in their literary works to draw the past into the present moment of the reader's consciousness so that we "seize hold" of historical memories.

Benjamin's observation on the imperfect, yet undeniable relation of memory to history also suggests the possibility of conceptualizing a complicated model of historical referentiality. This is a project that much of Cathy Caruth's influential work has addressed. The collection of essays Caruth coedited with Deborah Esch, *Critical Encounters: Reference and Responsibility in Deconstructive Writing,* addresses the problem of referentiality and history. In the introduction to this volume, Caruth argues that deconstruction has been misread "as denying memory, history, and all notions of truth."

Rather, Caruth insists, "the effect of deconstructive writing is not to eliminate the referential power of texts, but rather to offer a rethinking of the terms in which we have conceived it."[30] Expanding on these comments in her widely cited book *Unclaimed Experience: Trauma, Narrative, and History*, Caruth uses the concept of trauma to outline a deconstructive model of referentiality. Rereading Tasso's story of Tancred and Clorinda as Freud discusses it in *Beyond the Pleasure Principle*, Caruth theorizes trauma as the (re)experiencing of a wound that has not been forgotten but has been missed at the original moment of infliction; trauma occurs when the wound cries out belatedly, after the fact of the original wounding. Thus, for Caruth, trauma involves a double wounding and, in its inherent latency, trauma is simultaneously a displacement of that experience and an undeniable connection to it. The link between trauma and the initial missed experience leads to a model of reference that is not direct and immediate, but belated, displaced, and oblique. For Caruth, such a theory of trauma and its indirect referentiality suggests "the possibility of a history that is no longer straightforwardly referential."[31]

Where better to find an obliquely referential history than in literature, which by virtue of its figurative language constantly exceeds straightforward understanding? Lyrical excess, or intense lyricism, distinguishes the texts of Erdrich, Morrison, Klepfisz, and Kogawa and bears witness to the trauma of certain historical events in order to suggest the ways in which these events continually exceed direct or transparent representational strategies. This excess is productive in another, potentially more significant way too: intense lyricism compels the reader to listen to these painful histories and remember them. This move is crucial, for if the (counter)histories these authors narrate are to become anything more than marginalized, alternative — hence muted — stories in contemporary American culture, they need the support of collective memory.

*   *   *

Without memory can there be history?
— Marlene Nourbese Philip, *She Tries Her Tongue* (1989)

In contrast to the pessimism voiced by Jameson and other postmodern cultural critics, Erdrich, Morrison, Klepfisz, and Kogawa use their literary texts to struggle successfully against amnesia and toward historical memory. Their texts function in ways similar to the poems Carolyn Forché includes in her important anthology *Against Forgetting: Twentieth-Century Poetry of Witness*. Because of the extremities and atrocities of twentieth-century history, "the poem might be our only evidence that an event has occurred: it exists for us as the sole trace of an occurrence," Forché observes in her introduction. "As such, there will be nothing for us to base the poem on, no independent account that will tell us whether or not we can see a given text as being 'objectively' true. Poem as trace, poem as evidence."[32] Forché pinpoints here the sobering conditions of writing history in the twentieth century: given the absence of "valid" forms of evidence and the deaths of eyewitnesses in many instances, one must be willing to read traces of history in unorthodox forms, and one must be willing to accept a certain postmodern resignation that "what really happened" will always elude our efforts to know it or inscribe it in language. But, for Forché, this postmodern recognition does not lead to a lament about the relativism of history at the end of the twentieth century. Rather, she argues that these texts obligate the reader to respond actively to their calls for justice. "These poems will not permit us diseased complacency," Forché observes. "They come to us with claims that have yet to be filled, as attempts to mark us as they have themselves been marked." If poems can mark their readers as Forché maintains, then attentive readers will become implicated in the historical events and traumas surrounding the texts they read. This investment in the text, then, creates the possibility of transferring historical memory to a community of readers, a community with the potential to construct and nurture collective memory.[33]

While Forché turns to poetry as a significant cultural site for remembering, Andreas Huyssen emphasizes the potential value of museums in his 1995 book *Twilight Memories: Marking Time in a Culture of Amnesia*. The book takes its title from Huyssen's sense that the experience of temporality has been significantly transformed by postmodern high-tech culture, a culture in which traditional forms of memory have almost become obsolete and which is thus "terminally ill with amnesia." At the same time, Huyssen notes an important "memory boom" in contemporary American society, occurring most prominently in the proliferation of museums in postmodern culture, which he reads as "a potentially healthy sign of contestation," a means of resisting amnesia.[34] While acknowledging that museums as institutions are historically linked to the excesses of modernity—unabated elitism, capitalism, and imperialism—Huyssen maintains that sweeping institutional changes occurred in museums in the 1970s and 1980s. These changes, in Huyssen's view, have made it possible to regard contemporary museums as providing "a space for the cultures of this world to collide and to display their heterogeneity, even irreconcilability, to network, to hybridize and to live together in the gaze and the memory of the spectator."[35]

Huyssen thus rejects the claims of cultural critics who argue that contemporary museums, like television or other mass media, provide entertainment, not a real or profound sense of history. Museums, for Huyssen, offer something distinctive that television does not: "the material quality of the object." Huyssen goes on to explain: "The permanence of the monument and the museum object, formerly criticized as deadening reification, takes on a different role in a culture dominated by the fleeting image on the screen and the immateriality of communications. It is the permanence of the monument in a reclaimed public space, in pedestrian zones, in restored urban centers, or in pre-existing memorial spaces that attracts a public dissatisfied with simulation and channel-flicking." Huyssen's view of museums as potentially important cultural resources in postmodernity becomes especially crucial when he considers the proliferation of museums that commemorate the Holocaust. He asks, "How, after all, are we to guarantee the survival of memory if our culture does not provide memorial spaces that help construct and nurture the collective memory of the Shoah?"[36]

Huyssen's optimism that contemporary museums provide public spaces where the performance of memory can be facilitated and collective memory nurtured is very much like the optimism evident in this book, which argues that literary texts can produce a desire for historical memory that significantly resists the tendency toward amnesia in the broader culture. The individual chapters that follow discuss various traumatic moments in the particular histories of Native Americans, African Americans, Jewish Americans, Japanese Americans and Japanese Canadians, while also noting similar points of crisis and intervention in historical memory. To consider the larger cultural dilemmas that surround these texts, I read them along with other kinds of postmodern commemorative practices—photographs, museums and memorials, historical monographs, and films. A particularly productive dimension of the literary texts comes to the foreground when they are read against these other practices: literature has a significant capacity to direct the reader's attention to what cannot be articulated or made fully visible, and this insistence on reading silence and absence may be precisely what is needed in a postmodern age to sustain historical memory. Although some of the texts included in this study fit quite easily into conventional ideas of the historical novel, others treat their historical materials more elliptically. One of the central claims of *Against Amnesia* is that twentieth-century American history is marked by such extreme events and traumas that no one mode of representation or historical reference is sufficient or wholly adequate, and so the reader who wishes to follow Jameson's famous injunction "Always historicize!"[37] must be prepared to use multiple resources and analytical strategies.

And yet certain strategies or points of emphasis are evident in the diverse body of work included in this study. In contrast to mass culture, the literature by Erdrich, Morrison, Klepfisz, and Kogawa examined here offers a resistance to amnesia by providing sustained and extended — though not simplistic or linear — narratives. This is especially the case with Erdrich's and Morrison's decisions to write interlinked historical novels that begin to function as epics. Moreover, this literature presents a history that hurts, that does not merely entertain or facilitate the indulgence of nationalist fantasies. In contrast to conventional historical studies, the literary texts analyzed in this book explore things we will never know for certain. They imagine interior lives for people who have been rendered invisible or silent in the frames and documents of official history. But in contrast to other postmodern novels, these texts do not merely play with history. Their primary impetus is not only deconstructive, but also (re)constructive. They outline counterhistories to intervene in the painful amnesia that marks contemporary America and postmodern culture.

In his "Theses on the Philosophy of History," Benjamin warns, "Every image of the past that is not recognized by the present as one of its own concerns threatens to disappear irretrievably."[38] By providing challenging, yet compelling reading experiences, the literary texts examined in this study suggest the rigorous, yet pleasurable intellectual process required to think historically in a postmodern culture saturated with competing narratives and explanations.

Under these conditions, facts are not enough to produce "real" history—first the narrative must compel the reader to want to investigate further, to make the facts worth knowing. In asking, inviting, or obligating the reader to join in the performance of memory, these texts counter pessimistic forecasts concerning historical understanding in a postmodern age. We may very well be located in the "twilight of memory," as Huyssen observes, but the following chapters demonstrate that so long as authors like Erdrich, Morrison, Klepfisz, and Kogawa continue to insist on history and to provoke readers "to become *consciously* historical," as Rich urges, we will have significant cultural resources for vigorously resisting amnesia.

Chapter Two
"Haunted America"
Louise Erdrich and Native American History

In *Sweet Medicine: Sites of Indian Massacres, Battlefields, and Treaties*, photographer Drex Brooks has revisited the scenes of some of the most wrenching confrontations in the nineteenth-century Indian wars.[1] From the place where smallpox was introduced to native populations at Fort Union, North Dakota, to the location at Fort Pickens, Florida, where Apaches were held in captivity, from the graveyard of the Carlisle Indian School (now the U.S. Army War College) in Carlisle, Pennsylvania, to the Sand Creek Massacre site in Kiowa County, Colorado, Brooks asks his viewers to see what is and is not there. Some of the sites have historical markers; many do not. And even when a marker is present, it does little to tell the story of these physical, cultural, and psychological battlefields. Brooks gives us painful images of what Western historian Patricia Nelson Limerick calls, in her essay at the end of the volume, "Haunted America."[2] These locations are haunted not only by the spirits of those who died and those who survived, those who conquered and those who were conquered, but also by the inability of these spirits to be felt in the layers of twentieth-century development that have been constructed over the very ground that they haunt.

Limerick's essay focuses on the difficulties historians face when choosing a narrative or theme that will unite the complicated, or what she calls "muddled," stories of the West in the nineteenth century.[3] This muddled quality is found in Brooks's photographs as well. For instance, the site of the Mystic Massacre in Mystic, Connecticut, photographed by Brooks in 1991, is occupied by references to American capitalism: there are shiny cars, well-paved road-

Mystic Massacre Site, Mystic, Connecticut, 1991. Photograph © 1991 by
Drex Brooks.

ways, and wide sidewalks where an Anglo woman (a mother?) walks
holding the hand of a four- or five-year-old boy; retail venues line
the sides of these streets; a large American flag takes center stage in
the foreground of the shot, while a church occupies the center spot
of the background, situated on rising ground, its steeple crosscut by
the electric power lines. Facing this image, the viewer is prompted
to ask, where is the massacre site? Why is there no marker, at the
very least? How is it possible to occupy this space at the end of the
twentieth century without having to encounter the moment in history, in 1637, when British settlers killed 400 or 500, perhaps even
600, Pequots by slicing them with swords or by burning them alive?

Brooks's photographs on the right side, along with printed texts
from historical records and eyewitness narratives that face them
from the left side, take up the task of trying to bring Native American history into collective memory in the postmodern, commodified culture that dominates late twentieth-century America. Much

of contemporary Native American literature also testifies to this difficult task, but it is to the work of Louise Erdrich, who is of Turtle Mountain Chippewa and German ancestry, that I want to turn, for Erdrich has woven together five interlinked novels (so far) that span the twentieth century and thus move toward an epic portrayal of life in North Dakota similar to William Faulkner's fictional recreation of Mississippi. Like Faulkner's Snopeses, Bundrens, and Compsons, Erdrich's Morrisseys, Lamartines, Nanapushes, Kashpaws, and Adares are individuals who come to represent the history of an entire region. Because of their emphasis on Chippewas living on and off the reservation, Erdrich's novels offer versions of history that are marginal to the American story of declaring independence to reap economic progress.

Despite their attention to historical contexts and subtexts, Erdrich's first two novels became a source of some controversy regarding their commitment to native history. In a 1986 review of Erdrich's second novel, *The Beet Queen*, Leslie Marmon Silko argues that Erdrich is more interested in the kind of dazzling language and self-referentiality associated with postmodernism than in representing Native American oral traditions, communal experiences, or history. In Silko's view, the kind of "self-referential writing" Erdrich practices "has an ethereal clarity and shimmering beauty because no history or politics intrudes to muddy the well of pure necessity contained within language itself."[4] Whether or not one agrees with Silko's characterization of postmodernism, with her criticism of *The Beet Queen* as apolitical and ahistorical, or with the implicit agenda she proposes for Erdrich, it is true that mainstream reviewers of Erdrich's first two novels, *Love Medicine* and *The Beet Queen*, tended to praise her lyrical prose style and applaud her subtle, understated treatment of Native American issues.[5] *Tracks*, published in 1988, almost seems to be an answer to Silko's criticisms of *The Beet Queen* in that it overtly engages political and historical issues. But writing such a novel did not come easily to Erdrich: the original four-hundred-page manuscript for *Tracks* lay in a drawer for ten years, and it was not until she had already worked backward in time from *Love Medicine* to *The Beet Queen* that Erdrich returned to the manuscript and began to link it to her already completed novels about contemporary generations of Chippewa and immigrant settlers in North Dakota.

In fact, concerning *Tracks*, Erdrich commented to one critic, "I always felt this was a great burden, this novel."[6] Erdrich's choice of words in this comment is striking, for "burden" is precisely the term Hayden White uses to characterize history in a chapter titled "The Burden of History," where he argues that "it is only by disenthralling human intelligence from the sense of history that men will be able to confront creatively the problems of the present."[7] White's comments about history are an extension of Nietzsche's caution, in *The Use and Abuse of History*, that excessive historicism can lead to paralysis rather than action, that it can lead to carrying on traditions and values that have lost their utility. How might such an excess of history weigh on Erdrich, writing in *Tracks* about the forces dividing the Chippewa as a tribe in the early part of this century? One of the problems of Native American history is trying to record these losses and tragedies without falling into the predominant late nineteenth-, early twentieth-century image of vanishing Indians, of totally victimized and colonized natives on the verge of extinction.[8] On the other hand, the writer-historian cannot ignore the painful events of the past simply because they seem to lend themselves to being organized along the lines of a tragic narrative.

Facing this burden, this difficult responsibility, Erdrich takes a postmodern turn, invoking historical detail while simultaneously calling into question the very concept of "History." In this regard, her novels participate in the deconstruction of history to which White's career has been devoted. Radically calling into question the grounding assumptions of history in his seminal work *Metahistory*, White works against the burden of empirical, positivist conceptions of history by showing that literary patterns are inevitably present in historical narratives.[9] Since the publication of *Metahistory*, many philosophers of history and postmodern theorists have scrutinized history's claims to objective truth. While for White "getting out of history" (the title of one of his later essays) is emancipatory,[10] the resulting deconstruction of history has led to a crisis of referentiality that is felt in postmodern culture more broadly but has become focused on historical memory in particular. When Silko criticizes Erdrich for concentrating on language rather than history, then, she locates the troubling, unstable postmodern conditions within which contemporary history is written, within which, as I will argue, Native American history has to be written today. By discussing *Tracks* and *The Bingo Palace*,[11] this chapter shows how Erdrich paradoxically unites postmodern methods and Chippewa traditions to write a counterhistory that not only tells the other side of the story, but also makes a new ending possible for a history of dispossession and other traumatic losses.

The Wounds of History in *Tracks*

Tracks poignantly portrays the Turtle Mountain Chippewa's struggle to keep their land in the late nineteenth and early twentieth centuries.[12] Throughout the novel, a tribal elder, Nanapush, tries to change the course of events so that the contestation over land tenure between the tribe and white settlers, which culminates in the battle over Fleur Pillager's land, will not destroy the tribe. Fleur, one of the few unassimilated full-bloods among the Anishinabeg (Chippewa), has been allotted a valuable tract of timber-filled land adjoining the lake Matchimanito.[13] Although Nanapush does his best to retain Fleur's claim to the land, white lumber interests turn U.S. government policies to their advantage, and in the end, Fleur's land is lost.

Tracks opens with an elegiac description of the plight of the Chippewa at the turn of the century. Nanapush, one of the novel's first-person narrators, is telling Lulu, Fleur's daughter, the history of their people. This passage is significant, for it exemplifies the historical method Erdrich uses throughout the novel:

We started dying before the snow, and like the snow, we continued to fall. It was surprising there were so many of us left to die. For those who survived the spotted sickness from the south, our long fight west to Nadouissioux land where we signed the treaty, and then a wind from the east, bringing exile in a storm of government papers, what descended from the north in 1912 seemed impossible.

By then, we thought disaster must surely have spent its force, that disease must have claimed all of the Anishinabe that the earth could hold and bury.

But the earth is limitless and so is luck and so were our people once. Granddaughter, you are the child of the invisible, the ones who disappeared when, along with the first bitter punishments of early winter, a new sickness swept down. The consumption, it was called by young Father Damien, who came in that year to replace the priest who succumbed to the same devastation as his flock. This disease was different from the pox and fever, for it came on slow. The outcome, however, was just as certain. Whole families of your relatives lay ill and helpless in its breath. On the reservation, where we were forced close together, the clans dwindled. Our tribe unraveled like a coarse rope, frayed at either end as the old and new among

us were taken. My own family was wiped out one by one, leaving only
Nanapush. And after, although I had lived no more than fifty winters, I was
considered an old man. I'd seen enough to be one. In the years I'd passed, I
saw more change than in a hundred upon a hundred before.
  My girl, I saw the passing of times you will never know.
  I guided the last buffalo hunt. I saw the last bear shot. I trapped the last
beaver with a pelt of more than two years' growth. I spoke aloud the words
of the government treaty, and refused to sign the settlement papers that
would take away our woods and lake. I axed the last birch that was older
than I, and I saved the last Pillager. (*T* 1–2)

In these opening paragraphs, Erdrich lays tracks for a revisionist
history. Nanapush's speech is revisionist because it defamiliarizes
the popular narrative of American history as progress by showing
the costs of that "progress" for native peoples.[14] His speech to Lulu
presents an alternative narrative of certain past events — epidemics
("the spotted sickness," "consumption") and "government papers" (various federal treaties and legislative acts) — that led to
hardship and death for members of the tribe. Indeed, historical
sources document the fact that Nanapush's account corresponds to
past events: North Dakota was afflicted with outbreaks of smallpox
from 1869 to 1870 and of tuberculosis from 1891 to 1901. In fact,
historians today believe that European diseases such as smallpox,
measles, and tuberculosis were more deadly to native populations
across the country than Indian-white warfare was.[15]
    But Erdrich's work moves beyond documentation. Such histor-
ical facts do not fully acknowledge the horror of depopulation and
genocide, a horror that is registered in the opening passage by the
shift from "we" (the people) in the first paragraph to "I" (the
only surviving witness) in the last. The problem of communicating
this history is further addressed in the passage when Nanapush
instructs Lulu on the limits of his own narrative: "My girl, I saw the
passing of times you will never know." Without denying the referentiality or importance of his historical narrative, Nanapush acknowledges that the Real (or "what really happened") is that which Lulu
"will never know" — in other words, the complexity of the past exceeds his (and anyone else's) ability to re-present it fully.[16] Nonetheless, Nanapush insists on telling this history to Lulu, for only by
creating his own narrative can he empower her.
    The question of power and empowerment is central: Erdrich's
novel focuses not only on the limits of documentary history but also

on its politics. "Documents originate among the powerful ones, the conquerors," writes Simone Weil, a French Jew exiled to London during World War II. "History, therefore, is nothing but a compilation of the depositions made by assassins with respect to their victims and themselves."[17] Indeed, a documentary history of Native America would necessarily be based on treaties, legislative acts, and other documents written or commissioned in the name of the United States government and subsequently (ab)used to take land from indigenous peoples.[18] The history of treaty making and treaty breaking with Native Americans demonstrates that such documents are not autonomous, objective, or transparent statements but texts open to interpretation by whoever is in power.

The wounds of history, then, for Native Americans include not only the ways in which they were wounded by disease, warfare, genocide, and broken promises but also by the writing of standard documentary history. Because traditional written history represents a kind of discursive violence for Native Americans, *Tracks* emphasizes oral traditions and marks Nanapush's opening speech as oral, not written history: Nanapush does not name himself, as he would not in a face-to-face traditional storytelling situation, nor is the addressee named except to designate her relation to the narrator ("Granddaughter"); the last two paragraphs quoted above contain a rhetorical pattern typically associated with orality, repetition with variations ("I guided," "I saw," "I trapped"). Other oral markers signify Erdrich's rejection of the language of documents: Nanapush refers to "the spotted sickness" and not to smallpox or measles; he uses traditional oral tribal names — Nadouissioux, Anishinabe — rather than anglicized textual ones (Sioux, Chippewa); he speaks of "a storm of government papers" instead of naming specific documents affecting the tribe. The turn to oral history in *Tracks* signals the need for indigenous peoples to tell their own stories and their own histories.

But the evocation of the oral in a written text implicates this counterhistory in the historical narrative that it seeks to displace. *Tracks* renders a history of Anishinabe dispossession that moves within and against an academic account of this history. Indeed, the need to know history as it is constructed both orally and textually is indicated by the contextual phrases that begin each chapter: first a date, including the designation of season(s) and year(s), then a phrase in Anishinabe followed by an English translation. This information establishes two competing and contradictory frames of reference: one associated with orality, a seasonal or cyclic approach to history, a precontact culture; the other linked with textuality, a linear or progressive approach to history, a postcontact culture. Erdrich creates a history of dispossession that moves between these frames, that is enmeshed in the academic narrative of dates and of causes and effects concerning the loss of land. Indeed, only by knowing this narrative can the reader attach any significance to the fact that the first chapter begins in 1912.

The academic historical narrative that Erdrich uses and resists typically begins with the reservation period, when the federal government initially disrupted tribal ways of life by confining often nomadic tribes to strict boundaries, boundaries that sometimes did not even include their traditional homelands. Motives behind the establishment of reservations are complex, but one factor might be emphasized over others: confining tribes to specified areas enabled white settlers to claim more and more territory. Loss of native land was unfortunately facilitated under the Dawes Allotment Act of 1887, which codified a change in government policy, emphasizing the need to divide land formerly held in common on reservations and allot it to individual Indians.[19] The point of this policy was to convert tribes such as the Chippewa from communal hunting and gathering organizations to capitalistic, individualistic agricultural economies. To achieve this transition, the allotted tracts were to be held in trust for twenty-five years (according to the original plan), during which time the owners would be encouraged to make a profit from the land (by farming, selling timber rights, and so on) but would not be required to pay taxes on their tracts. The goal was to use the trust period to assimilate the Indians into the white man's way of life so that by the end of it they would be productive capitalists, capable of assuming the responsibilities of landholding—such as paying taxes—without further governmental intervention. But in 1906 Congress passed the Burke Act, which allowed the Commissioner of Indian Affairs to shorten the twenty-five-year trust period for "competent" Indians. Under this act, those deemed competent were issued a fee patent rather than a trust patent for their land, which meant they could sell or lease—or lose—their allotments. Then, in 1917, Commissioner of Indian Affairs Cato Sells announced a "Declaration of Policy" defining as competent all Indians of one-half white blood or more, thus making them U.S.

citizens and granting them fee patents for their allotments. Although the professed original intent of allotment was to maintain Indian land ownership, the policy had the opposite effect: "Before allotment 139 million acres were held in trust for Indians. In 1934 when allotment was officially repealed, only 48 million acres of land were left and many Indians were without land."[20] Some Indians lost their allotments because they could not pay the taxes after the trust period ended; others were conned into selling their allotments at a price well below the land's real value; still others used their allotments as security to buy goods on credit or to get loans, and then lost the land after defaulting on the repayment.[21]

By opening in 1912 and proceeding through the disastrous consequences of Sells's 1917 declaration, *Tracks* dramatizes the tenuousness of land tenure for Native Americans. Although Nanapush tells Father Damien, " 'I know about law. I know that 'trust' means they can't tax our parcels' " (*T* 174), the map Father Damien brings along — with its little squares of green, "pale and rotten pink," sharp yellow — shows that the agent's office is busy levying taxes and calculating who will not be able to pay them. As Fleur, Nanapush, Eli, Nector, and Margaret work to raise money to pay their taxes, native traditions are forced into a new economic context: the Pillager-Kashpaw family gathers and sells cranberry bark, just as Turtle Mountain women sold herbs and roots to raise money, while Eli traps and sells hides, activities that Turtle Mountain men engaged in.[22] At the end of all these efforts, they count the money and discover they have sufficient funds to cover the levies on all their allotted tracts. But when Margaret and Nector go to pay the taxes, they are told they have enough money to pay the taxes only on their own tract. No doubt Fleur's land is too valuable to be left to Indian ownership; the lumber on it alone is worth too much to the encroaching capitalists to leave it unharvested. As Nanapush recognizes, the late payment fine levied by the agent is probably illegal, yet greed and desire divide the Anishinabeg, turning some, such as Bernadette Morrissey and Edgar Pukwan Junior, into "government Indians," while others — Margaret and Nector — learn to look out for their personal welfare at the expense of communal values.

Erdrich's novel presents a turning point in the history of Anglo-Indian land conflicts. But the absence of names for the dates, acts, and other specifics attached to this kind of history displaces this narrative even as it is invoked. That is, the tension and conflict at the heart of *Tracks* become utterly clear only when readers have some knowledge of the Dawes Allotment Act of 1887, but the text significantly does not make direct reference to the act.[23] The documentary history of dispossession that the novel uses and resists functions as an absent presence; the text acknowledges the way in which this historical script has impinged on the Anishinabeg but does not allow this history to function as the only story that can be told.

Moreover, by refusing to participate in such documentation, Erdrich's novel refocuses attention on the emotional and cultural repercussions that the loss of land entails. In one of the final events of the novel, the trees on Fleur's tract are razed, and what happens to her trees, her land, becomes the extreme wound of history in the course of the narrative. In part, the trauma of her dispossession is intensified because Fleur has already lost so much: almost all her family members are dead from disease when the novel opens; she is raped in Argus, a town adjoining the reservation, by men from the butcher shop where she worked; her husband, Eli, is unfaithful to her; her second baby dies soon after birth; and her daughter, Lulu, is taken off to government boarding school. Fleur uses her shamanic, totemic powers to redress some of these wrongs: for instance, she causes a tornado in Argus that maims and kills the men who raped her, she turns Boy Lazarre's speech to babbling because of his voyeurism, and she asks the manitou of Matchimanito to drown men who cross her. But her powers cannot ward off the loss of her land, the land that Pillager spirits haunt.

This final loss is so excruciating that the narrative of Fleur's life takes the shape of tragedy by the end of the novel. So, too, does part of the historical narrative Erdrich's novel develops; it is because traditional Anishinabeg like Fleur and Nanapush are dispossessed, consequently fragmenting Native American clans and tribes, that the tracks of Native American history and culture are so difficult to discern. Thus at the end of the novel Fleur is said to walk "without leaving tracks" (*T* 215), a foreboding description considering that earlier in the novel Pauline calls her "the hinge" between the Chippewa people and their manitous (*T* 139) and Nanapush describes her as "the funnel of our history" (*T* 178). Her disappearance as the novel closes marks the end of the possibility of living solely according to Anishinabe traditions. But her tracklessness also indicates the impossibility of recording traditional Anishinabe lives and stories of the past in a form like documentary history, a genre that has historically placed Native Americans in the margins and has paid little attention to native women's lives.[24] Erdrich's historical novel, however, renders Fleur's dispossession and tracklessness as absences that haunt the narrative,[25] and so the novel calls for a kind of Native American history that both refers to the past and makes a space for what can never be known of it, that conveys the tragedies of history while desiring a different ending to this story.

"Native" Voices

Though Fleur is arguably the central character of *Tracks*, Erdrich does not use her as a narrator. What we learn of Fleur's powers, perspectives, and experiences comes to readers through the voices of the novel's two very different narrators: Nanapush and Pauline. In this way, *Tracks* demonstrates that historical narrative is a problematic representation, for it cannot give voice to the (precontact) past directly as figured specifically in the character of Fleur. Is it then possible at all to envision or write *Native* American history? And if it is, given that history is not an objective or unbiased narrative, but a story constructed out of personal and ideological interests, then what would compel us to give credence to one particular version of history — say the native version — over another? By juxtaposing Nanapush's and Pauline's narrative perspectives, *Tracks* explores these crucial issues.

Nanapush's narration begins and closes the novel, but Erdrich has carefully structured *Tracks* so that the narrators alternate chapters. The plot primarily continues to unfold chronologically as the narration shifts from Nanapush's voice to Pauline's, but it soon becomes clear how dependent the story is on the storyteller. In contrast to Nanapush's tribal allegiance, Pauline is a mixed-blood, alienated from both the tribe and Anglo society. She is also orphaned, lacking parents as well as tribal elders to give her direction. This lack of community is especially distressing, since Pauline is also a young woman trying to make sense of the beginnings of her sexual desire. She eventually resolves this psychological crisis by converting to Catholicism and becoming a nun, but this happens only after she becomes pregnant, tries to force a miscarriage, and then forgets about the illegitimate baby after she is delivered. To become a nun, Pauline must pass: she has a vision in which "God" appears to her to tell her that she is not part Chippewa, that she is "wholly white" (*T* 137).[26] Pauline's narrative voice thus reproduces a phenomenon bell hooks describes in *Black Looks*: "Too many red and black people live in a state of forgetfulness, embracing a colonized mind so that they can better assimilate into the white world."[27] Furthermore, as her name suggests, Pauline is linked to St. Paul's anxious gospel messages about the body as open to corruption, the threat of uncontrollable sexual urges, and the need for women in church to veil their hair and remove all ornaments that call attention to their bodies. Pauline embraces Catholicism to repress her sexual desire and to forget her connection to pagan (tribal) culture, but the perverseness of her repression becomes apparent in the novel when she begins masochistically punishing herself for being unworthy — wearing her shoes on the wrong feet, allowing herself to urinate only once a day, and practicing various other sorts of bodily mortification.[28]

Given the considerable differences in their identities and allegiances, it is inevitable that Nanapush and Pauline narrate contrasting interpretations of the historical moment that unfolds in *Tracks*. Nanapush's elegiac historical saga runs contrapuntally with Pauline's assimilationist version, which interprets the Anglo settling of America as progress. Whereas Nanapush sees the allotment policy and the concomitant conversion of the Anishinabeg from hunters and trappers to farmers as the cause of starvation, poverty, and land loss, Pauline suggests that "many old Chippewa did not know how to keep" — that is, farm — their allotments and thereby deserved to lose them. In addition, while Nanapush views the destruction of Anishinabe society and culture as tragic, Pauline sees it in terms of Christian millenialism:

A surveyor's crew arrived at the turnoff to Matchimanito in a rattling truck, and set to measuring. Surely that was the work of Christ's hand. I see farther, anticipate more than I've heard. The land will be sold and divided. Fleur's cabin will tumble into the ground and be covered by leaves. The place will be haunted I suppose, but no one will have ears sharp enough to hear the Pillagers' low voices, or the vision clear to see their still shadows. The trembling old fools with their conjuring tricks will die off and the young, like Lulu and Nector, return from the government schools blinded and deafened. (*T* 204–5)

Pauline assumes a prophetic voice in this passage, repeating the verb "will" to reveal a future in which Christianity along with interventions by the federal government dispossess the people of their land and culture. Pauline, by teaching at St. Catherine's, becomes one of those agents who blind and deafen children to their native language and culture. She sees the eventual outcome of Indian-white conflict and wants to align herself with the victors for both personal and political reasons.[29] Nanapush, in contrast, takes an oppositional stance: he rescues Lulu from boarding school and its inevitable racism; he refuses to reveal his name to Anglo authorities. Pauline, on the other hand, is eager to be renamed and reborn as Leopolda—a name given to her as she accepts her vows as a "wholly white" nun.

Significantly, Erdrich's novel holds Nanapush's and Pauline's antithetical views in tension. While it is easy to critique Pauline's historical perspective as accommodationist and self-mutilating, it is also clear that her voice has to be reckoned with and cannot be too easily dismissed if for no other reason than the fact that she narrates almost half of the story of the novel. More importantly, however, Pauline's prophecy of the Anglo conquest of the Anishinabeg indeed comes to pass and is corroborated by Nanapush's own narrative. Because historical events caused intact tribes and bands like the Turtle Mountain Chippewa to become split at the root, both Nanapush's and Pauline's points of view are necessary to convey an "indigenous" account of what happens in *Tracks*.

Read together, Pauline's and Nanapush's narratives also suggest the need to comprehend both textual and oral history. Nanapush tells his story to Lulu, but Pauline addresses no one in particular, which means essentially she is addressing a reader, not a listener. The lack of an immediate audience signifies her distance from oral tribal culture. But Nanapush himself has to move beyond a purely oral perspective. On the one hand, Nanapush participates in the construction of a binary opposition by which one might measure the distance between his narrative and Pauline's: oral "tribal" values in contrast to textual "Anglo" values. In the novel, an Anglo-American worldview is figured in terms of money and writing, systems of representation that historically were not native to the Anishinabeg. Nanapush recognizes that money and writing pose a threat to the tribe: "I've seen too much go by—unturned grass below my feet, and overhead, the great white cranes flung south forever. I know this. Land is the only thing that lasts life to life. Money burns like tinder, flows off like water. And as for government promises, the wind is steadier" (*T* 33). He sees that money is an unstable system of value: for white capitalists, it is the measure of progress, but for his people, "Dollar bills cause the memory to vanish" (*T* 174). Writing as representation similarly threatens the Anishinabeg. The white settlers need written words and documents to prop up their oral promises, whereas the Anishinabeg trust that spoken words and oral agreements are binding in themselves. Nanapush alone foresees that the white man's written promises are unstable texts, not fixed documents:

Once the bureaucrats sink their barbed pens into the lives of Indians, the paper starts flying, a blizzard of legal forms, a waste of ink by the gallon, a correspondence to which there is no end or reason. That's when I began to see what we were becoming, and the years have borne me out: a tribe of file cabinets and triplicates, a tribe of single-space documents, directives, policy. A tribe of pressed trees. A tribe of chicken-scratch that can be scattered by a wind, diminished to ashes by one struck match. (*T* 225)

Nanapush performs a literal deconstruction of written words in this passage. Linking bureaucratic policies and the paper they are written on to the destruction of mature trees on Indian tracts like Fleur's, Nanapush foresees how unstable, how open to quick destruction, paper and paper promises are, as well as the tribes who rely on them.

My reading of Nanapush, up to this point, has emphasized his role as the conservator of Anishinabe history and worldview. Erdrich's novel, however, points out that conservatism alone is not a successful political strategy given the threat of Anglo colonialism. Hence the contrast between Fleur's trust in tradition to prevent her land from being taken — "She said the paper had no bearing or sense, as no one would be reckless enough to try collecting for land where Pillagers were buried" (*T* 174) — and Nanapush's recognition that paper must be fought with paper. Paradoxically, his ability to adapt to these new conditions in part comes from his traditional namesake: the Chippewa trickster Naanabozho.[30] In fact, episodes in the story of Naanabozho parallel episodes in Nanapush's story. Both share the ability to come back to life after death or near death, both are powerful storytellers, both are noted for their keen ability to track people, and both avenge wrongs committed on family members.[31]

Most important, perhaps, is that Nanapush and Naanabozho as

tricksters are sometimes tricked by others, but are at other times triumphant. For instance, when underwater manitous kill his nephew, Naanabozho finds and wounds the manitous, but they escape. He tracks them, however, and tricks the old woman who is doctoring them back to life into divulging not only where the manitous are, but how to get past the guards in order to kill them. He then kills the woman and skins her; putting on her skin, he disguises himself to look like the enemy. His trickster tactics succeed, and he avenges his nephew's death.

Like Naanabozho, Nanapush puts on the guise of the oppressor to effect justice. He does so when he decides to allow Father Damien to write a letter recommending him as a tribal leader, for instance. In making this concession to writing, Nanapush does not leave behind his earlier skepticism concerning the written word; rather, he increasingly realizes that it is politically necessary for him not to stay outside the system of written discourse, but to use the technology against itself. In fact, he becomes a bureaucrat and uses the authority of the written word to save Lulu from her exile to boarding school. Producing the birth certificate filed by Father Damien, which names Nanapush as Lulu's father, Nanapush gains the power to call her home. Ironically, Lulu's birth certificate—recognized as an authentic document by white authorities—is a false document, for Nanapush is not her biological father. And yet, from a tribal view, Nanapush is certainly Lulu's spiritual father, the one who mentors her and teaches her the old ways.[32] Thus, the piece of paper—both fiction and fact—becomes a clever tool used to save Lulu from assimilation.

The final paragraph of *Tracks*, describing Lulu's return home from school, thus strikes a note of cautious optimism. As Lulu emerges from "the rattling green vehicle" of the government, she bears the marks of her encounter with Anglo-American cultural authority: hair shorn, knees scarred from attempts to make her docile, attired in the shameful "smouldering orange" of a runaway, Lulu at first seems alien to Nanapush and Margaret (*T* 226). As they watch, however, Lulu's prim school-taught walk becomes a leap forward, and her face becomes electrified with Fleur's bold grin and white hot anger. Marked by her encounter with the shapers of mainstream American history, Lulu is only "half-doused" (*T* 226) and will carry a trace of Anishinabe history and myth forward.

Nanapush's negotiation between the old ways and the exigencies

of the present is the significant legacy he passes on to Lulu. He recognizes that it is no longer possible to rely solely on the oral tradition to pass down narratives of the past. To do so would be to end up
like Fleur, the funnel of oral history silenced by Anglo economic
and cultural conquest. As pure Indian, Fleur is nearly a mythic
figure — a source of inspiration for Lulu, but one that seems beyond
emulation. (And this is perhaps why Erdrich does not give Fleur a
direct voice in the narrative.) Neither does Pauline, Fleur's opposite, offer a model to Lulu, for Pauline's assimilation into the dominant culture results in a voice that echoes hegemonic history. Moreover, by forgetting the past and radically rewriting her own identity
and experience, Pauline signifies a sense of history as pure fiction,
without any referential linkage whatsoever. *Tracks* ultimately rejects
such a position by following Pauline into ever increasing torments.

   In the last chapter she narrates, Pauline takes a leaky boat into
the middle of the lake Matchimanito while a wild storm rages. Her
risky voyage is an attempt to free herself from memories of her
former lover, Napoleon; of Russell Kashpaw, Dutch James, and the
horror of what happened to Fleur in Argus; of Fleur's infant who
died; and of anything connected to Margaret, Nanapush, and Fleur.
She cannot control her desire to be connected to Fleur, however,
and so she screams to Fleur on shore only to watch Fleur turn her
back and walk away. Pauline has been drawn to Fleur throughout
the narrative, but has been unable to articulate this desire for connection (for a mother? for a lover?) to Fleur or to herself. The pain
of her unfulfilled longing for Fleur in this scene is marked only by a
sentence fragment — "A crushing sadness" — followed by the possibility of forgetting: "I was glad when at last night approached"
(*T* 200). Pauline then resorts to biblical narratives to explain her
pain: comparing her ordeal on the water, as night falls and as the
cold water seeping into the sinking boat numbs her body, to Christ's
ordeal in the desert for forty days and forty nights, Pauline grows
ever more deluded. She prepares to be tempted by Satan himself
and arrives on shore, naked, carrying a rosary as her only defense,
and ends up believing she has strangled the devil with her rosary
beads. As it turns out, she has killed not the devil but her former
lover, Napoleon Morrissey, and Pauline's initial anguished reaction
to the killing is quickly supplanted by denial: "I felt a growing horror and trembled all through my limbs until it suddenly was revealed to me that I had committed no sin. There was no guilt in this

matter, no fault. How could I have known what body the devil would assume?" (*T* 203). Pauline's inability to admit her culpability, as well as her "increasing madness" as Erdrich has described it,[33] render her an unreliable narrator as the novel closes, and thus her condemnatory attitude toward the Anishinabeg and her affirmation of white progress are called into serious question.

By presenting Pauline's historical vision as ultimately inadequate, *Tracks* begins to work toward a complicated vision of Native American history. Participating in the radical skepticism articulated in postmodern theory about the transparency of historical evidence and the objectivity of traditional history, *Tracks* simultaneously calls into question the conflation of fiction and history that has become one of the defining characteristics of postmodernism. To put it in the terms of the novel, this kind of conflation is dangerous, for it ultimately leads to the easy translation of Napoleon's murder as a defeat of Satan. By affirming the connection between Lulu and Nanapush, *Tracks* moves toward a kind of history writing and telling that neither relinquishes its referential debt to the past nor oversimplifies it, that is grounded in native traditions and ready to adapt to postmodern conditions.

Moreover, the alignment between Lulu and Nanapush at the end of the novel creates the possibility of writing a different ending for this story, for this history. Unlike the tragic narrative endings associated with Fleur's disappearance and Pauline's eventual madness, the novel dwells at the end on an image of Lulu, having just returned from boarding school, running toward Nanapush and Margaret. The final line reads, "We gave against your rush like creaking oaks, held on, braced ourselves together in the fierce dry wind" (*T* 226). Nanapush's opening speech in the novel lapses into "I" as it proceeds, but his final words on the last page are of "we." The image of oaks that hold on also suggests the ability of the people to survive the wounds of history. Despite the razing of the trees on Fleur's land at the end, *Tracks* envisions a historical narrative that is not completely tragic, that does more than represent the Anishinabeg as vanishing victims of white conquest. By emphasizing Nanapush's connection to Lulu around the issue of tribal history, *Tracks* points out that the telling is as important as the tale. Ultimately, the only history that must be seen as tragic is that which is irrecoverable because there are no elders to tell it or younger generation to hear it and pass it down to those who will come after. *Tracks* shows, in contrast, that telling the history of Anishinabe dispossession can paradoxically make it possible to narrate a history of Anishinabe survival and cultural continuance.

Righting History in *The Bingo Palace*

Toward the end of the nineteenth century, the Lakota were faced with circumstances similar to those affecting Erdrich's Anishinabeg in *Tracks*: the loss of the buffalo, the loss of land through treaties, and the splintering of the people. But they also had ceremonies to ease the pain caused by these losses. The *heyoka* ceremony is particularly interesting, for it emphasizes laughter and humor as ways of reckoning with loss, and it is this precise tension that becomes a significant concern in Erdrich's sequel to *Tracks, The Bingo Palace*.

Black Elk Speaks gives perhaps the best-known description of the heyoka ceremony. At the point in the narrative when Black Elk describes this ceremony, the Lakota have lost most of their land in what is now South Dakota, including the Black Hills; the people have been divided between those who are willing to negotiate with the white military authorities and those who are not; Crazy Horse has been murdered. These traumatic events, and others, lead up to the ceremony, which is performed by sacred fools or comedians called heyokas. Black Elk paints his body red with streaks of black lightning; he shaves the right side of his head and leaves the hair on the left side hanging long; he carries a bow and arrows that are so long and crooked as to be unusable. The heyokas perform various antics to make the people laugh, to restore their spirits. Black Elk explains that only those who have had visions of the west — that is, of the immensely powerful and destructive Thunder Beings — can become heyokas, for they are able to see the sacred, potentially terrifying truth and share it with the people in a benign way:

The heyoka presents the truth of his vision through comic actions, the idea being that the people should be put in a happy, jolly frame of mind before the great truth is presented. When the vision comes from the west, it comes in terror like a thunderstorm, but when the storm of [the] vision has passed the whole world is green and happy as a result. In the ceremony of the heyoka this order is reversed, the creation of the happy frame of mind in the people preceding the presentation of the truth.[34]

As Black Elk describes it, the heyoka ceremony has a complex dynamic: it is designed to elicit laughter from a people who are already in despair, and by lifting their spirits, the ceremony prepares them to face other sacred, potentially terrifying truths.

Black Elk's analysis of sacred laughter, of laughter that heals, offers a valuable way to articulate the relation of *The Bingo Palace* to *Tracks*. *The Bingo Palace* has a strong comic dimension; it elicits a kind of healing laughter to alleviate the wrongs of history that are so pointedly dramatized in *Tracks*. Erdrich has commented in various interviews that Indian humor is a kind of pantribal ceremony, enabling tribal peoples to deal with the terrible hands they have been dealt. "Ironic survival humor," as Erdrich calls it in a 1989 interview conducted by Bill Moyers, "enables you to live with what you have to live with." One of the things native peoples have had to learn to live with is injustice; after her comments about humor, Erdrich informs Moyers that "when you grow up and see your people living on a tiny pittance of land or living on the edge, surrounded by enormous wealth, you don't see the world as just."[35]

Erdrich's comments anticipate one of the most significant observations in *Indi'n Humor: Bicultural Play in Native America*, in which Kenneth Lincoln argues that Indi'n humor is fundamentally connected to the wounds of history: "After five hundred years of dispossession — germ and conventional warfare, bounty hunting, guns, plows, telegraph poles, trains, barbed wire enclosures, land swindles, and outright stealing — native peoples still persist on some 53 million acres of reservation land left over from the great dirt grab. . . . Clearly, humor both targets and takes some fatal sting out of history."[36] One of the ways to survive such a tragic past and to be able to narrate something other than tragic history is to hold onto and develop the capacity for laughter. The prevalence of Indi'n humor in *The Bingo Palace* makes it clear that Erdrich's Chippewa are not tragic victims, like the impassive and sad-faced Indians portrayed in some of Edward Curtis's well-known photographs from the early part of this century.[37] Erdrich's characters are contemporary survivors, able to see the ironic, humorous side in even the bleakest situations. It is necessary to read *The Bingo Palace* in relation to *Tracks* to make visible the meaningful connections between history and humor, between tribal fragmentation and cultural renewal. Following the postmodern trickster tactics of Nanapush in *Tracks*, *The Bingo Palace* suggests that contemporary Chippewa tricksters can turn to legal discourse and bingo justice to right the wrongs of history.[38]

The Bingo Palace is punctuated by comic incidents, most of them involving Lipsha Morrissey, who has been drifting physically and psychologically since his days in *Love Medicine* and who returns home to the reservation without a clear sense of identity or direction near the beginning of the novel. Almost immediately, Lipsha falls for Shawnee Ray, who has had an affair and a baby with his uncle Lyman, a successful entrepreneur and respected tribal member. Lipsha's desire for Shawnee Ray and his contest with Lyman to win her affection furnish the novel with some hilarious scenes. On his first date with Shawnee Ray, Lipsha's adrenaline rush turns to embarrassment at the U.S.-Canadian border, when he is arrested for drug possession—which might turn into material for serious consideration had the border patrol not mistaken an old-time pemmican fruitcake (that Zelda had given Lipsha and that he did not want in the first place) for hash! Later in the novel, a verbal confrontation between Lipsha and Lyman over Shawnee Ray breaks out into an impromptu food fight at a Dairy Queen. "Doing a flying drop kick," Lipsha explains, "I knock into an entire large-size family who are carefully turning from the ice cream counter and balancing five-topping sundaes with whipped cream and cherries. The cherries explode into the air, the walnut bits zing sideways, the ice cream blobs collide at super speed," and the Dairy Queen erupts with "one big explosion" (*BP* 167). Driving away from the scene of the food fight, though, Lipsha and Lyman do not continue their battle but instead forge lines of connection, and Lipsha discovers that "mixing it up with Lyman doesn't unwedge either my friendship feelings for him or my love for Shawnee Ray" (*BP* 169). Because of their friendship, it is perhaps not so surprising that Lipsha and Lyman subsequently go together to Xavier Toose's to participate in a sweat lodge ceremony and to fast for a spiritual vision. Even this very serious ceremonial endeavor, however, produces comic results: while Lyman has a vision that reconciles him to his brother Henry's suicide, Lipsha is visited by a skunk—literally. That their competition results in comedy and an unlikely bonding, rather than violence and tragedy, is explained by Lipsha in terms of their Indianness: "Reading is my number-one hobby," Lipsha confesses, "and I have browsed a few of the plays of the old-time Greeks. If you read about a thing like Lyman and me happening in those days, one or both of us would surely have to die. But us Indians, we're so used to inner plot twists that we just laugh" (*BP* 17). As individual men in love with the same woman, Lipsha and Lyman are adversaries, but as Indians, accustomed to dealing with ironies and the twisted plots and words of the federal government, Lipsha and Lyman know how to recognize an absurd situation and laugh about it rather than come to blows.

Lincoln's treatment of Indi'n humor pays particular attention to the bicultural dynamics evident in Lipsha's remark. As "a form of public teasing to raise Indian-white issues," Indi'n humor mediates conflicts between the dominant culture and Native America. Drawing on Freud's analysis of jokes as making sense out of nonsense, combining bewilderment and amazement, Lincoln demonstrates that Native American jokes are both playful and deliberate: jokes about Indian-white relations have to be taken "not too seriously, so as not to wreck the playful construct on the rocks of reality, and yet seriously enough to engage the mind in unpuzzling the real."[39] In other words, like the heyoka ceremony Black Elk speaks of, Indi'n humor enables the participants to laugh and lift their spirits, but it also prepares the participants to face a sobering reality—the reality of living in a society that privileges whiteness at every turn. An unnerving episode in *The Bingo Palace* illustrates what is at stake in this kind of joking: Lipsha encounters a bigoted Anglo gas station-convenience store clerk when he enters the store to buy condoms so that he and Shawnee Ray can have their first intimate moment. He is so nervous about the purchase and dazzled by the numerous choices that he quickly picks up two boxes of economy size, setting in motion the verbal combat that follows. When the clerk asks him if he is on a "heavy date," Lipsha—having already noticed that the clerk is wearing a T-shirt with "Big Sky Country" written on it—sees the clerk's ugly grin and responds: " 'Not really. Fixing up a bunch of my white buddies from Montana. Trying to keep down the sheep population' " (*BP* 70). The humorous jousting gets more intense, with Lipsha following up on the sheep innuendoes and the clerk resorting to racist innuendo, at one point asking Lipsha which species he belongs to. As Lipsha turns to leave the store he hears the clerk mutter "prairie nigger"—a phrase so wounding Lipsha can hardly believe he hears it right. " 'What?' " Lipsha turns and asks, " 'What'd you say?' " There is a standoff at this point, until Lipsha gets to the door of the store and cries out " 'Baah. . . .' " (*BP* 71). He gets the last line and the last laugh, at least for the moment, and triumphs to the extent that he gets the upper hand in a potentially devastating and dehumanizing situation.

Joking under these conditions becomes a way to turn pain into pleasure, as Lincoln suggests. But what are the limits of such joking? Can jokes effectively renegotiate Indian-white power relations? *The Bingo Palace* takes on this issue in the subsequent meeting between Lipsha and the Big Sky Country clerk. After Lipsha has the amazing fortune to win the grand prize at bingo — a fully equipped van — he cannot help but want to show it off. With Shawnee Ray unavailable, Lipsha heads for a party in Hoopdance and unfortunately encounters the same clerk with some of his friends. To put Lipsha in his place, they decide to force him to get the state of Montana tattooed on his buttocks. Although Lipsha tries to inject humor into the situation, even pleading for a different form of retribution ("'Just beat me up, you guys. Let's get this over with'" [*BP* 80]), the whites are the only ones who laugh at this moment in the encounter. Luckily, for Lipsha, the tattooist is a fellow Chippewa, Russell Kashpaw. Kashpaw listens attentively while the Anglos describe what kind of map they want Lipsha to have — like "'those maps we did in grade school showing products from each region. Cows' heads, oil wells, missile bases, those little sheaves of wheat and so on'" — and then gravely instructs the Anglos to tie Lipsha up and "'leave this place.'" After they leave this ominous scene, Lipsha is surprised to have a vision of Russell as his "twin" — someone who has "the same thoughts in another brain" (*BP* 81). As they exchange glances, Russell "suddenly grins" and says, "'I don't have a pattern for Montana'" (*BP* 82) — as if this were the only reason he doesn't follow through on the tattoo. Bonding together, Russell and Lipsha create a comic conclusion to what has threatened to become a vicious joke. But violence is not entirely averted in Lipsha's encounter with the Anglos: his prized bingo van is destroyed by the group. This final outcome serves as an important reminder that although joking can be a useful way to assuage the painful history of white oppression and racism, it is not enough for Lipsha just to crack jokes. In order to enjoy laughter without the threat of violence erupting, the unequal power relationship between the parties has to be addressed.

The title of Erdrich's novel points to one way of leveling the playing field: bingo. Bingo and other forms of gaming have become increasingly significant—and controversial—sources of revenue for Indian nations across America. Proponents argue that bingo and casino games make it possible to end the terrible impoverishment that has afflicted most reservations; critics argue that this economic boon comes with hidden price tags, and they contend that native involvement with gambling is detrimental to tribal traditions and values. There is no clear consensus among native peoples, although the establishment of bingo palaces and casinos on reservations across America has increased exponentially since the late 1980s. In recent essays, Gerald Vizenor has been vocal in his criticisms of bingo and gambling, arguing that these contemporary games are not in any way connected to Indian traditions like the moccasin game, that the legal circumstances permitting casinos on reservations could impinge on tribal sovereignty in the future, that the debates about bingo and gambling casinos have led to disturbing intratribal rifts.[40] Vizenor's criticism of contemporary Indian gaming is also ethical in nature: "Casino avarice with no moral traditions is a mean measure of tribal wisdom."[41]

In contrast to Vizenor's openly critical stance on this issue, Erdrich's novel exhibits ambivalence about bingo as an economic tool. The novel presents a critical view by following Lipsha's attachment to bingo. He wants to win money and the bingo van, not to end impoverishment on the reservation, but to impress Shawnee Ray. With the help of his mother's spirit (June, who died at the beginning of *Love Medicine*) and her notebook of winning bingo numbers, Lipsha begins to win money at bingo regularly. But by winning this money, he loses his touch—the mysterious power concentrated in his hands, which he had formerly used to heal people—altogether. As in *Tracks, The Bingo Palace* questions whether economic gains for Indians ought to be arrived at by any means necessary. Except for Lulu, who is one of the few players who actually makes money playing bingo and who seems untainted by its excesses, the other players have a difficult time reconciling bingo and gambling with their traditions. The link between gambling and the corruption of tradition is most apparent in the novel when Lyman, in a wagering fever, puts up Nector's peace pipe as collateral to get more money for gambling at a Las Vegas casino: he loses the money as well as the pipe.

Lyman is also unduly influenced by dreams of casino cash as he plans to build an even grander bingo palace than the one he already owns and operates. He, in fact, is so interested in profits and his plans for this building that he cons Lipsha into allowing him to be a co-signer of the savings account into which Lipsha is depositing his bingo earnings. When Lipsha goes to withdraw money from this account, he discovers the balance is zero — Lyman has taken all of his money, he has stolen from his own nephew. Because of these events, Lipsha and Shawnee Ray (and Erdrich's readers) become increasingly concerned about the location of the bingo palace Lyman plans to build, for his bingo palace is destined for the shores of Matchimanito, to be located on Pillager land. Once more Fleur will be displaced: not by white lumber interests this time, as happens in *Tracks*, but by her own grandson. The desire for bingo dollars allows Lyman to contemplate an unthinkable act of injustice, directed at someone of his own people, of his own family.

Fleur's reaction to her impending dispossession is curious, though. When Lipsha asks to visit with her, she "smiles . . . showing her sharp old teeth," registering on her face what Lipsha calls "fierce pleasure" (*BP* 132). When Lipsha reveals that the purpose of his visit is to ask for a potion that will make Shawnee Ray love him, Fleur instead transforms herself into a bear and with her "hot rasp[ing]" voice (*BP* 137) tells Lipsha "her bear thoughts, laughing in tongues" (*BP* 151). What does Fleur, who knows she is on the verge of being dispossessed, once again, have to laugh about? Why does she acquiesce in the taking of her land for a bingo palace? The answers to these questions indicate the complexity of Erdrich's handling of bingo in the novel.

To understand Fleur's laughter, we have to be able to conceive of the almost inconceivable: the possibility of Indian victory. Because of the dismal outcome of the Indian wars of the nineteenth century, any image of Indian victory has come to be charged with irony. Irony also lies at the heart of Lincoln's exploration of bicultural Indi'n humor: laughter as a survival strategy is created precisely out of defeat, out of something painful. But what about the possibility of conceiving a laughter that emerges from triumph and justice? Because of the tragedies of Indian history in America, we initially have to look elsewhere, outside of native culture, for such a prospect. "The Laugh of the Medusa," Hélène Cixous's often-cited essay, proposes such a kind of laughter, a laughter that occurs at a time of rupture, when "the new breaks away from the old." In this essay, Cixous calls for a radical reconceptualization of woman's position in Western culture modeled on the black power slogan of the sixties ("we are black and we are beautiful"), so that what has been repressed or defined as a negative for woman can be reevaluated and seen as having extraordinary value. The essay takes its title from Cixous's feminist revision of the myth of Medusa: "You only have to look at the Medusa straight on to see her. And she's not deadly. She's beautiful and she's laughing."[42]

While not going so far as to claim that Erdrich's novel is straight-forwardly "feminist," I do want to suggest a connection between Cixous's Medusa, whose laughter marks her empowerment and vision, and Fleur's "laughing in tongues."[43] Concerns of triumph and justice are linked to Fleur throughout the novel. In a flashback, the novel relates the incident when Fleur coyly maneuvers the agent who took possession of the Pillager land around Matchimanito into playing cards and losing badly. Erdrich's narrator tellingly comments on Fleur's strategy and success: "Fleur was never one to take an uncalculated piece of revenge. She was never one to answer injustice with a fair exchange. She gave back twofold" (*BP* 145).[44] Fleur's bear laughter, then, voices not just survival but triumph; in the encounter with the agent, she got her land back. The implication is that she can laugh at the loss of her land to the bingo palace because she is able to envision a kind of bingo justice — a justice that will enable the Chippewa to get their land back twofold or more. Appearing to Lyman in a dream — a dream that first arises while he is "staring into the lighted face of [a] video slot machine" (*BP* 147), gambling away all his money and Nector's sacred pipe — Fleur speaks in her rasping bear voice, repeating Nanapush's important words from *Tracks*: *"Land is the only thing that lasts life to life. Money burns like tinder, flows off like water, and as for the government's promises, the wind is steadier"* (*BP* 148). She then adds her own words of advice: *"This time, don't sell out for a barrel of weevil-shot flour and a mossy pork. . . . Put your winnings and earnings in a land-acquiring account. Take the quick new money. Use it to purchase the fast old ground"* (*BP* 148–49). Fleur shapes Lyman's vision of the importance of bingo money: it ought not to be used to create red versions of white capitalists but should buy back the land — acres and acres of it. In effect, she becomes a trickster figure, showing Lyman how to cunningly take a new technology and use it to restore the tribe's vital connection to the land.[45]

As Lipsha describes it later in the novel, "temporary loopholes in the law" (*BP* 221) have made it possible for bingo palaces and casinos to spring up on reservations around the country. The legal background that the novel refers to shows that trickster maneuvers can be very effective even in contemporary America. In 1987, the U.S. Supreme Court ruled in *California v. Cabazon Band of Mission Indians* in favor of the Indians.[46] The Cabazon Band had been running bingo games with prizes up to two hundred times higher than what was allowed by California state law; they also had conducted poker and other card games. When California attempted to enforce state laws on Indian reservations, which typically fall under the jurisdiction of the federal government and tribal self-rule, the Cabazon Band fought back in court. In its ruling, the U.S. Supreme Court decided that a state has no right to *regulate* gaming on Indian lands, although it could *prohibit* gaming on Indian lands if similar kinds of gaming were prohibited in the state. If, however, a state permits a form of gaming (in the case of California, the state allowed bingo and other kinds of gaming to raise money for charitable purposes), then tribes could operate such games and do so without state interference. Bingo parlors run by tribes had been allowed before the Cabazon decision was handed down (federal agencies had, in fact, promoted bingo as a means of economic development for tribes), but the decision changed the playing field by giving tribes access to more lucrative forms of gaming. More important to many tribal members, however, was the way in which the Cabazon decision reaffirmed the principle of tribal sovereignty by treating the tribes as independent nations within the United States.

Because the Cabazon ruling made it possible for high-stakes bingo and other forms of gaming to be located on reservations throughout the country, Congress almost immediately sought to codify the decision in the Indian Gaming Regulatory Act of 1988 (IGRA). This act divided kinds of games into three tiers, each tier involving a different level of regulation. The IGRA declared that all "class I gaming" — traditional Indian games played for social or ceremonial purposes — was to fall under "the exclusive jurisdiction of the Indian tribes" and thus was not subject to any of the provisions of the act. "Class II gaming" — including bingo, poker, and other "non-banking" card games — was to fall under the jurisdiction of Indian tribes but would be subject to IGRA regulations. "Class III gaming" — slot machines, roulette, blackjack, baccarat, video poker, and other kinds of casino gaming — would be permitted only if "located in a State that permits such gaming for any purpose by any person, organization, or entity."[47] To establish class III gaming on a reservation, tribes were required to negotiate "compacts" with the state, but to make these negotiations equitable, the IGRA set a strict time period for conducting them, and if an agreement was not reached within the time limit or if the state did not negotiate in good faith, the tribe could ask for federal intervention.[48] In any court action arising from failed negotiations, the IGRA declared that "the burden of proof shall be upon the State to prove that the State has negotiated with the Indian tribe in good faith."[49]

Although the IGRA was meant to establish clear guidelines for the appropriate regulation of gaming on Indian reservations and lands, it created some interesting loopholes. Because the language for "class III gaming" includes the phrase "for any purpose," a tribal attorney in Wisconsin — surely a trickster in his own right — was able to convince a federal judge that "since Wisconsin has a state lottery and since the lottery consisted of prize, chance, and consideration, and since all casinos had games consisting of prize, chance, and consideration, therefore, Wisconsin had to negotiate a compact with the tribes which would allow Indian casinos."[50] In other words, the wording of the IGRA and the outcome of the *Lac du Flambeau Indians v. State of Wisconsin* case of 1991 allowed Indians to establish casinos in states that did not have casinos per se, but which allowed occasional "Las Vegas nights" to be staged by charities and churches. This ruling has led directly to the proliferation of casinos on reservations across the United States.

Another kind of loophole concerns the definition of "Indian lands." The IGRA defines them as "all lands within the limits of any Indian reservation; and any lands title to which is either held in trust by the United States for the benefit of any Indian tribe or individual or held by any Indian tribe or individual subject to restriction by the United States against alienation."[51] What happens, though, if tribes — using their bingo and casino earnings — buy land? Can casinos or bingo parlors be set up on these newly purchased lands which are often not contiguous to their reservations? Although one court case has suggested the answer is no (*Siletz Tribe v. the State of Oregon*), other tribes continue to raise this issue in court.[52] Because of the revolution in Indian gaming over the past decade, tribes are now poised to demand or buy back some of the land forcibly taken from them in the nineteenth century. No wonder Fleur laughs at the loss of her land to Lyman's bingo palace. When she laughs as a bear manitou, Fleur is surely thinking several moves ahead in the game; she is foreseeing conditions beyond the story told in this novel, conditions under which contemporary legal tricksters have been able to effect a kind of bingo justice.[53]

Erdrich's tricksters in *The Bingo Palace* are most successful when, like Fleur in *The Bingo Palace* and Nanapush in *Tracks*, they figure out how to set in motion traditional strategies and goals adapted to contemporary conditions. Erdrich's characters in *Tracks* are in the process of being redefined as Chippewa, and not as Anishinabeg; that is, they confront the various ways in which the dominant culture is defining their land, their identity, and their political status. To assert any measure of agency under these conditions, Nanapush learns to create false documents and learns to participate in alien and alienating discursive systems to achieve tribal goals. In *The Bingo Palace*, Erdrich's contemporary Chippewa learn to manipulate mass media and various postmodern technologies for their own purposes. In other words, Erdrich's novels suggest that postmodernism and native traditionalism are not incompatible and may, in fact, work together to create significant oppositional strategies.[54]

Erdrich's Chippewa live in a society driven by mass media, technology, and global commodification — a society and culture so saturated with images and representations that any connection with the Real — let alone Native American traditions — seems tenuous at best. But out of what some might call a dismal situation Erdrich creates new possibilities; her strong characters learn to put the new technologies to good use. Lipsha is one of those who learns to straddle the worlds of Native American traditions and postmodern technology. Waiting for spiritual insight on his vision quest, Lipsha finds that his head has become a tape deck: he "plays" audiotapes and videotapes in his mind, sometimes stopping to rewind and listen to or watch a particular moment again. Here is a contemporary version of oral memory.[55] Similarly, when the skunk from his vision quest later reappears to him, Lipsha invokes the language of both tradition and postmodernism: " 'Excuse me,' " Lipsha addresses the skunk, " 'I got the wrong vision. Could you change the channel?' " (*BP* 220). But the vision turns out to be the right one, for the skunk is a manitou who keeps repeating in slang "*This ain't real estate"* (*BP* 200, 218) to enable Lipsha to evaluate critically Lyman's plans for the bingo palace. Lipsha is able to see that "the money life has got no substance, there's nothing left when the day is done but a pack of receipts." And yet, he also glimpses Fleur's vision of bingo as a kind of trickster justice, in which "a clever operator . . . can use the luck that temporary loopholes in the law bring to Indians for higher causes, steady advances." Seeing this situation from two opposing vantage points, Lipsha significantly comments, "It's not completely one way or another, traditional against the bingo. You have to stay alive to keep your tradition alive and working" (*BP* 221).

Lipsha's both-and vision might be seen from a conventional standpoint as a wobbly ethical stance, but it closely resembles the version of postmodern ethics Jean-François Lyotard articulates in *Just Gaming.* Like Lipsha, Lyotard works against universal concepts of justice, asserting that "one must judge case by case."[56] Similarly, the language associated with bingo in Erdrich's novel—gaming, chance, play—is also the language of Lyotard's postmodernism. Moreover, Erdrich's concept of trickster justice is analogous to the double entendre of Lyotard's title, *Just Gaming,* meaning merely playing, but also meaning a playful kind of justice. For Lyotard, "Justice . . . does not consist merely in the observance of the rules; as in all . . . games, it consists in working at the limits of what the rules permit, in order to invent new moves, perhaps new rules and therefore new games."[57]

The invention of a new game happens literally in Erdrich's novel. Lipsha wins his van by playing a form of bingo that does not exist in practice: he chooses his own numbers (actually the numbers June's spirit has given him) and writes them down on a blank bingo card. If bingo players were allowed to do so in real games, certain players could—by studying the distribution of numbers called in games over time and by analyzing the most favorable array of numbers—create cards that would be much more likely to win; hence, the even-handed luck that characterizes bingo would be undermined. (In fact, this sense of impartial fairness is so important to the game that most bingo parlors will not allow players even to look through a stack of preprinted cards to select their own.) Moreover, as the efforts to amend the IGRA and to restrict gaming on Indian reservations suggest, bingo and casino income has enabled contemporary tribes to play if not a new game, then at least a game using new rules in their negotiations with state and federal governments.

Playing an old game by new rules through the combination of postmodern conditions and native traditions becomes extremely important in Erdrich's novel at the end when Lulu toys with the federal agents who are searching for her son, Gerry Nanapush, who has escaped from prison officials once again, this time via a "lucky" plane crash.[58] As they question her for information about Gerry, Lulu gives them the impression she is playing their game: she acts the part of a senile old Indian lady who doesn't quite have her wits about her and must circle around and around a subject before getting to the point. It takes forever for the agents to realize that Lulu might be leading them on a wild goose chase; meanwhile the communal "we" that narrates this episode is laughing and smiling behind the agents' backs, clearly understanding Lulu's machinations. Eventually, the duped agents decide to arrest Lulu — presumably for harboring stolen government property since she has taken and framed a post-office wanted poster of Gerry and has it on display in her apartment — but readers suspect they arrest her simply to save face and assert their authority. Again, however, Lulu gets the upper hand: as she walks handcuffed out of the old people's home, surrounded by muscle-bound agents, she wears full ceremonial dress and clutches her eagle-feather fan — and TV cameras record the moment to broadcast on "the six o'clock news, everywhere, all through the country" (*BP* 265). Lulu as a postmodern trickster in this final scene manipulates the situation so that the television cameras reproduce an image of police brutalizing a frail, old Indian lady — a representation that is both true, in the sense of the abusive treatment tribal people have experienced and continue to experience in that hands of legal officials and courts, as well as false, because readers know and respect Lulu's strength and cleverness.

While the cameras continue to roll, Lulu "dances the old-lady traditional, a simple step, but complex in its quiet balance, striking. She dances with a tucked-in wildness, exactly like an old-time Pillager" (*BP* 265). Her image functions as a spectacular reminder to viewers watching the six o'clock news across the country that Indians and their traditions continue to live and survive in the twentieth century, that the people are not docile victims who vanished at the end of the nineteenth century. And as the cameras continue to roll, Lulu begins "the old-lady trill, the victory yell that runs up our necks" (*BP* 265), prompting her tribal kin to join her. Lulu is clearly using the news media for her own purposes to circulate an electrifying image of triumphant native peoples. This image is efficacious not only for the audience of these newscasts but also for her own people: it is her trickster tactics, as well as her willingness to begin the trill by herself, that lift the people's hearts and move them to join her.

This moment of triumph, unprecedented in Erdrich's other novels, points to the possibility of a future for native peoples in which traditions and tribes are revitalized and strong, where the wheel of history—like the sacred hoop Black Elk speaks of—has revolved and is putting Native Americans on top. But Erdrich's novel does not end with Lulu's victory; her moment of triumph is only one of the five separate final chapters that bring the novel to a close. In these last chapters, Zelda finally recognizes her love for Xavier Toose, Lipsha is left in the middle of a blizzard in a stolen car cuddling a baby he has accidentally kidnapped, Shawnee Ray has left Lyman and dreams of Lipsha returning to her, and Fleur leaves Matchimanito to begin the journey toward the land of the spirits. In embracing such narrative complexity, Erdrich's novel resists a clear or firm resolution and strikes a balance between rebirth and death that is analogous to the situation of contemporary Native Americans. In fact, in contrast to the end of *Tracks* when Fleur leaves Matchimanito without leaving tracks, at the end of *The Bingo Palace*, Fleur's journey to the land of the spirits is marked, and uncannily her tracks remain: "Her tracks should have filled with snow," the collective narrator marvels. "They should have blown away with those rough songs from the wild dead we cannot hush. . . . And yet on clear and brilliant days and nights of black stars they are sometimes again left among us, Fleur's tracks, once more, so it is said that she still walks" (*BP* 273).

But as the collective narrator continues to reflect on Fleur's haunting presence, the possibility arises that the people are falling away from the traditional vision Fleur is associated with. The last reference to bingo and gaming for tribal peoples in the novel is ominous: "as we drown our past in love of chance" (*BP* 274). The phrase raises the critical question of how far traditions can be adapted to postmodern conditions and still be thought of as traditions. This dilemma is explored further in the very last paragraph of the novel as the collective narrator continues to meditate upon Fleur's presence in their lives: "You have heard the bear laugh — that is the chuffing noise we hear and it is unmistakable. Yet no matter how we strain to decipher the sound it never quite makes sense, never relieves our certainty or our suspicion that there is more to be told, more than we know, more than can be caught in the sieve of our thinking" (*BP* 274). Erdrich's novel does not end on a note of certainty or security; it ends with intense questioning — of what strategies are possible and appropriate for contemporary tribal peoples who wish to affirm their sovereignty and traditions in a postmodern world. The novel points toward the kind of postmodern local justice that Lyotard calls for in *Just Gaming*, by affirming the need not for secure and absolute answers, but for continual collective analysis of what is best for the people.

Like Erdrich's novel, Paul Pasquaretta's 1993 essay on the relation of bingo and gambling to "Indianness" ends with a question rather than a secure answer: "Will gambling provide a means to support the independent life of an indigenous community or contribute to the erasure of its boundaries and the complete assimilation of its people?"[59] In his detailed essay, Pasquaretta narrates the story of gambling at two different reservations, the tragic controversy at Akwesasne in New York state and the great success story of the Mashantucket Pequots in Connecticut. What is striking about the Pequot story is not just that the Pequots run the most successful gaming facilities in this country,[60] but that they were on the verge of extinction as recently as the 1940s when only one family lived on the reservation. In fact, the amazing rebirth story Pasquaretta narrates concerning the Pequots takes us back to Drex Brooks's photograph of the Mystic Massacre site discussed at the beginning of this chapter: the massacre of the Pequots in 1637 did not extinguish the people, despite the selling of able-bodied survivors into West Indian slavery and the distribution of the rest among neighboring tribes, nor despite the wording of the treaty they were forced to sign, a treaty "that declared them extinct as a people and forbade the use of their name forever."[61] The history of the Pequots is a story of despair and survival, of racist violence and Indian victory, of traditions that have been adapted to fit postmodern conditions. The history of the Pequots, like the history of the Chippewa that Erdrich's novels relate, cannot be told as a single story along clean lines; it is just as inadequate to dwell too much upon the massacre as too much upon economic success. The history of Native America, as the Pequot story and Erdrich's novels so compellingly demonstrate, continually exceeds conventional frames of reference, and so postmodern strategies become a necessary means for narrating and refiguring the past so that native identity, traditions, and spirits have a continuing vital presence in contemporary America.

Chapter Three
Toni Morrison and the Desire for a "Genuine Black History Book"

Toni Morrison, like Louise Erdrich, has devoted much of her career to crafting an extraordinary series of interconnected historical novels. The desire to create linked novels might be traced in part to the influence of William Faulkner on both authors. But there is an urgency to the projects Morrison and Erdrich are carrying out, a desire for history that is quite distinct from the tragic or nostalgic overtones of Faulkner's Yoknapatawpha. For Morrison and Erdrich, a keen sense of history is crucial for their characters and for their readers, not to be burdened by the past, but to tell a story of the past that can revitalize the present moment.

This chapter focuses on the particular dynamics and strategies Morrison employs in her historical trilogy: *Beloved* (1987), *Jazz* (1992), and *Paradise* (1998). Like Erdrich, Morrison strikes a useful and unusual mediatory stance between the claims of historical referentiality and the exigencies of postmodern culture. By exploring and retelling African American and Native American history through a series of linked novels, Morrison and Erdrich have charged these novels with epic intentions. An epic at the most basic level is the tale of the tribe, and by creating historical narratives that exceed the covers of any one book these authors are able to communicate the painful complexities, the sharp twists and turns of history for their people. Epics also hold great cultural weight; by aspiring to a comprehensive, or epic, view of history offered through their novels, Erdrich and Morrison are able to claim a cultural authority for their historical reconstructions that might not otherwise be available. And yet, there are considerable risks involved in laying claim to epic intentions in contemporary American culture. As authors aware of writing in a postmodern era characterized by twenty-second sound bites, glitzy images, and prepackaged narratives, Morrison and Erdrich face a serious struggle to command the sustained attention of an audience. Readers must be willing to journey through several novels, to commit the time to reckon with several hundred pages of intricate narrative lines and beguiling prose, often to arrive at tantalizing but ultimately open-ended conclusions. In such a context, Morrison's and Erdrich's epic impulses might seem to be sheer folly. But both authors remain keenly aware of what official histories do not record and of the limits of contemporary efforts to reconstruct "what really happened." As women writers of color endeavoring to make the silences of history speak, to make the absences of history palpable, Morrison and Erdrich necessarily rely on unorthodox and postmodern methods, methods that have led to criticisms of their novels as inaccurate or incomplete histories.

The title of Morrison's acclaimed essay "Unspeakable Things Unspoken: The Afro-American Presence in American Literature" signals her commitment to exploring the limits of official histories and the limits of memory. Some things are unspoken because reigning ideologies do not consider them worthy of notice. Other things are unspeakable because they are too traumatic to be remembered. Morrison's brilliant interpretation of Herman Melville's *Moby-Dick* in this essay, as well as her dazzling commentary on the opening lines of her own novels, demonstrates her emphasis on reading between the lines, on reading silence, absence, and words together. Originally delivered as the Tanner Lecture on Human Values at the University of Michigan on October 7, 1988, Morrison's essay appeared in a 1989 issue of *Michigan Quarterly Review* accompanied by two responses: one from Hazel Carby, the other from Eric Foner.[1] These responses function as supplements to Morrison's text, taking up and further developing certain strands of her lecture. Carby, not surprisingly, follows up on Morrison's remarks about canon building in the essay by providing compelling examples from her own teaching and research. If it is possible to miss the sometimes biting tone of Morrison's lyrical prose, Carby's analysis adamantly addresses what is at stake in the politics of canonization for the study of African American literature and culture. Merely including African American literature in the canon, as Carby points out, is not the goal, for it can too easily lend itself to mere accommodation; rather, a good faith inclusion of African American and other minority studies would lead to a profound, radical transformation of the exclusionary structures of power and knowledge that universities continue to operate under.

Like Carby, Foner begins his response by commending Morrison's observations about canon building and discussing their relevance to the field of American history and various efforts to revise that canon. But as his response unfolds, Foner veers away from the subject of canonization and into a critique of *Beloved*. The peculiar twist in Foner's argument occurs on the fourth page of his six-page response: just after criticizing Allan Bloom's and Lynne Cheney's efforts to promote the positive accomplishments of American history while suppressing or misremembering the horrors, Foner turns to *Beloved* as an articulation of Morrison's dissatisfaction with "the thrust of current writing about slavery."[2] As it turns out, Foner ironically becomes aligned with Bloom and Cheney in finding fault with the bleakness of Morrison's historical narrative.

Foner at first tries to explain his reaction by drawing distinctions between the kind of history historians write versus the kind novelists write: "Historians today stress the resiliency of the slave community, the creativity of blacks in forging a quasi-independent life for themselves within the oppressive confines of slavery, and their success in creating families and a sense of family tradition. Morrison's latest novel, *Beloved*, is in part a meditiation [*sic*] on the legacy of slavery, but she dwells more on disruption and degradation than resiliency and creativity."[3] Foner's distinctions are descriptive at first, but his analysis quickly becomes evaluative: "Morrison [does not] present anything but a pessimistic picture of the post-emancipation society her black characters inhabit. . . . As one who has studied this period for many years now, I see Reconstruction in a rather different light — as a remarkable time of hope, of accomplishment, of dreams, soon to be shattered, of a brighter future. Nothing that Morrison relates is 'untrue,' but she offers the reader no hint of the remarkable achievements of blacks in the *public* world in these years." The problem for Foner is that Morrison's bleak view is only a partial history; he would have her mention not only harsh realities such as rise of the Ku Klux Klan, economic exploitation of blacks, and denial of their basic rights, but also the hopeful achievements that were part of such an era. In fact, Foner's discomfort with Morrison's pessimistic historical reconstruction in *Beloved* becomes so acute that he can only weakly surmise what the point of this historical novel might be: "The book's lesson, *I suppose*, is that we cannot live in the past" (emphasis added).[4]

My purpose for looking closely at Foner's reaction to Morrison is not to criticize his views, but rather to use his ambivalent response to *Beloved* to suggest the ways in which boundaries between history and literature, between fact and fiction, have become destabilized under contemporary postmodern conditions. It is fascinating, after all, that Morrison's "Unspeakable Things Unspoken" essay should have responses from both a (black feminist) literary critic and a (white liberal) historian. Foner's response indicates the high level of anxiety that attends the destabilization of the lines between history and literature that a novel like *Beloved*, and its sequels *Jazz* and *Paradise*, embrace. As an academic historian, Foner is invested in documenting "what really happened" in the era of Reconstruction, and his response to *Beloved* betrays an anxiety that Morrison's novel might be (mis)taken as history (reality/fact), rather than as literature (imagination/fiction). Of course, the very origins of the novel, though he does not mention them, would reinforce such an anxiety, since Morrison's novel was inspired by newspaper accounts of the slave mother Margaret Garner, who became a cause célèbre of the abolitionist movement. *Jazz*, too, has its origins in documented history: Morrison was struck by the story behind a funereal photograph taken by the now-famous Harlem photographer, James Van Der Zee. And the impetus for *Paradise* arose from a recurring headline in a black newspaper, "Come Prepared or Not at All," that Morrison came across in her research for the novel.[5]

Despite his dismay that Morrison's historical sense in *Beloved* is (in his opinion) inaccurate and partial, Foner's analysis of the novel is extremely valuable in giving serious attention to *Beloved* as a history book — not just as fiction, in other words, but as "real" history. Like Foner, Morrison takes historical reconstruction seriously. Indeed, her novels have always demonstrated an interest in retelling African American history, but this reconstruction has taken a different turn in her most recent works. The characters in *The Bluest Eye* (1970) and *Sula* (1973) are defined by their history and trapped in their historical moment (the first novel opens in 1941, the year the United States entered World War II, and the second opens in 1919, just after the end of World War I); thus, they never find a way to create a life in the present that is not already determined by the past. *Song of Solomon* (1977), Morrison's third novel, represents a breakthrough in this respect: Milkman does not merely discover his family's history—he reconstructs it so that knowledge of the past functions not as a fixed explanation for the characters' present behavior, attitudes, and situations, but as a useful, dynamic construct. As in her subsequent novel *Tar Baby* (1981), it is significant in *Song of Solomon* that Morrison uses mythic sources to conceive of the past as dynamic and not fixed; myth allows the development of a historical consciousness that is not only factual or objective but constructive and fictional. In *Beloved, Jazz,* and *Paradise,* Morrison tries out her vision of a dynamic historical consciousness using more recalcitrant materials: actual historical accounts.

Like *Beloved, Jazz* is a historical novel that "fails" to represent its epoch properly: set in Harlem, the novel opens in 1926, in the heyday of the Harlem Renaissance, but it offers for full view almost none of the artistic, cultural, or political milestones that African Americans achieved in those years. In his brief review of the novel, Henry Louis Gates, Jr., notes this unexpected treatment, describing *Jazz* as "so near to—yet so far away from—the black literary movement known as the New Negro, or Harlem Renaissance."[6] Gates, perhaps feeling an urgency to fill in the details "missing" in Morrison's novel, spends the next two paragraphs providing references to some of the great black artistic accomplishments of 1926. He, for instance, cites Langston Hughes, who published both *The Weary Blues* and his influential essay "The Negro Artist and the Racial Mountain" in 1926, as well as Countee Cullen and Zora Neale Hurston, who launched *Fire!!* in that same year; he mentions Duke Ellington and Josephine Baker, who were incredibly popular in the mid twenties. And if we move beyond Gates's list, we might also observe that Morrison's novel does not name great black leaders, like W. E. B. DuBois and Marcus Garvey, who so passionately spoke out about civil rights and equality in those years. Though he praises Morrison's novel, Gates is like Foner in being perplexed by a historical novel that is set in such a significant era and yet ignores public history, "real" history, almost all together.

Paradise, which takes place between 1968 and 1976, follows this same strategy of bracketing the events of public history: the assassinations of Martin Luther King, Jr., and Robert Kennedy, the Watergate scandal, the rise of Black Power, the war in Vietnam—all are mentioned in passing in the novel without any elaboration or explanation. Astutely, in her review of *Paradise*, Christine Bold draws a connection between Morrison and Erdrich on this point, writing "The novel's action itself — much like Louise Erdrich's novels of Ojibway life — displaces not only whites but recognizable public history to its margins."[7] The question remains, however, as to why these writers, who ostensibly are interested in writing historical novels, in reshaping historical memory, would be almost deliberately antihistorical in their approach.

One way to begin to understand this paradox is to note that Morrison, like Erdrich, demonstrates great ambivalence about the practices of history. On the one hand, by using actual historical events and documents in *Beloved, Jazz,* and *Paradise,* Morrison brings attention to the traumas of history that have been rendered "unspeakable" and "unspoken." On the other hand, Morrison sees clearly the inadequacies of conventional historiography for reconstructing an African American history that will be profoundly meaningful or vital to her readers, especially her black readers. In fact, more than a decade before she began work on her own historical trilogy, while she was a senior editor at Random House, Morrison became involved with designing, assembling, and publishing an unconventional historical text called *The Black Book.* A close look at this project, and Morrison's statements about it, provides a valuable framework for understanding the choices Morrison would subsequently make regarding her own historical reconstruction in *Beloved, Jazz,* and *Paradise.*

The Black Book and African American History

The Black Book (1974) resembles a scrapbook: it assembles a wealth of visual and verbal materials, such as news clippings, photographs and etchings, quotations from black leaders and writers, bits of folk wisdom, songs and poems, jokes, sayings, and gossip. Its implicit definition of what counts as history is expansive, as it includes not only the kinds of documents that are the basis of conventional historical accounts, but also materials from popular culture — posters, ads, songs, sheet music, and so on — as well as nuggets of black folk wisdom — recipes, household hints, and various instructions on how to interpret dream visions to play the numbers or how to cast a hex or assemble a good luck charm, for instance. In one of the essays she published at the time she was working on this project, Morrison explained why it was important that *The Black Book* be so inclusive in its selections: "Historians must necessarily speak in generalities and must examine recorded sources: statistics on income earned, books by activists and leaders, dates, etc. . . . They habitually leave out life lived by everyday people. History for them is what great men have done. But artists don't have any such limitation, and as the truest of historians they are obligated not to." A few paragraphs later, Morrison describes *The Black Book* as "a genuine Black history book — one that simply recollected Black Life as lived."[8]

Why was such an alternative history text necessary? Why was "Black Life as lived" in such danger of being unrecorded? Morrison's comments on this project suggest the limitations of the kind of public history both Foner and Gates seem to want her to engage in: public history is so ideologically invested in the accomplishments of great white men that such a history would miss the ordinary black people — like the black men and women in Morrison's novels — trying to have a "livable life" (*B* 198).[9] In fact, *The Black Book* is so concerned with conveying "Black Life as lived" that the final section presents six pages of photographs and sketched portraits of various black men and women and children from all walks of life; remarkably, not one of these individuals is identified or named. The anonymity of these faces in the final pages of *The Black Book* reinforces Morrison's insistence on everyday life and ordinary black people as the foundation for a genuine black history.

These faces also suggest the subtle, yet significant pedagogical imperative of *The Black Book*. It was deliberately created as a collective enunciation, a gathering of information that would traditionally be passed along orally from one generation to the next in a thriving black community. But the status of this knowledge as written (not oral) text indicates that the transmission of such wisdom was becoming erratic and unreliable, and so *The Black Book* was designed to pass along African American collective memories that were in danger of being forgotten. As Morrison explains in an essay entitled "Rediscovering Black History" from 1974 (the same year *The Black Book* appeared), black history was in need of rediscovery in part because scholarly accounts of American history continued to focus on Anglo-Americans and thus failed to recognize black people as central to the story of America. But in this same essay Morrison also criticizes "the new black history" that grew out of the

Black Power movement as a kind of history more interested in "exoticism" than "reality." She argues that in abandoning the past to try "to cure the cancer of slavery and its consequences, some healthy as well as malignant cells were destroyed." Black revisionist history, Morrison points out, thus repudiated not only slavery, but any knowledge of "those qualities of resistance, excellence, and integrity" that were also a significant part of the African American past.[10]

One important function *The Black Book* served was to recover from obscurity positive and admirable qualities of ordinary black people in America. It includes pages of notable accomplishments: numerous patents taken out by black inventors for such things as overshoes, an "air-ship," a telephone system, an improved fountain pen, a corn harvester, a street sweeper, an egg beater; stories and photos of great successes, including black millionaires, the black physician (Dr. Daniel Hale Williams) who performed the first successful open heart surgery in 1893, talented performers such as Count Basie and Lena Horne, outstanding athletes like Joe Louis and Satchel Paige; records showing that blacks were significant landholders in New York in the 1600s; photographs of amazing quilts and other handiwork created by slaves. It also recovered historical incidents almost too painful to bear witness to. *The Black Book* did not flinch when it came to including traumatic materials — photographs of lynchings, a notice announcing that all the "cells" in a lunatic asylum for blacks were filled, an excerpt from a letter written to W. E. B. DuBois from a white scholar at Clark University inquiring "whether the Negro sheds tears," ads that depict crude caricatures of blacks to promote various products (the one for Sunlight Soap features a plump black girl in a dazzling white dress and a slogan extolling the product's virtues — "so clean and white").[11] Considering these images, it is no wonder the "new black history" wanted to wipe out the past. *The Black Book* also includes records that complicate racial relations: documents of black slaveholders; stories of whites who were beaten, branded, and killed for helping blacks escape; and records of black infantrymen attacking American Indians.

In addition to its content, the most stunning quality of *The Black Book* is its unique, unconventional design. "It has no 'order,' no chapters, no major themes," Morrison warns prospective readers. "But it does have coherence and sinew. It can be read or browsed through from the back forwards or from the middle out, either way."[12] Although it is a history text, *The Black Book* interestingly eschews the conventional chronology and organization of typical history books. It is organized according to narrative or thematic clusters — such as the slave trade, blacks on the frontier, and black music — and within each of these sections, visual and verbal texts are placed next to each other without any authorial or narrative commentary to make transitions or connections, or to tell readers what to think. On one page, for instance, readers are told about the struggle of black doctors to gain professional respect and recognition through the following snippet: "In 1919, after a bitter struggle, a black physician was placed on the staff of Harlem Hospital, situated in the heart of the black capital of the world and serving a predominately black clientele." Despite its brevity, this anecdote is richly ambiguous. Is the narrative voice reporting this 1919 event as an accomplishment or sardonically calling attention to the irony that for many years black doctors were not allowed to treat black patients in Harlem, of all places? The reading of this small clipping becomes even more resonant when considered along with the item that follows it: "In the early 1930's, the wife of W. C. Handy (Father of the Blues), died on the doorstep of Sydenham Hospital, which refused to admit her on the ground that it was a private hospital and that she would have to be taken to a city hospital."[13] Despite the reportorial tone of this item, we can discern that racism, and not a private/public distinction, lies behind the failure to take care of this woman. Comparing the dates of the two anecdotes is also useful: evidently the breakthrough accomplishment at Harlem Hospital in 1919 did not lead to unmitigated progress for black people, since more than a decade later, Handy's wife — despite his fame — could not gain admission to a private white hospital even to save her life. *The Black Book* is filled with similarly revealing juxtapositions like this one. Without any clear narrative pattern to the text or the voice of a single authoritative author/narrator, the reader must learn to reckon with "Black Life as lived" in all of its fascinating and heartbreaking contradictions. The unorthodox historiographical practices of *The Black Book* produce a reading experience that is complex and intense, that can take very different shapes and directions, and that is accompanied by a wide range of emotions — laughter, anger, joy, shock, dismay, pride.

With its unusual design and range of topics, *The Black Book* serves as a valuable primer for reading black culture and history—a text that could perhaps supplant the all-too-familiar and disabling Dick-and-Jane primer passage that Morrison uses to open *The Bluest Eye*. Clearly, *The Black Book* as a history text was intended to address a kind of historical amnesia in America, and it succeeds tremendously at repairing gaps in the historical record. But what about historical memory? Even if records of the past are recoverable and are recovered, they do not necessarily become part of collective historical memory, particularly when they are as painful as some of the material included in *The Black Book*. When Morrison began to create her own historical fictions, she faced this dilemma: Is it enough for genuine black history to rediscover records, documents, and information concerning the all-too-often invisible presence and value of African Americans in America? Or does black history have to do more—to enable black people to face the past and remember it so that they can have a present and future worth living? As she began to work on *Beloved* and the intensely painful historical case that inspired it, Morrison found a way to address these questions and to create her own anguished, but "genuine Black history book."

The (Im)Possibility of Historical Recovery in *Beloved*

The Black Book and *Beloved* are connected projects in several ways.[14] Morrison came across the story of Margaret Garner's desperate act of infanticide when she was working on *The Black Book*.[15] This story about an escaped slave's decision to slit the throat of her baby and to try to kill her other children rather than see them returned to slavery came to haunt Morrison, and in one of the essays she wrote about *The Black Book*, Morrison describes the overwhelming impression this story had on her: "I . . . lived through a despair quite new to me but so deep it had no passion at all and elicited no tears."[16] This profound and inarticulate response would prompt Morrison to fashion a language and form that could penetrate and communicate such despair, and so the gripping story of Margaret Garner became the narrative core of the novel Morrison worked on a decade later.

The Black Book did not just furnish the central story of *Beloved*, however; it also provided a particular model of how to reconstruct

African American history, a model to which *Beloved* subscribes. There are, for instance, moments of extreme discomfort and utter despair in *Beloved*; like *The Black Book*, Morrison's novel does not avoid depicting the brutalities of slavery.[17] The terrors of the Middle Passage, during which African women are raped by white crew members; the torturing of slaves who refuse to become docile and subservient (Sethe's mother, Sixo); the administration of beatings so severe that they leave permanent indelible marks on a person, like the "tree" on Sethe's back; the "neck jewelry" Paul D is forced to wear; the dehumanizing "bit" that was placed in the mouths of disobedient slaves — these are the unspeakable things unspoken of in most nineteenth-century slave narratives that *Beloved* dares to put forward. In this sense, Morrison's novel aims to set the historical record straight by bringing to consciousness such terrible realities, which understandably might be willfully forgotten.[18] And given these historical exigencies, Sethe's "rough motherlove" is perhaps not so monstrous as it might seem outside of such a context.[19]

But Morrison's novel does not dwell only on the victimizing of blacks under slavery (as Stanley Elkins's infamous analysis does); like *The Black Book*, *Beloved* brings into view tremendous acts of resistance and courage alongside moments of utter dehumanization. Sixo roams beyond the confines of Sweet Home, joins his "Thirty Mile Woman" at night, and learns of the Underground Railroad that might take them all to freedom. A trickster in his own right, Sixo takes a young pig from the plantation under schoolteacher's reign and spectacularly argues that he is entitled to it in order to make schoolteacher's property increase. Even as he burns alive, Sixo shouts out jubilantly "Seven-O" to announce the continuation of his spirit in the baby that the Thirty Mile Woman is carrying. Collectivity is another means of resistance and sustenance that *Beloved* shares with *The Black Book*. The collective enunciation of black people is felt in the Clearing where Baby Suggs urges her listeners to love themselves; it is felt in the community of slaves at Sweet Home and in the group of singing women in Ohio who prevent Sethe from being overwhelmed by Beloved's needs and from repeating another act of murder. Both *Beloved* and *The Black Book* give culturally significant instructions on the necessity of community and collective action for African Americans.

Thinking of the community and not just self-advancement is a hard lesson to articulate in the capitalist economies of late twentieth-century America during which Morrison has come to prominence, and so *Beloved*, like *The Black Book*, explores experimental forms to find a language adequate to this task. *Beloved* is a magically simple story, like a myth or fairy tale, and, at the same time, a deliberately difficult, convoluted narrative. In her 1984 essay "Rootedness: The Ancestor As Foundation," Morrison argues that "the novel is needed by African-Americans now in a way that it was not needed before. . . . We don't live in places where we can hear those stories anymore; parents don't sit around and tell their children those classical, mythological archetypal stories that we heard years ago." The novel takes up the traditional function of oral tales and mythic legends to convey the inherited wisdom of a people, but Morrison also adds that since the novel has its origins in European culture and values, black writers must employ "unorthodox novelistic characteristics" to convey the "discredited knowledge" of black people.[20] And so Morrison's *Beloved* eschews linear plot and progressivist teleology; it brings a dead baby back to life (as a ghost?) and creates exquisite lyrical prose to enunciate the passionate reclaiming of black mother and daughter bonds, despite the legacy of slavery.[21]

One kind of discredited knowledge that *Beloved* is particularly interested in exploring is historical knowledge. In "The Site of Memory," Morrison observes that her "job" as "a writer in the last quarter of the twentieth century, not much more than a hundred years after Emancipation, a writer who is black and a woman," is "to rip that veil drawn over 'proceedings too terrible to relate' " in nineteenth-century slave narratives. But Morrison also points out that because of certain discursive constraints (genre conventions, the interests of abolitionists, and so on), "the unwritten interior life of these people" can only be accessed through the imagination.[22] These comments suggest the interesting paradox that drives *Beloved*: a commitment to historical recovery and referentiality (encountered immediately in the novel's controversial epigraph, "Sixty Million / and more")[23] along with an incisive critique of the possibility of carrying out such recovery efforts.[24] From its opening moments, *Beloved* demonstrates the slippage between the past and our memories of it: while a great deal of attention has been given to its representation of slavery, the novel, in point of fact, opens in 1873 — a decade after the Emancipation Proclamation and nearly twenty years after Sethe and Paul D have left Sweet Home.

The discrepancy between history as a record of the past and history as a reconstruction of the past creates the rich texture of Morrison's historical novel and implicates Morrison's project in the larger battles over history that have emerged in the late twentieth century. *Beloved*, despite being set in the nineteenth century, works toward a problematic view of historical reconstruction that we have come to associate with twentieth-century postmodernism.[25] *Beloved* strikingly demonstrates that historical reconstruction is always already compromised, that any attempt to recover African American history will inevitably be haunted by that which can never be recovered. Like the cut that severs Beloved's neck, there are wounds that cannot be sutured, gaps that cannot be filled, losses that can be mourned but not transcended.

One limitation on the possibility of recovering nineteenth-century African American experience that *Beloved* calls attention to involves discursive constraints. *Beloved* dramatizes the numerous ways in which the white slavocracy exercises its power to define the experience and identity of slaves. Even a benevolent slaveholder like Mr. Garner employs this privilege of definition: he boasts to other slaveholders that unlike them he has "men" who work for him. His power to name his slaves "men," however, calls into question their very experience of "manhood," as Paul D later reflects: "For years Paul D believed schoolteacher broke into children what Garner had raised into men. And it was that that made them run off. Now, plagued by the contents of his tobacco tin, he wondered how much difference there really was between before schoolteacher and after. Garner called and announced them men — but only on Sweet Home, and by his leave. Was he naming what he saw or creating what he did not?" (*B* 220). This final question is ultimately undecidable; Garner's words constitute a discourse that constructs and determines Paul D's vision of his own experience so that he cannot subsequently ascertain whether he indeed was a man at Sweet Home or not. No amount of contemplation on the past will provide a secure answer to this haunting question. Asking the question in the present moment, however, does enable Paul D to reflect critically on the past and to arrive at his own model of black manhood, a model that creates the conditions under which he and Sethe join together to look for a future with one another.

A more pernicious example of the power of whites to define coercively the terms of African American experience is embodied in the character of schoolteacher. As many scholars have noted, schoolteacher is associated with the power of writing and documentation. The documents he instructs his nephews to produce are part of various Euro-American "scientific" and "objective" practices such as law and history, which conveniently become the means for asserting white colonialist interests. " 'No, no. That's not the way. I told you to put her human characteristics on the left; her animal ones on the right. And don't forget to line them up' " (*B* 193) — overhearing schoolteacher's instructions makes Sethe so profoundly ill that she does not speak of this trauma to anyone, not even Halle, her husband, until years later when she tries to explain herself to Beloved. As she tells this story to Beloved, Sethe emphasizes that, after overhearing these instructions, they should have made plans immediately to leave Sweet Home. Sethe recognizes schoolteacher's words and "logic" as almost a greater threat to blacks than the material conditions of slavery itself; she discerns that his instructions promote an unspeakable terror and violence. This moment in the narrative also has a significant metahistorical purpose: a history based on the records schoolteacher instructs his nephews to prepare is utterly useless for understanding African American history, and so Morrison's novel pointedly deconstructs conventional Euro-American scientific historiographical practices.

Given the degree to which any understanding of African Americans in the nineteenth century is necessarily compromised by the ways in which whites defined, recorded, and interpreted the lives of black men and women — not just to other whites but to blacks themselves — Morrison's historical account is inevitably marked by absences and silences. Sethe's two sons, Howard and Buglar, walk off one day and disappear; their names are mentioned throughout the novel, not to anticipate their return, but to remind the reader continually of huge gaps that can never be filled. Years after Baby Suggs's death, Sethe longs to return to the Clearing where Baby preached, not to re-create Baby's voice but "to listen to the spaces that the long-ago singing had left behind" (*B* 89). Such absences and silences are caused not just by epistemological limits, but also by the trauma of the past. In her 1990 essay " 'Somebody Forgot to Tell Somebody Something': African-American Women's Historical Novels," Barbara Christian points out that contemporary black women writers such as Morrison create historical fictions to present stories of the past that have been forgotten or ignored not only by the white dominant society but also by the black community. Drawing on comments from Morrison's 1977 interview with Ntozake Shange, Christian notes that the "upwardly mobile African-Americans of the forties and fifties" did not want to pass down stories of enslavement, dispossession, and despair to their children, thus leaving gaps in their children's understanding of African American history that novels such as *Beloved* attempt to redress.[26]

This problem of narrating a traumatic past is at the heart of the novel: Sethe is willing to tell Paul D of the painful incident when schoolteacher and his nephews hold her down and steal her milk, but she does not or cannot tell him of her decision to take the life of her "crawling already?" baby rather than see her returned to slavery. So Paul D learns of Sethe's infamy from the newspaper article that Stamp Paid shows him,[27] and Stamp Paid begins to wonder "How did information that had been in the newspaper become a secret that needed to be whispered in a pig yard?" (*B* 169). Memory as trauma also surfaces in the image of Paul D's heart as a "tobacco tin buried in his chest . . . its lid rusted shut" (*B* 72–73) and in the story of his imprisonment in Alfred, Georgia, which he cannot tell anyone, not even Sethe. The problem of memory becomes so acute that Sethe realizes early on that "she could not remember remembering" (*B* 39). Given the trauma of remembering, it is not possible for *Beloved* merely to rediscover or recover black history; the novel, like *The Black Book*, must confront the problem of locating and articulating "genuine" black history.

The concept of "rememory" is one way in which the novel addresses the problem of "disremembering" and absence. Early in the novel, Sethe tells Denver, " 'Some things you forget. Other things you never do. . . . Places, places are still there. If a house burns down, it's gone, but the place — the picture of it — stays, and not just in my rememory, but out there, in the world. What I remember is a picture floating around out there outside my head. I mean, even if I don't think it, even if I die, the picture of what I did, or knew, or saw is still out there. Right in the place where it happened.' " Denver eagerly grasps the potential of Sethe's description of rememory as a thought-picture that exists independently in the world and immediately wants to know, "Can other people see it?" Sethe answers:

"Oh, yes. Oh, yes, yes, yes. Someday you be walking down the road and you hear something or see something going on. So clear. And you think it's you thinking it up. A thought picture. But no. It's when you bump into a rememory that belongs to somebody else. Where I was before I came here, that place is real. It's never going away. Even if the whole farm — every tree and grass blade of it dies. The picture is still there and what's more, if you go there — you who never was there — if you go there and stand in the place where it was, it will happen again; it will be there for you, waiting for you. So, Denver, you can't ever go there. Never. Because even though it's all over — over and done with — it's going to always be there waiting for you." (*B* 36)

The description of rememory as a "thought picture" suggests that memories are not unmediated recollections of the past, but narratively (re)constructed images. The power of such narrative reconstructions — time capsules of past moments, as it were — is made clear in this passage. Rememories are potentially dangerous for Denver in that the experience of slavery, an experience which she has not directly encountered and which Sethe struggled so tragically to prevent her children from ever having, might be conferred upon her through rememories of Sweet Home. (Here the "cancer" of slavery that the new black history worked so hard to excise is unavoidably malignant.)

Walter Benn Michaels reads this potential somewhat differently: he sees it as symptomatic of a misguided, naïve contemporary American obsession with gaining access to or claiming experiences we have not had.[28] But Morrison's concept of rememory does not offer any direct, or unmediated access to these experiences or memories: as "re" — the unusual prefix that Morrison appends to the root word "memory" — suggests, rememories are always already narrative constructions. Rather than trying to make available to readers experiences which they have not had and cannot have directly, rememory offers a strategic negotiation into a slightly different contemporary preoccupation: the crisis of referentiality that surrounds history in a postmodern era. Rememories remain, even when all witnesses to an event are dead, even if the landscape and buildings and scenery of a momentous event are eradicated or fall into oblivion. Morrison's concept of rememory insists that some narratives of the past can be so powerful that they can (productively or dangerously) haunt the living.

In her evocative reading of haunting and history in *Beloved*, Avery Gordon writes, "To be haunted is to be tied to historical and social effects."[29] In Morrison's novel, the most concrete instance of a rememory that comes to haunt the living involves the character of

Beloved. She is first of all a figure of uncertain status—Is she real or a figment of the imagination? Is she Sethe's murdered baby returned or a delusional young black woman escaped from sexual abuse at the hands of white masters? And if she is the "crawling already?" baby returned, is she alive or a ghost? Her ambiguous position or substance in the novel makes visible and tangible the problem of historical memory. Beloved is the past brought to life fictionally and metafictionally. Interestingly enough, though, Beloved's return as a literal figure of the past does not provide firm answers or clear resolution. She sets in motion certain paths of self-exploration for Sethe, Paul D, and Denver, but she can speak and think of only herself and her own needs. As a figure of/for the past, Beloved warns against a kind of history based solely on the recovery of past details or the repetition of one monologic story (a point Morrison develops much further in *Paradise*). Near the end of the book, Paul D tells Sethe, " 'me and you, we got more yesterday than anybody. We need some kind of tomorrow' " (*B* 273). In this way, Morrison's novel signals the need for a kind of history that is not solely obsessed with analyzing the past in itself (a kind of antiquarianism), but explores the past in order to create some kind of livable present and future.

If *Beloved* ended at this point—when Paul D and Sethe begin to join together to create the possibility of a future for themselves—the novel might be read as a positive statement about reconstructing African American history by facing the past directly and taking it into account. But it does not end at this moment. Rather, the last two pages of the novel create a coda that calls into question many of the premises of historical recovery.[30] The repeated phrase "It was not a story to pass on" (*B* 274, 275) might be taken to advocate both the need to remember and the need to forget. This potential contradiction in meaning signals the fundamental ambivalence of the novel regarding historical memories attached to traumatic events. In other words, the story of Beloved is so agonizing that to remember and understand it fully simultaneously sets in motion an urgent desire to forget. Under these conditions, historical memory must necessarily be imperfect, and the narrative created from it will be occupied by irreparable gaps and silences.

The coda also calls attention to a perplexing mystery in the novel involving Beloved's name. "Everybody knew what she was called, but nobody anywhere knew her name. Disremembered and unaccounted for, she cannot be lost because no one is looking for her, and even if they were, how can they call her if they don't know her name?" (*B* 274) — everyone wants to disremember Beloved in this passage from the coda, and the most convenient way to do so is to forget her name so that they cannot even call out to her. Furthermore, by drawing a key distinction between "what she was called" and "her name," the passage follows up on a brief but significant recollection of Denver's — that she recognized Beloved as "soon as she spelled her name — not her given name, but the one Ma'am paid the stonecutter for" (*B* 208). Given this evidence, readers have to wonder, What is Beloved's given name? Why is it never revealed in the novel? And why does Sethe have the tombstone engraved with the name "Beloved" (taken from the phrase "Dearly Beloved" that the preacher says at the graveside ceremony) and not with Beloved's given name? Although it is possible that the naming of a baby might not be coincident with birth, surely a "crawling already?" baby would be old enough to have been given a personal name.[31] Sethe, evidently, has forgotten the name she gave this child, which might be read as a willful, though understandable and initially therapeutic, forgetting. The coda, thus, reminds us that the name Beloved bears witness to a part of the past that will never be fully recovered.

Moreover, the coda offers a glimpse into the future when even the returned Beloved (and not just her name) is eventually forgotten:

> They forgot her like a bad dream. After they made up their tales, shaped and decorated them, those that saw her that day on the porch quickly and deliberately forgot her. It took longer for those who had spoken to her, lived with her, fallen in love with her, to forget, until they realized they couldn't remember or repeat a single thing she said, and began to believe that, other than what they themselves were thinking, she hadn't said anything at all. So, in the end, they forgot her too. Remembering seemed unwise. (*B* 274)

In this passage, there is no difference between those who have direct experience of Beloved and those who do not; both parties eventually dismiss her from their personal memories and collective memory — it simply takes a little longer for those who knew her to complete this process. Morrison's novel thus undercuts the idea that witnesses of events are reliable sources of "what really happened," and in this way *Beloved* calls into question one of the foundations of conventional history.

At the same time, however, Morrison's novel makes an appeal similar to that of *The Black Book* in terms of urging the community to hold on to its memories, no matter how traumatic they might be. Despite the willful amnesia that occurs in the novel and especially in the coda, something remains to register the existence of Beloved: "Sometimes the photograph of a close friend or relative — looked at too long — shifts, and something more familiar than the dear face itself moves there" (*B* 275). An otherworldly spirit — a familiar — appears in the familiar photograph, marking the liminal presence of Beloved, as do the footprints "in back of 124" that "come and go, come and go" (*B* 275). Though the penultimate paragraph of the novel evokes what can never be re-remembered, it too moves on to notice something that lingers: "By and by all trace is gone, and what is forgotten is not only the footprints but the water too and what it is down there. The rest is weather. Not the breath of the disremembered and unaccounted for, but wind in the eaves, or spring ice thawing too quickly. Just weather. Certainly no clamor for a kiss" (*B* 275). Even without a trace marking her now-forgotten existence, some part of Beloved remains as weather — as the very climate or conditions in which we take breath. No one clamors yet for her return or to embrace her memory, but the final word of the novel, set off in its own paragraph — "Beloved" — attempts to initiate such a clamor with its double meaning — "Be loved."[32]

The project of embracing a traumatic past, however, is ultimately beyond the scope of *Beloved*. Morrison's first novel in her historical trilogy concentrates on the traumatic memories that surface in any attempt to reconstruct African American history: *Beloved* demonstrates only too well why the "new black history" that Morrison criticized in her essays from the 1970s for shunning "the cancer of slavery" would be motivated to do so. But a solution to this denial is not so easy to reach, for cancer / slavery and a traumatic past are not willingly embraced. *Beloved*, ironically, is as pessimistic as Foner claims it is: its pessimism, however, is not just confined to its representation of Reconstruction but extends to the larger project of reconstructing African American history. But along with this pessimism is desire — the clamor for Beloved's kiss — that is summoned up as a lack at the end of the novel. It will be the project of Morrison's second novel in the trilogy, *Jazz*, to create the conditions out of which "a clamor for a kiss," a collective embracing of the past, may arise.

Jazz and Collective Rememory

Morrison originally thought the stories that form the narrative core of *Beloved* and *Jazz* would be told in the same novel.[33] In her interview/conversation with Gloria Naylor from 1985, Morrison explained that Margaret Garner's decision to kill her children to keep them out of slavery became intertwined for her with the story behind James Van Der Zee's funereal photograph of a young black woman, beautifully dressed and coiffed, resting in a satin-lined coffin. The woman had been shot by her former lover at a party, but did not tell anyone of the shooting, and the people surrounding her noticed only when she collapsed that there was blood on her. She refused medical treatment and refused to summon the police, evidently in order to let her lover escape, and so she died. In both of these stories, Morrison explains to Naylor, "a woman loved something other than herself so much. She had placed all of the value of her life in something outside herself."[34]

Morrison was very familiar with Van Der Zee's photographs; in fact, she wrote the foreword to his 1978 collection of death portraits called *The Harlem Book of the Dead*, in which the photograph and the compelling story behind it were published. It is striking, however, that when Morrison discusses the subject with Naylor, she dwells on the story and not the image. Van Der Zee's funereal portrait is marked by his characteristic attention to aesthetics: the framing, the lighting, the composition of the scene engage the viewer in such visual pleasure that the mournful subject matter of the photo and its underlying narrative can almost be overlooked. Perhaps it was the dissonance between the beauty of this photo and the singular story of the young black woman featured in it that captured Morrison's attention, for in her foreword, Morrison draws attention to the paradoxical qualities of Van Der Zee's death portraits: "The narrative quality, the intimacy, the humanity of his photographs are stunning, and the proof, if any is needed, is in this collection of pictures devoted exclusively to the dead about which one can only say, 'How living are his portraits of the dead.' "[35] Morrison focuses neither on the aesthetic or compositional aspects of these harmonious photographs, nor on their historical or documentary dimensions in recording a common practice in Harlem of the twenties and thirties. Rather, she emphasizes their "narrative quality" — their ability to tell a story that makes a picture come to life. Mor-

"I'll Tell You Tomorrow" (1926), from *The Harlem Book of the Dead*. Photograph by James Van Der Zee. © Donna Mussenden Van Der Zee.

rison's observations about Van Der Zee are significant in locating the emphasis of her own historical practice, which dwells not on the photograph but on the story that accompanies it, not on mere facts or documents but on the narrative that makes use of them.

The opening of *Jazz* illustrates this distinction. In the first few pages we are given almost all the facts pertaining to the tragic triangulated relationship at the center of the novel. We learn that Joe and Violet Traces' thirty-some-year marriage is troubled: Violet, who has been childless by chance and perhaps by choice, desires a baby now that it is biologically too late for her to have one of her own, and Joe, who has become distanced from her, begins an affair with Dorcas, a young woman of eighteen who seems too self-indulgent for most of the novel to be worthy of Joe's passion and devotion. And most important, we are told immediately that a desperate Joe has shot and killed Dorcas, after learning that she was stepping out on him, and that Violet, shocked by the knowledge of Joe's betrayal, has become violent, going to Dorcas's funeral with a knife in hand to cut her rival's face. Just when we might think there is nothing left to find out about this story, the narrative takes a peculiar twist: Violet decides to learn everything she can about the dead girl, going so far as to visit Dorcas's aunt, Alice Manfred, and to bring home a picture of Dorcas that she sets prominently on the mantle.

The photograph of Dorcas that Violet and Joe gaze upon is not a stable image, but is changeable, like the image of the photograph that shifts familiarly as the viewer contemplates it in the closing pages of *Beloved*. Taking turns in their restless nights to get out of bed and look at the photograph, Joe and Violet catch very different glimpses of Dorcas:

If the tiptoer is Joe Trace, driven by loneliness from his wife's side, then the face stares at him without hope or regret and it is the absence of accusation that wakes him from his sleep hungry for her company. No finger points. Her lips don't turn down in judgment. Her face is calm, generous and sweet. But if the tiptoer is Violet the photograph is not that at all. The girl's face looks greedy, haughty and very lazy. The cream-at-the-top-of-the-milkpail face of someone who will never work for anything; someone who picks up things lying on other people's dressers and is not embarrassed when found out. It is the face of a sneak who glides over to your sink to rinse the fork you have laid by her plate. An inward face—what it sees is its own self. (*J*12)

The image in the photograph literally remains the same for both viewers, but clearly its meanings shift, contingent on the interests Joe and Violet bring to it. Both Joe and Violet use this photograph to try to find secure answers to the questions and anxieties that plague them, but the photograph as an object in itself (like any fact or document) does not provide useful explanations. Like the uncanny photograph that appears at the end of *Beloved*, however, the photograph of Dorcas in *Jazz* does create a sharp desire for some kind of critical understanding, and so Joe and Violet begin to reach back into the more distant past to re-collect the stories that will enable them to comprehend their present situation.

The problem for them, as it is for Sethe and Paul D in *Beloved*, is that Joe and Violet have spent most of their lives forgetting or, as Morrison calls it in *Beloved*, "beating back the past" (*B* 73). Having left Vesper County, Virginia, in 1906 aboard a train called the Southern Sky heading north, Joe and Violet hoped to leave behind past disappointments and dispossession and begin a new, brighter life. They eventually arrive in Harlem, the promised land for "the wave of black people," like them, "running from want and violence" (*J* 33). By 1926, when the novel opens, Harlem seems to be the site of a new historical epoch. The narrator describes the feeling in the air: "Here comes the new. Look out. There goes the sad stuff. The bad stuff. The things-nobody-could-help stuff. The way everybody was then and there. Forget that. History is over, you all, and everything's ahead at last" (*J* 7). "History" in this passage is understood as the bad stuff that has happened (in the South) in the past; like slavery, it is something to be gotten over, to be left behind literally in the Great Migration, to be forgotten (like Beloved). Despite the promise of Harlem to be posthistorical, however, Joe and Violet find that the past comes along to haunt them, that they have to reckon with "the sad stuff," "the bad stuff" in order to resuscitate themselves as individuals and as a couple. This narrative movement does, and should, remind us of *Beloved*.

Morrison's historical novels are structured recursively; that is, the narration of present events is continually interrupted by the telling of "background" stories. The nature of these stories from the past tells us something about Morrison's definition of historical. Neither *Beloved* nor *Jazz* is much interested in narrating fictionalized stories of monumental events. In fact, the tendency in both novels is simply to make passing references to History with a capital H, as this passage from *Beloved* shows: "No more discussions, stormy or quiet, about the true meaning of the Fugitive Bill, the Settlement Fee, God's Ways and Negro pews; antislavery, manumission, skin voting, Republicans, Dred Scott, book learning, Sojourner's high-wheeled buggy, the Colored Ladies of Delaware, Ohio, and the other weighty issues that held them in chairs, scraping the floorboards or pacing them in agony or exhilaration" (*B* 173). By creating such a list, Morrison is not dismissing the significance of these public and political issues for African Americans, but she is insisting that a useful black history not be solely concerned with such matters. At the same time, Morrison continually prompts her readers to consider what does not get recorded about the realities of black life in America, as Stamp Paid's anguished reflections from *Beloved* suggest: "Eighteen seventy-four and whitefolks were still on the loose. Whole towns wiped clean of Negroes; eighty-seven lynchings in one year alone in Kentucky; four colored schools burned to the ground; grown men whipped like children; children whipped like adults; black women raped by the crew; property taken, necks broken. He smelled skin, skin and hot blood. The skin was one thing, but human blood cooked in a lynch fire was a whole other thing. The stench stank" (*B* 180).[36] Passages in *Jazz* also summon up images of racist violence against blacks that goes unmentioned in the mainstream newspapers and hence does not become part of the public record or monumental history. These terrible events remain visible only because of the collective memory that people like Stamp Paid and Ella and Baby Suggs in *Beloved*, or Joe Trace and Felice's father and Alice Manfred in *Jazz* sustain. Morrison's emphasis is thus on the myriad individual lives and the "background" stories attached to them, for they form the substance of a vital African American history.

Morrison has described her goal in *Jazz* as wanting "to tell a very simple story about people who do not know that they are living in the jazz age, and to never use the word."[37] Like *Beloved*, *Jazz* does refer to various public events of the time, such as the July 1917 East St. Louis riots; the much celebrated return of the 369th Regiment (an all-black unit) in 1919 from World War I;[38] the vital presence of clubs, leagues, and societies in Harlem during the twenties (the Universal Negro Improvement Association, the National Negro Business League, the Civic Daughters, and so on); and the emergence of print media targeted specifically to a black audience (*The Crisis*, *Opportunity* magazine, the *Amsterdam News*, the *Messenger*). More often, though, the novel conveys a strong sense of Harlem as a mecca, a promised land for African Americans in the 1920s, through generalized descriptions such as this one: "Everything you want is right where you are: the church, the store, the party, the women, the men, the postbox (but no high schools), the furniture store, street newspaper vendors, the bootleg houses (but no banks), the beauty parlors, the barbershops, the juke joints, the ice wagons, the rag collectors, the pool halls, the open food markets, the number runner, and every club, organization, group, order, union, society, brotherhood, sisterhood, or association imaginable" (*J* 10). This passage acknowledges the inequities that remained in Harlem even during the Renaissance years, but the parentheses set them to the side, and so the predominant impression here is of Harlem as a self-sufficient community of black people, the largest community of its kind in America and the world in the twenties.[39] Morrison's novel thus performs an important act of historical recovery by bringing to mind for contemporary readers this exceptional era of African American history, when it seemed that for the first time, blacks would have access to a range of economic, educational, and social opportunities that had previously been denied them.[40]

But in *Jazz*, as in *Beloved*, Morrison's emphasis always moves away from the big picture and returns to the everyday lives of black people. Joe declares himself "a new Negro," for instance, which is a reference that might be connected to Alain Locke's important collection of 1925, but Locke himself is never mentioned in Morrison's narrative and so the phrase remains local in its meaning. Most of the novel, in fact, consists of individual stories of the past related to Violet and Joe, Dorcas and Alice Manfred: Violet reckons with her mother's suicide and what it meant to grow up hearing glorious stories of the light-skinned, fair-haired mulatto child (Golden Gray) that her grandmother helped to raise; Joe meditates on his unsuccessful attempts to have Wild acknowledge him as her son; Dorcas sifts through the traumatic memories of her father's and mother's deaths; and Alice faces the intensity of her repressed feelings about her husband's infidelity of thirty years ago. As they recount the stories of their past, Morrison's novel suggests that history is never over, that a conscious historical connection is absolutely necessary for the psychological well-being of the individual and community.[41]

This connection is particularly tenuous because of the historical era in which *Jazz* is set. A time of mass migration from the South to the North along with a newly conceived image of black selfhood — the New Negro as someone who is self-assertive and militant, who refuses a Booker T. Washington conciliatory stance, who has freed himself from the power of whites to define his life and goals — the Harlem Renaissance might also be seen as a time of rupture, when newness became a cultural dominant that marked not only progress, but trauma.[42] Nathan Huggins suggests that the problematic metaphor of "the New Negro" offered a limited and unstable model of assertive black manhood: "Whatever promise the new man has for the future, his name and the necessity for his creation imply some inadequacy in the past. Like the New Year's resolution or the 'turning over a new leaf,' the debut of the New Negro announced a dissatisfaction with the Old Negro. And since the New/Old dichotomy is a mere convenience of mind — Afro-Americans were really the same people all along — the so-called Old Negro was merely carried within the bosom of the New as a kind of self-doubt, perhaps self-hate."[43] In Huggins's analysis, this self-doubt eventually contributed to the implosion of the Harlem Renaissance as a movement.

Black men were not the only ones who found themselves unsettled by the cultural, social, and political transformations of these years. In *Workings of the Spirit*, Houston Baker, Jr., focuses on the generation of black women writers who came of age in the Harlem Renaissance. Writers such as Nella Larsen and Jessie Fauset, Baker argues, understandably wanted to depart from the constraining images of black women in nineteenth-century literature but ended up completely sundering all connections to their roots in southern folk wisdom and black vernacular, leaving only the possibility of adopting northern "white-faced minstrelsy" on which to model their literary expressivity. Because of the "daughters' seduction" into "whitemale patriarchy," Baker asserts, "passing" became the predominant trope of their literature.[44]

Although Baker proposes theoretical interventions to suture the gaping wound between northern and southern, urban and rural, male and female black experience, Morrison, it would seem, suggests a different kind of intervention, an intervention involving history and rememory. What is passing if not the repression of one's personal history? Morrison's novel emphasizes historical rememory precisely to move away from passing as the trope that governs contemporary views of the Harlem Renaissance as a historical era. Both Joe and Violet yearn for some kind of connection with their previous selves in order to deal with the trauma brought on by migration and urban life. Joe cannot tell his best male friends in Harlem, Gistan and Stuck, things he would easily have said to his boyhood friend and near-brother, Victory. He admits, "I changed once too often. Made myself new one time too many. You could say I've been a new Negro all my life" (*J* 129) — such continual newness and self-renewal, while made attractive by the rhetoric of the Harlem Renaissance, prove to be problematic and painful. Cut off from Victory and any other connection to his past life in the South, Joe urgently needs someone to listen to all of his unspoken dreams and memories.[45] Violet, who suffers from her own psychological amputations, cannot fulfill this role, and so Joe directs his tremendous neediness toward an eighteen-year-old self-absorbed young woman who reminds him vaguely of Wild, who, perhaps, is his mother. His desire for Dorcas involves not only sex or beauty or youth — perhaps more importantly it involves his desire to articulate, to narrate, memories and stories that might connect the past to the present in a meaningful way.

The urgency to make these kinds of connections is also felt by Violet and Alice. Violet suffers "public crazinesses" and "private cracks" in Harlem (*J* 22) — fissures in her own self-concept that the novel registers with names signifying her split self: "Violent" and "*that* Violet." She begins to heal these fractures by creating a historical narrative for herself. Violet says to Alice, midway through the novel, "Everybody I grew up with is down home" (*J* 111), and to Felice, late in the novel, she remarks, " 'Before I came North I made sense and so did the world' " (*J* 207). Her ability to recognize the profound geographic and emotional dislocations migration entailed and to articulate these traumatic effects allows Violet to move forward.[46] It is also important that Violet's healing occurs as a result of the bond she and Alice form after Dorcas's death. Violet initially comes to Alice's apartment to find out what Dorcas was like in an attempt to understand Joe's betrayal, but instead finds herself growing attached to the dead girl and to Alice. Likewise, as Alice stitches up Violet's frayed and torn dress, then her coat, she listens closely and repairs Violet's tattered sense of self. Together they figure out that "sisterhoods" are necessary between black women if they are to avoid becoming wild, armed, and dangerous (*J*78).

As Morrison observed in a 1977 interview with Ntozake Shange, "What [black] women say to each other and what they say to their daughters is vital information."[47] Without this passing down of wisdom, the daughters cannot have "livable" lives and an entire generation of African Americans will be affected adversely because of the wounds these motherless or sisterless black women carry with them.[48] Morrison's novel dramatizes this predicament by presenting numerous instances of orphaned or abandoned children: Dorcas is raised by her aunt, Alice, after being orphaned; Sweet is raised by his aunt, Malvonne, but despite her best efforts, he joins a gang, robs postal boxes, disappears from Harlem; Violet's mother, Rose Dear, jumps in a well and drowns herself to escape her pain, and so Violet vows never to have children of her own; Joe's mother is possibly Wild — he never knows for sure — and his father is unknown, so Joe too does not want children of his own. To be sure, young black women like Alice and Violet have learned to exercise a certain kind of strength and will power to become mature women who have relatively comfortable lives, but their emotional lacks are profound. By giving such close attention to the traumatic lives of Alice and Violet, Morrison's novel both points to the necessary resilience and creativity of black women in trying to make lives for themselves and their families amid tremendous adversities, while it also suggests the pain that is the underside of such achievement. In this way, Morrison's novel implicitly provides a much more complicated and compelling explanation of the fractures and fissures in black families than sociological-historical accounts such as Stanley Elkins's 1959 book, which argued that slavery totally dehumanized blacks, or the Moynihan Report of 1965, which produced the cultural image of a controlling and emasculating black matriarch.[49]

Morrison's novel deliberately avoids such broadly laid out, neatly organized socio-historical analyses and, in fact, dramatizes the failures of monumental histories. By taking a comprehensive view of an era, a monumental history must necessarily oversimplify and condense. To arrive at a coherent narrative, a monumental history inevitably eliminates local, individualized, or contradictory stories. Moreover, in a monumental history, the outcome of the events has already been decided, and so individual players are unimportant except as they contribute to the final, already determined conclusion. Individual lives, outside of such a grand narrative, however, are much more chaotic, contradictory, and unpredictable; by emphasizing individual stories, Morrison's novel creates a necessary space for resistance, agency, and counternarratives. This issue is taken up specifically in *Jazz*, as the narrator suggests that the City with a capital C — an echo of the idea of Harlem during the Renaissance as the capital of the world — predetermines what will happen to Joe: "Take my word for it, he is bound to the track. It pulls him like a needle through the groove of a Bluebird record. Round and round about the town. That's the way the City spins you. Makes you do what it wants, go where the laid-out roads say to. All the while letting you think you're free. . . . You can't get off the track a City lays for you" (*J* 120). But does the City really have the power to define and prescribe individual lives? If it does, Morrison would be close to Richard Wright's naturalism or to totalizing constrictive accounts of black life in America such as Moynihan's or Elkins's. The dominant image of the passage quoted above — the groove of a Bluebird record — suggests a recognition of coercive and oppressive conditions that have adversely affected African Americans, yet by being associated with black music, the image also evokes resistance and resilience.

The Bluebird label was known for its blues recordings,[50] and blues as a genre is founded on the principle of repetition with subtle variation. The initial line or lyric is seldom repeated exactly in the same way in the blues, and so operating from within a blues sensibility means that we are not condemned merely to repeat the past (to invoke George Santayana's famous line). Jazz offers another example of a (narrative) line that resists predetermination: although a jazz composition has a set melody, the room for improvisation and the spontaneity of performance create a fluid and shifting text. Jazz as a genre revisits its own past melody to claim what is useful and make possible further development. It is, in other words, a model of a useful black history. Hence the title of Morrison's novel can be read not only as a reference to its historical setting but more importantly as the model for her historical reconstruction. Like the narrator's description of the grooved Bluebird record, Morrison's own novel lays down seemingly inescapable tracks — lines of type that logistically must be read on the page from left to right, top of the page to bottom — but contains narrative impulses that are patterned after jazz, where breaking away from and improvising on previous melodic lines is the hallmark of achievement. This is seen most vividly in *Jazz* at the beginning of each chapter, when the narrator picks up and improvises on a key image or phrase from the end of the previous chapter.

Along with the novel's jazz-based improvisational moves, its numerous individual stories require such intricate and complicated maneuvers to unfold that *Jazz* defies any single totalizing description.[51] Part of this intricacy is created by Morrison's curious narrator, who has the detachment and overarching knowledge typically associated with a reliable omniscient narrator, but who also has the limited knowledge, biases, and involvement associated with an unreliable first-person narrator. The narrator, for instance, somehow has knowledge of parts of Joe's past and Violet's past that they have never told anyone, let alone each other. At the same time, however, the narrator bluntly admits to many instances of not knowing; remarks like "Anyway, Joe didn't pay Violet or her [boy]friend any notice. Whether she sent the boyfriend away or whether he quit her, I can't say" (*J* 4–5), or "I've wondered about it" (*J* 71) and "If I remember right . . ." (*J* 71) are typical of this narrator. The status of the narrator becomes even more curious, though, when it becomes clear that this narrator will play a greater role in the novel than simply relating the stories of the various characters. She, in fact, unlike any of the narrators found in Morrison's other novels, becomes an individual voice, a quasi-character, one who shapes the story as she tells it.[52] At times, she has the voice of a gossip, as in the opening line of the novel: "Sth, I know that woman." Other times, she bluntly interjects her own feelings into the story, exclaiming, for instance, "I'm crazy about this City" (*J* 7) early in the novel and beginning a sentence later on with "My own opinion was . . . " (*J* 118). Her voice as narrator has a wide range of inflections and levels, moving fluidly from relatively straightforward narrative reportage to lyrical prose to slang to blues lyrics.

One of the most startling attributes of this narrator, however, is her self-reflexivity: she confesses to having serious inadequacies as narrator. Questions about her ability to narrate become particularly pointed in the elaborate story of Golden Gray that unfolds in the novel. The Golden Gray episode is the longest "background" story told in the novel, for various reasons. It reveals parts of Joe's and Violet's past that help to explain the drift and loneliness of their lives in Harlem in 1926.[53] The episode is also a stunning reworking of various Faulknerian motifs, such as long kept secrets revealed and anxieties about miscegenation (Morrison's master's thesis at Cornell explored the theme of alienation in Faulkner and Woolf). But perhaps most important, the episode highlights the problems of narrating such a complex story: the narrator begins to tell the saga of Golden Gray's search for his father, Henry LesTroy (or Le*story*), who is called familiarly Hunters Hunter (*J* 143), but the story for various reasons eludes her, and so she begins again several pages later (*J* 150).

One of the problems in narrating Golden Gray's story is that he is a racist. Raised by Miss Vera Louise into an ideology of whiteness, Golden Gray is repulsed by black flesh, and so when he witnesses Wild's mad dash into a tree, knocking her unconscious, he can barely bring himself to touch her. And when he arrives at Henry's house, his first concern is to get his trunk inside before he returns to his carriage to see about Wild. These character deficiencies are so glaring that the narrator, who like Violet is attracted to the golden young man, begins to loathe him — until she tells the story a second time and adds some slight but influential details: "That is what makes me worry about him. How he thinks first of his clothes, and not the woman. How he checks the fastenings [of his trunk], but not her breath. It's hard to get past that, but then he scrapes the mud from his Baltimore soles before he enters a cabin with a dirt floor and I don't hate him much anymore" (*J* 151). These intimate details create a much more complicated picture of Golden Gray, one that makes it impossible to simply dismiss him. The narrator continues to relate the contradictions of Golden Gray's character, how he tries to make up a story for himself or for his father that will exonerate him, that will make him a hero for saving a "wild black girl" (*J* 154). The narrator bluntly calls him a "hypocrite" for these efforts (*J* 154), but goes on to look at him so closely that she can understand how fear drives his racism and his hypocrisy:

Aw, but he is young, young and he is hurting, so I forgive him his self-deception and his grand, fake gestures, and when I watch him sipping too quickly the cane liquor he has found, worrying about his coat and not tending to the girl, I don't hate him at all. He has a pistol in his trunk and a silver cigar case, but he is a boy after all, and he sits at the table in the single chair contemplating changing into fresh clothes, for the ones he is wearing, still wet at the seams and cuffs, are filthy with sweat, blood and soil. (*J* 155)

It is not that the narrator is willing to overlook Golden Gray's faults, but her commitment to look again brings more details into the picture and poses new contradictions; thus, her former narrative with its desire for neat evaluations will no longer suffice.

But as the narrator continues to try to tell Golden Gray's story, she once again gets stuck and soon laments, "What was I thinking of? How could I have *imagined* him so poorly? Not noticed the hurt that was not linked to the color of his skin, or the blood that beat beneath it. But to some other thing that longed for authenticity, for a right to be in this place, effortlessly without needing to acquire a false face, a laughless grin, a talking posture. I have been careless and stupid and it infuriates me to discover (again) how *unreliable* I am" (*J* 160, emphasis added). The narrator's self-reflexive commentary might cause readers to wonder if any of the versions of the Golden Gray story is to be trusted: after all, here is a narrator who confesses to imagining Golden Gray and to her own (repeated) unreliability. These questions become even more acute when the narrator reveals how she will arrive at a version of Golden Gray that is fair: "Now I have to think this through, carefully, even though I may be doomed to another misunderstanding. I have to do it and not break down. Not hating him is not enough; liking, loving him is not useful. I have to alter things" (*J* 161). How, indeed, will *altering* things lead to a full, complete, or fair story of Golden Gray?

The narrator in the Golden Gray episode is like a historian confronted with various pieces of evidence. This evidence can be used to construct many different explanations or stories: the story of Golden Gray as a repulsive racist, the story of Golden Gray as a fearful and confused young man, and so on. But narratives such as these, constructed in a tidy logical way, prove dissatisfying to the narrator as she continues to contemplate past events. She, paradoxically, is unreliable as a narrator-historian, not because she uses her imagination but because she does not make good enough use of it — she does not alter things enough to create a narrative that could be genuinely useful or informative. In fact, the narrator's dilemma and resolution here are strongly reminiscent of the comments Morrison has made about her own goals as an African American writer. In "Memory, Creation, and Writing," Morrison distinguishes between memory — "the deliberate act of remembering," "a form of willed creation" — and research — "an effort to find out the way it really was."[54] Morrison, of course, does research herself as part of writing her novels, so it is not that she wants to dismiss research altogether. But research material in itself does not provide an intelligent or useful understanding of the past, as Morrison's comments in a later essay, "The Site of Memory," suggest: "The crucial distinction for me is not the difference between fact and fiction, but the distinction between fact and truth. Because facts can exist without human intelligence, but truth cannot." To dwell too much or too soon on the facts, Morrison adds, is to miss the opportunity to explore the "mystery" of the interior lives that she is trying to reconstruct. Fiction offers a kind of truth because, by connecting the world of facts to the world of imagination, it provides a vital understanding of "two worlds — the actual and the possible."[55]

The necessity to create a narrative that is faithful to the actual and yet points toward the possible is what the narrator learns in the Golden Gray episode. She demonstrates that she has learned this lesson when, later in the novel, she corrects the mistaken prediction she made in the opening chapter. In the first few pages, when the narrator is supposedly telling readers what will happen to Joe and Violet after Dorcas's death, she sees a bleak picture as they reestablish another triangle substituting Felice for Dorcas. According to the narrator, only one thing changes: "What turned out different was who shot whom" (*J* 6). So we read the entire novel waiting for a second shooting that never happens. Instead, by the end of the novel, Joe and Violet have worked through their problems, and the narrator comes to understand her own fallibility:

I was sure one would kill the other. I waited for it so I could describe it. I was so sure it would happen. That the past was an abused record with no choice but to repeat itself at the crack and no power on earth could lift the arm that held the needle. I was so sure, and they danced and walked all over me. Busy, they were, busy being original, complicated, changeable — human, I guess you'd say, while I was the predictable one, confused in my solitude into arrogance, thinking my space, my view was the only one that was or that mattered. (*J* 220)

The narrator sees the limits of her earlier attempts to narrate the past: she has been an overly confident historian, focusing so concertedly on the big picture and its predictable patterns that she has forgotten to take into consideration human agency and the mystery of individual lives. The narrator's confession is a key moment in the novel. Elsewhere Morrison links the ability to learn from one's mistakes to jazz as a genre: "In a performance you make mistakes, and you don't have the luxury of revision that a writer has; you have to make something out of a mistake, and if you do it well enough it will take you to another place where you never would have gone had you not made that error. So, you have to be able to risk making that error in performance."[56] The narrator not only risks making mistakes, but she integrates these mistakes into the performance of her role as narrator.

Joe too takes such a risk when he reaches out of his loneliness to speak to Dorcas, but rather than trying to move on to a new place, he tries to reenact the past by conflating Dorcas and Wild. Trying to touch Wild/Dorcas, Joe shoots his lover: "I had the gun but it was not the gun — it was my hand I wanted to touch you with" (*J* 130–31). The narrator thinks that the appearance of Felice at the end of the novel will also lead to a scene of dangerous reenactment, hence her prediction in the opening chapter. This prediction, however, significantly does not hold true: despite the fact that Felice was Dorcas's best friend and resembles Dorcas so remarkably that Violet at first mistakes her for the dead woman, Violet, Joe, and Felice do not reenact the lover's triangle that previously led to tragedy. They instead make possible a future for themselves. Though Felice initially comes to the Traces' apartment to get some help in recovering the opal ring from her mother that she had lent to Dorcas and to tell Joe not to be so broken up about Dorcas, this passing encounter turns into a promising relationship as they reconstitute the black family: Felice gains surrogate parents in Violet and Joe whom she can talk to and learn from; Violet gets a surrogate daughter to receive some of her hard earned pearls of wisdom and affection; and Joe is reborn as father and lover, able to leave behind his unbearable sadness when Felice passes on Dorcas's final words: " 'There's only one apple. . . . Just one. Tell Joe' " (*J* 213).

Morrison's novel emphasizes the role of narration in achieving this bond. By talking about their individual lives and pasts, Felice, Joe, and Violet heal themselves through a collective and reciprocal effort to face, tell, and renegotiate what has happened to them. Watching their felicitous companionship, the narrator learns that a past of trauma, pain, and unfulfilled longings does not have to continue on into the present or the future — if one can arrive at a narrative that will enable reflection and renegotiation. This point is critical for Morrison's efforts to reconstruct African American history. Through the use of a self-reflexive narrator, who can provide commentary on the usefulness of certain kinds of narratives, and through the intricate retelling of past events, *Jazz* emphasizes that history is first of all a story—a set of stories African Americans need to tell and retell in order to create the foundation for a livable life and a viable future. By insisting on the narrative and fictive—the storytelling—aspects of history, Morrison's novels align themselves with current trends in the postmodern novel, a genre so obsessed with history that theorist Linda Hutcheon defines postmodernism as "historiographic metafiction." While the historical content of novels like *Beloved* and *Jazz* should be taken seriously, it also seems clear that Morrison strategically emphasizes narrative patterns in her novels that work against the construction of a new monolithic black history. *Jazz*, for instance, does not attempt to present one clear picture of the Harlem Renaissance or the Jazz Age from a black perspective, but self-consciously re-presents the past in order to emphasize that historical understanding must be dynamic and constantly reworked if it is to be useful.

Nowhere is this more clear than in the final paragraphs of the novel. The narrator, who has been observing the newly found tenderness Joe and Violet have for each other, begins to meditate on love and intimacy. She confesses, "I envy them their *public* love" (*J* 229, emphasis added). The odd choice of "public" to modify "love" might recall the words of Baby Suggs in the Clearing in *Beloved*, urging her audience of black people to love themselves, to love their own bodies and flesh (*B* 88). This collective act of self-love cannot be sustained in *Beloved*, for Baby Suggs is shattered after whitefolks enter her yard and precipitate Sethe's fatal embrace of her baby. Neither could this self-love be sustained in the literary movement of the Harlem Renaissance, as analyses such as Baker's and Huggins's suggest. *Jazz*, however, as a historical novel revisits these past traumas and refigures them, closing with an articulation of the kind of public or collective self-love these other texts long for:

I myself have only known it in secret, shared it in secret and longed, aw longed to show it—to be able to say out loud what they have no need to say at all: *That I have loved only you, surrendered my whole self reckless to you and nobody else. That I want you to love me back and show it to me. That I love the way you hold me, how close you let me be to you. I like your fingers on and on, lifting, turning. I have watched your face for a long time now, and missed your eyes when you went away from me. Talking to you and hearing you answer—that's the kick.* (*J* 229)

This passage evokes the intimacy, the connection through communication, the joining together that the narrator has just observed between Joe, Violet, and Felice. And it stands in marked
contrast to the "no clamor for a kiss" that ends *Beloved*.

This passage also surprisingly suggests a new identity for the narrator of *Jazz* as the book itself, talking to the reader, describing a
reading experience that is intimate, passionate, and dynamic.[57]
Reminiscent of "the talking book" that Gates discusses in *The Signifying Monkey*, the self-reflexivity of postmodern fiction, and the
nonlinear design of *The Black Book*, the narrator as the book itself
invites the reader to participate in the construction of the story: "If
I were able I'd say it. Say make me, remake me. You are free to do it
and I am free to let you because look, look. Look where your hands
are. Now" (*J* 229). Books literally do not speak to readers, and
paradoxically, the narrator manages to say what she has just said she
is not able to; somewhere in the course of the novel, the typical
story, the typical history has gotten off track. In this dazzling puzzle
lies an insight that has repercussions for Morrison's historical reconstruction — (black) history books have no life, no meaning, unless they engage readers and compel them to "make" and "remake" the story in order to locate something useful for living today
and tomorrow.

This making and remaking does not mean, though, that anything
goes: just as the improvisational sections of a jazz piece must make
recognizable reference to a previous phrase if listeners are to per-
ceive the passage as improvisation and not as something entirely
new, so, too, would playing fast and loose with the details make
Morrison's historical novel illegible as history. Morrison's emphasis
on the mutual and collective construction of the story is not an
invitation to radical historical relativism, but an insistence on a
necessary, collective support for counternarratives in order for
them to become something other than marginalized or alternative
or muted perspectives.[58] In the final paragraphs of *Jazz*, as in the
concept of rememory so central to *Beloved*, Morrison claims the
power of wonderfully engaging narratives and stories to contest and
displace disabling hegemonic narratives in a culture's memory. In
essence, *Jazz* repairs the dislocations and traumas of the past for
African Americans so stunningly portrayed in her other novels by
beginning a communal, collective project, the ongoing reconstruction of a "genuine" and useful African American history.

"Deafened by the Roar of Its Own History": *Paradise*

The imperative of *Jazz* to re-collect and retell communal and personal histories is understood only too well by the denizens of Ruby in *Paradise*, the third novel of Morrison's historical trilogy. The townspeople know by heart the story of their ancestors' migration from Mississippi and Louisiana in 1889, their shunning by whites and Indians when they arrived in Oklahoma Territory, the Disallowing in Fairly when lighter-skinned blacks refused to allow them to join their community, and the founding of their own all-black town first in Haven, then in Ruby. Indeed, at the center of the town of Ruby stands the Oven, an ever-present, monumental reminder of the past and the authorized, official history of those events. In sharp contrast to *Beloved* and *Jazz*, in *Paradise* Morrison develops characters who are completely connected to their past, to history, to memory. So what could be wrong, or as the novel asks, "How could so clean and blessed a mission devour itself and become the world they had escaped?" (*P* 292). This is the unspoken story, the unspeakable history of Ruby, that unfolds in Morrison's novel.

Something has come so unhinged in Ruby that *Paradise* begins with a dramatic scene of violence: nine men invade "the Convent" (which they think of as a "coven") and kill—or try to—the five women living there. The opening chapter reveals such venom, rage, and loathing among these men that *Paradise* at first seems to be a magnificently inappropriate title for the novel.[59] How the women of the Convent come to be targeted by the men of Ruby—men who pride themselves on having established a town where no woman ever has to worry about being "prey"—is the conundrum that supplies the narrative energy of the novel. To comprehend this twist, this reversal, requires following the complicated narrative lines the novel traces and weaves together, including the personal histories of the women of Ruby—Soane, Dovey, Billie Delia, Arnette, Patricia Best, Lone DuPres—and of the Convent women—"Mother," Consolata, Mavis, Gigi, Seneca, Divine—as well as the history of Ruby, the history of black towns in Oklahoma, and the displacing and dispossession of Native Americans as Oklahoma went from being "Indian Territory" to statehood. This narrative emphasis on history is important to note, since it might otherwise seem that Morrison has taken a sudden turn away from the imperative to remember and to recover black history that lies at the heart of *The Black Book*,

Beloved, and *Jazz*. What afflicts the community of Ruby is not history per se, but a history that has become official and monolithic, and hence dangerous to the well-being of the community.

The rigidity of this history is made brilliantly clear in the serious disputes that recur over the inscription on the Oven. Forged by the grandfathers to unite and strengthen the community after the Disallowing, the Oven was inscribed, using a precious supply of nails, with a biblical motto; unfortunately, sometime during the intervening eighty years and the move from Haven to Ruby, the nails forming the first word were lost. Deacon and Steward Morgan insist that the original inscription reads "Beware the Furrow of His Brow," signifying the heroic obedience to God exemplified by the grandfathers who founded the community. For the younger generation of Ruby, however, such obedience is anathema, for in their eyes it indicates a kind of Booker T. Washington subservience to white hegemony. Thus, they paint a raised fist on the Oven ("jet black with red fingernails" [*P* 101]) and insist that the first word of the inscription is "Be." "Be the Furrow of His Brow" signifies for them the possibility of divine retribution, of rejecting separate but equal racist thinking, while insisting on black power and equal rights. The fierceness of this public debate becomes apparent when the town meets to discuss the problem of the inscription. Steward Morgan gets the last word and ends the discussion by threatening the disputers: " 'Listen here. . . . If you, any one of you, ignore, change, take away, or add to the words in the mouth of that Oven, I will blow your head off just like you was a hood-eye snake' " (*P* 87). Despite Steward's vehement warning, some of the people to improvise (privately) upon the inscription, and by the end of the novel, readers are left with several inventive possibilities: "Be the Furrow" (*P* 143), "Be the Furrow of *Her* Brow" (*P* 159), and "We Are the Furrow of His Brow" (*P* 298).

By playing with this inscription, at the narrative level *Paradise* follows *Jazz* in emphasizing the need to make and remake the story, the history. Or as Morrison wrote in a 1984 essay, "If my work is to be functional to the group (to the village, as it were) then it must bear witness and identify that which is useful from the past and that which ought to be discarded; it must make it possible to prepare for the present and live it out, and it must do that not by avoiding problems and contradictions but by examining them."[60] These comments about the usefulness of history and memory anticipate the central tensions found in *Paradise*. The founding families of Ruby certainly bear witness to the past, but they do not have a critical and dynamic relation to it. They have raised the history of their exodus and disallowing to biblical status so that any attempt to tell a new story is akin to blasphemy and can only evoke the armed hostility Steward demonstrates in the town meeting. At the very beginning of the novel, readers learn that Deacon and Steward, the town's twin patriarchs, "have powerful memories. Between them they remember the details of everything that ever happened — things they witnessed and things they have not" (*P* 13). Throughout the novel, the brothers exert an overly controlling, conservative force on the community and collective memory. The elevation of town history to scripture that Deacon and Steward insist on becomes most obvious at the school Christmas pageant where the story of Mary, Joseph, and the baby Jesus is conflated with the Disallowing. In the school's Christmas story, there are seven holy families who are turned away from the inn, representing the seven founding families of Ruby who are currently respectable; there are four innkeepers, signifying the light-skinned blacks of Fairly who do not allow the group to join their community; and there is a wise man who puts his gifts back in his sack at the pageant, reenacting the grandfathers' refusal to accept food from the people of Fairly (*P* 208–16). It is not just the repetition of the same story/history, year after year, that is the problem here; the people of Ruby have forgotten the need to experience and to tell new stories, and thus they have no communal resources to create the conditions for a livable life. Near the end of the novel, Reverend Richard Misner puts his finger precisely on the problem when he thinks to himself, "deafened by the roar of its own history, Ruby, it seemed to him, was an unnecessary failure" (*P* 306).

Without any self-reflection or engagement with the present moment, the people of Ruby experience a peculiar situation: no one has died in Ruby for more than twenty years, and it is not until after the men invade the Convent and shoot the women that a natural death occurs in Ruby. In this fantastical way, Morrison's novel dramatizes the way that history can be used to seal off the present and the future. Richard Misner notices, for instance, that the people of Ruby are great storytellers — that is, if they are telling stories about the past: "Over and over and with the least provocation, they pulled from their stock of stories tales about the old folks, their grands

and great-grands; their fathers and mothers. Dangerous confrontations, clever maneuvers. Testimonies to endurance, wit, skill and
strength. Tales of luck and outrage. But why were there no stories to
tell of themselves? About their own lives they shut up. Had nothing
to say, pass on" (*P* 161). An echo of the ending pages of *Beloved*
resonates here: the people of Ruby have nothing of their own lives
to pass on (or pass down) because they have passed on (ignored or
failed to see) the opportunities for living in the present moment.
As in *Beloved*, this is a dangerous situation for the characters in
Paradise.

Just as the characters in *Paradise* must learn to negotiate the need
to remember and the need to move forward, Morrison's novel as a
whole enacts a complex engagement with black history. On the one
hand, the novel works to restore historical memory of the all-black
towns in Oklahoma and elsewhere at the beginning of this century
and thus recovers an important moment of African American history. On the other hand, the novel dramatically suggests that obses-
sive and insistent historicizing has deadly effects. One way the novel
maintains a useful contradiction regarding these approaches to
history is by providing two different locations for the founding
families—the establishment first of a promising community in
Haven, followed by the decision to move the group and become cut
off from the rest of the world by founding Ruby. In this way, Morrison's novel both recovers the forgotten history of all-black towns
in Oklahoma, while it also advances a critical look at the problems
of that time. Similar to Morrison's complex treatment of Harlem in
Jazz as a mecca or promised land and as a site of historical rupture,
in *Paradise*, Morrison presents both the promise and the shortcom-
ings of all-black towns.

Morrison's own research for the novel reflects a similar productive tension. She was fascinated enough with the historical epoch to
read numerous newspapers from the all-black towns. And she was
particularly taken with the "Come Prepared or Not at All" headline
that appeared in the *Langston City Herald* during 1891–1892. The
all-black towns of Oklahoma often distributed pamphlets, ran ads,
and used other methods to promote their towns. Historian Kenneth M. Hamilton points out, however, that not all black people
were equally welcome. The boosters of such towns were particularly
interested in "blacks with capital." In fact, while the *Langston City
Herald* promised " 'rest, liberty, and plenty' " to those with money, it

discouraged prospective migrants if they could not " 'bring enough money to support themselves and families until they could raise a crop.' " Indeed, the newspaper took a hard stance against reports of poor blacks planning or trying to settle in Oklahoma.[61] In an interview with Carolyn Denard, Morrison talks at length about how this particular material gripped her imagination:

I read a lot of newspapers about the people who went to Oklahoma. About soliciting people to settle Black towns all over Kansas and Oklahoma, particularly Oklahoma. And I got interested in one little sentence, which was in a column in one of the Black newspapers, encouraging people to move, work your own land, etc.; and it had an ad that said "Come prepared or not at all." It encouraged people to come with a year or two or three of supplies or money, so that if things didn't go right they would be able to take care of themselves. And the newspaper articles indicated how many people came with fifteen thousand dollars and so on, but there was a little paragraph about two caravans of Black people who got to Boley or Langston, or one of those towns, and were turned away because they did not come prepared; they didn't have anything. So I thought about what it must feel like to make that trek, and be turned away by some Black people — maybe for good reasons but nevertheless turned away by Black people — because they were too ragged and too poor to come into their town and homestead.[62]

Provoked by this incident of black settlers refusing to help or even to welcome a prospective group of poor black migrants, Morrison crafts a novel that explores the repercussions of this troubling moment in African American history. The result is that Ruby, which might have been a paradise, a haven from white racism and lynching, which might have provided black people with unprecedented economic, political, and cultural opportunities based not on the color of their skin, but on their own self-worth, turns out to be a failure.

For historian Norman L. Crockett, this is the sad story of many all-black towns of Oklahoma and Kansas; while they "offered a social paradise with freedom to walk the streets without encountering the thousand subtle reminders of membership in a subordinate class," they also became "a prison without walls" — cut off from the larger industrial world they could no longer compete economically, and cut off from the larger political sphere some black-town citizens became psychologically trapped, "rigidly hostile and defensive."[63] This is precisely what happens in Morrison's novel. Richard Misner comments to Anna Flood that the town stands on shaky economic ground, since everyone is "prospering on credit" (*P*116). The town not only discourages white visitors (a lost white couple facing a winter blizzard is met with Steward's open hostility, and they leave town only to perish in the storm), but it also takes a hard-line stance against those of their own who do not follow the unwritten code of color. As Patricia Best realizes watching the Christmas pageant with Richard Misner, there were originally nine holy families in the play, but now there are only seven. She can puzzle out the disallowed families: the Catos and her own father. Both have refused to follow the unspeakable, unspoken rule of the founding families: blacker is better. Once disallowed by other blacks, the town families have now become disallowers themselves. Or, as Richard Misner reflects, "They think they have outfoxed the whiteman when in fact they imitate him. They think they are protecting their wives and children, when in fact they are maiming them" (*P* 306).

Ruby's only hope lies in breaking loose of that frozen history and reentering the contemporary, outside world. That it takes an act of terrible violence to do so indicates the paralysis that has plagued the community. One moment of hope occurs when Patricia Best, after spending years tracing the genealogical lines of Ruby's families, asking difficult questions about names with lines drawn through them in family Bibles, and adding her own personal annotations to the compiled material, burns all her ledgers. As a result of keeping these records, Patricia has been able to piece together parts of town history no one wants to speak of. She, for instance, notices the lines of colorism and, in fact, designs her own shorthand to follow the lineage of skin color. Next to those individuals with the darkest skin, Patricia writes "8-R," meaning "eight-rock, a deep deep level in the coal mines" (*P* 193). She also notices that while it is easy to trace male ancestors, it is not so easy to trace the women because their full or maiden names are unknown, unrecorded: "Who were these women who, like her mother, had only one name? Celeste, Olive, Sorrow, Ivlin, Pansy. Who were these women with generalized last names? Brown, Smith, Rivers, Stone, Jones. Women whose identity rested on the men they married" (*P* 187). Clearly, there are limits to the official records, to the official histories. And so Patricia also keeps records of things no one will talk about directly: she recognizes the existence of "stolen children," abandoned children who were taken in by the families during their migration; she sees clearly that the Morgan family, without heirs, is in danger of dying out; and she discovers through her careful recordkeeping that no one, since the deaths of Ruby and her mother, has died in Ruby. Assembling this material is useful for Patricia: it allows her to understand that her father is ostracized by the community not for embalming his own wife's body but because he married a light-skinned woman ("a wife of sunlight skin, a wife of racial tampering" [P 197]) and brought this outsider home to Ruby. At the same time, Patricia is able to remember that the women of Ruby, despite the hostility of their husbands and brothers, did genuinely try to help her mother, who died from complications in childbirth, and this rememory is very comforting. Most important of all, compiling this material allows Patricia crucial moments of self-reflection: she sees that by keeping this material she has become complicit in the town's own secretive, exclusionary practices, and she no longer wants to be implicated in this painful history. Having learned the history by heart, she recognizes when it is time to discard it in order to move into the present moment and make new stories possible. Patricia ultimately represents the critical engagement with history that Morrison calls for in her novels and essays.

Like Patricia, the women of the Convent discern when it is time to move forward and stop reliving their own traumatic histories. They do so under Connie's direction by telling and retelling their stories to themselves and each other. This collective narration is similar to the trialogue between Sethe, Beloved, and Denver in *Beloved*, which Stamp Paid overhears as cacophony; in *Paradise* "the loud dreaming" enables the women to enter each others' separate pasts and rememory these moments so that the hurt and trauma are shared (*P* 264). Together they face the heat of the Cadillac and the motionless sleep of the babies in the back; together they swim, panic-stricken, away from male pursuers; together they relive the pain of rape, abandonment, betrayal, and heartbreak. But unlike in *Beloved*, where Sethe and Beloved become locked in telling stories of a past for which there can never be recompense, in *Paradise* this collective enunciation allows real healing to begin.[64] Soane, who visits the Convent after this cathartic narration has taken place, tellingly notices that "unlike some people in Ruby, the Convent women were no longer haunted" (*P* 266).

Because they have directly faced their traumatic pasts, because they have narrated their personal histories together, the break the Convent women make with those histories is hard earned and ethical. They do not evade painful histories; rather, they struggle through them and they reckon with them. And so they know when it is the right time to begin shedding their stories of the past and to begin writing new stories. It is no small matter that it is these women who are able to imagine paradise — not some transcendent, heavenly Paradise, but paradise as a welcoming home here on earth.[65] Breaking loose from their frozen histories, they discover what they really hunger for and are not afraid to explore and satisfy that hunger. No wonder they pose such a threat to the men of Ruby. No longer following the rules, these women are "Improvisational. Daring, disruptive, imaginative, modern, out-of-the-house, outlawed, unpolicing, uncontained and uncontainable. And dangerously female."[66]

In her Nobel Prize lecture, Morrison laid the seeds for her vision of paradise by telling a revised story of the Tower of Babel:

> The conventional wisdom of the Tower of Babel story is that the collapse was a misfortune. That it was the distraction, or the weight of many languages that precipitated the tower's failed architecture. That one monolithic language would have expedited the building and heaven would have been reached. Whose heaven, she wonders? And what kind? Perhaps the achievement of Paradise was premature, a little hasty, if no one could take the time to understand other languages, other views, other narratives. Had they, the heaven they imagined might have been found at their feet. Complicated, demanding, yes, but a view of heaven as life, not heaven as postlife.[67]

In Ruby, under the rigid control of Deacon and Steward, there is only one official monolithic story, and it leads to failure — a failure to achieve real community, a failure to connect heaven and earth, even in the potentially liberatory space of an all-black town. In contrast, at the Convent through the ceremony Consolata leads the women in, they are allowed the opportunity to babble, to express their own views and painful stories, to share the narratives of other women, and hence they gain the capacity to imagine a heaven here on earth.

Like the end of *Beloved*, however, the end of *Paradise* leads to a haunting absence. "The white woman" and Consolata are shot and killed when the Convent is invaded by the men of Ruby, and the fate of the rest of the Convent women remains ambiguous: Does Gigi actually appear and talk to her father? Does Mavis indeed reconcile with her daughter over lunch? Does Jean find Seneca? Does Dee Dee really see her daughter (Pallas/Divine) outside her window?

Whether or not these are real sightings is beside the point. What is certain is that the Convent women have come to occupy a prominent place in the minds and imaginations of some people, and so they continue to have a vital life, if not a bodily existence. At Save-Marie's funeral, for instance, Billie Delia, missing the Convent women, wonders "When will they return?" and as she thinks about her own predicaments in life, she sees and hears them: "The Convent women would roar at that. She could see their pointy teeth" (*P* 308).

Although women like Billie Delia are prepared and willing to rememory the Convent women, the novel complicates the situation by depicting troubling attempts to "sanitize" (*P* 298) what really happened when the men of Ruby invaded the Convent. Even the witnesses to the events do not agree on what happened: Dovey and Soane, standing side by side, witness Steward's shooting of Consolata, but they do not see the same thing, and because of their differing perspectives, their friendship from then on is irrevocably altered. Another split perspective appears when K. D. and the men of Ruby look at the drawings and paintings the women have made on a basement floor as pornography and blasphemy; when Anna Flood takes a good look, however, she sees a much more sympathetic picture — "the turbulence of females trying to bridle, without being trampled, the monsters that slavered them" (*P* 303). Given that the witnesses do not agree on what indeed happened at the Convent, it is not surprising that very divergent stories emerge. Two versions, in particular, begin to take official status, and as Patricia Best recounts them for Richard Misner, readers quickly recognize that they are both inadequate:

One, that nine men had gone to talk to and persuade the Convent women to leave or mend their ways; there had been a fight; the women took other shapes and disappeared into thin air. And two (the Fleetwood-Jury version), that five men had gone to evict the women; that four others — the authors — had gone to restrain or stop them; these four were attacked by the women but had succeeded in driving them out, and they took off in their Cadillac; but unfortunately, some of the five had lost their heads and killed the old woman. Pat left Richard to choose for himself which rendition he preferred. (*P* 296–97)

Richard Misner is discerning enough to believe neither of these stories, and Morrison's novel offers an important lesson about always scrutinizing official stories when they become too neatly narrated.

Paradise, itself, could never be described as an orderly, neatly legible narrative, and in its beautifully complex intricacies, the narrative form of *Paradise* models the twists and turns, the indirections and contradictions, that a genuinely useful engagement with history will produce. For instance, immediately after Patricia tells Misner about the violent encounter at the Convent, the novel goes on to relate her own private theory about what happened there: "nine 8-rocks murdered five harmless women (*a*) because the women were impure (not 8-rock); (*b*) because the women were unholy (fornicators at the least, abortionists at most); and (*c*) because they *could*—which was what being an 8-rock meant to them" (*P* 297). By providing such a full, complex picture of what happens at the Convent—from the men's perspective, from Soane and Dovey's view, from Lone's perspective, from an omniscient narrator's vantage point—Morrison re-creates the contradictory and chaotic conditions of history making and reporting. To make this point, the novel also dramatizes the way in which nice official stories can lead to silence and amnesia. Lone DuPres, for instance, tries to tell her story of what she heard and saw, a story that tells how the men of Ruby planned coldly and strategically to kill the Convent women. But the threat of official, sanitized monolithic histories is such that the community calls Lone unreliable in order to discredit her story, and readers learn that Lone "became unhinged by the way the story was being retold; how people were changing it to make themselves look good" (*P* 297). She, like the Convent women, like Billie Delia, deserves better.

Despite the ominous implications that the fraudulent official story will silence other narrative possibilities, will silence women's truths, the novel also suggests that attempts to sanitize the story will never be entirely successful. By ending with sightings of the Convent women after they presumably have been killed, and by voicing Billie Delia's longing for the reappearance of the Convent women along with her certainly that they will return again, the novel makes the rememories of the Convent women so powerful and vital that they will remain no matter how strong the efforts to deny or forget them. *Paradise*, thus, presents a more affirmative position on rememory than does *Beloved*. In the earlier novel, the autonomous existence of rememories is potentially dangerous, since they may involve Denver in the trauma of slavery that she has never experienced directly and entangle Sethe in a cycle of guilt for which there can be no adequate expiation (she is, in fact, nearly consumed by the rememory of her killing of Beloved). Rememories haunt the living in *Beloved*. But in *Paradise* the rememories of the Convent women are a positive haunting; they ensure that the disruptive, inventive, creative life force represented by these women cannot be forgotten or erased entirely.

The traces that remain make it possible for the novel to end with a lyrical and thoroughly amazing story/picture of paradise. This final narrative twist, though strikingly affirmative in comparison to the two-page coda that unsettles the happy ending for Sethe and Paul D in *Beloved*, is at the same time every bit as disjunctive as *Beloved*'s coda. For on the last page of *Paradise*, readers find themselves not in Oklahoma but somewhere by the sea, find themselves located not with the Convent women or the people of Ruby but with Piedade, a female character who has been mentioned only briefly in the novel prior to this point. On this last page, Piedade is singing a song so remarkable that it remains in Connie's memory from childhood until death, so remarkable that Connie has been able to confer the memory of it upon the Convent women — and so too does the novel confer this memory upon Morrison's readers: "There is nothing to beat this solace which is what Piedade's song is about, although the words evoke memories neither one has ever had: of reaching age in the company of the other; of speech shared and divided bread smoking from the fire; the unambivalent bliss of going home to be at home — the ease of coming back to love begun" (*P* 318). Like Piedade's song, Morrison's novel evokes memories in her readers that we have not (yet) had, and in *Paradise* these memories are of home, love, true companionship, and connection.

The first two novels of Morrison's historical trilogy, *Beloved* and *Jazz*, vividly dramatize the costs of amnesia, of historylessness, but *Paradise* notably suggests that remembering the past and retelling the history are only part of the solution. At the end of *Paradise*, Morrison goes beyond the open invitation "Say make me, remake me" extended at the end of *Jazz* to give readers a brilliant picture of what a dynamic relation to history might produce. Working through the history of slavery, of emancipation and Reconstruction, of great migrations both north and west, Morrison's historical trilogy ultimately ends not by reiterating the tragedies and the traumas of history, but by trying to imagine shimmering possibilities, a new story of life "down here in Paradise" (*P* 318).

Chapter Four
Remembering Holocaust History

In fields across Poland, the Ukraine, and other locations in Eastern Europe, especially after it rains, fragments of human bones surface, small but resilient traces of the devastation that has come to be called *der khurbn*, the Shoah, or the Holocaust.[1] Historians will never know exactly how many Jews (or how many other victims) perished at the hands of Nazis and anti-Semites, for genocide means that (most of) the witnesses are dead, and the dead bodies, even in their silence, do not remain to testify to the magnitude of the atrocity. The fragments of bone, while they bear witness to destruction, also testify to the crises of memory and history in a postmodern age; shards, they offer only a partial glimpse into an enormous tragedy that exceeds all frames of reference and comprehension. In fact, one might say that the fragmentation of metanarratives (or master narratives) that Jean-François Lyotard has emphasized in his characterization of postmodernism occurred literally in the Nazi death camps, where ideals of citizenship, human compassion, and justice collapsed.[2] What we are left with are fragments, localized details, individual stories (Lyotard's *petits récits*) — and an intense desire to somehow comprehend what happened.

The trauma of the Holocaust, in other words, includes the subsequent, and ongoing, crisis of remembering and witnessing that destruction, as well as the destruction that occurred in the 1930s and 1940s. No other tragedy of the twentieth century cries out so urgently for a sense of clear historical truth, the kind of truth attached to now belated assumptions of historical documentation and objectivity, assumptions that have been radically called into question by poststructuralist and postmodern theory. But a post-

Auschwitz age is a postmodern age,[3] and there can be no return to a time of grand narratives, where historians could be charged with the obligation to discover "what really happened" and to fit these "facts" into a cohesive narrative frame. Indeed, Holocaust historian Saul Friedlander warns against "naïve historical positivism" and "simplistic and self-assured historical narrations and closures" that would erase the "excess" of the Holocaust.[4]

And yet, historian Jane Caplan, in an essay that otherwise speaks favorably of various theoretical challenges to the conventional practices of academic historians, writes:

> It is one thing to embrace poststructuralism and postmodernism, to disseminate power, to decenter subjects and all in all let a hundred kinds of meaning contend, when *Bleak House* or philology or even the archaeology of knowledge [is] the issue. But should the rules of contention be different when it is a question, not simply of History, but of a recent history of lives, deaths, and suffering, and the concept of a justice that seeks to draw some meaningful relation between these?[5]

Alluding to the Holocaust in this question, Caplan suggests that a thoroughgoing deconstruction of history does not allow for the moral or ethical stance that must be taken with regard to the Holocaust.[6] We are left with unsettling contradictory claims: we cannot retreat from postmodernism, and we must not shirk the ethical obligations that follow in the wake of the Holocaust.

In previous chapters, I have explored the ways in which Toni Morrison and Louise Erdrich negotiate the need to tell the history of their people and to correct the historical record, even while working within a postmodern skepticism regarding historical representation and historiography. Their creation of interconnected novels, as I have argued, produces an epic effect to repair the historical record, to convey the complexities and limitations of history, and to impress readers to take up the imaginative histories depicted in their novels and remember them. In contrast to the often-forgotten moments of Native American and African American history that Erdrich and Morrison call attention to, the Holocaust has become part of public and official discourse in America. Because of this attention, the Holocaust as a momentous historical event precipitates a series of crises surrounding history and memory that are somewhat different from the exigencies Erdrich and Morrison face. As a historical tragedy, one might say that the Holocaust is both overwritten and underwritten: it holds such stature both in public consciousness and in official histories that a useful, pliable knowledge and a living memory of "what really happened" are in danger of being forgotten. It may be that, in the face of so much historicizing, a genuine and useful history of the Holocaust needs to avoid the epic resonances Erdrich and Morrison invoke. What is clear is that strategic, critical interventions are necessary to address the specific crises in witnessing and memory attached to the Holocaust. It is my argument that Holocaust history written today must speak a language of fragments — fragments of evidence, fragments of knowledge, fragments of stories — to articulate a vital and appropriate response to these crises. For when a part of history becomes so engrained in public consciousness, the quality of historical knowledge may, paradoxically, be eroded. Something that comes to memory or consciousness too easily may lose a sense of dynamic contradiction and complexity. Fragments and gaps serve to disrupt neat lines of narrative, of comprehensibility, and so they can revitalize historical memory and knowledge.

The fragility of Holocaust memory and history has become acutely evident: the survivors of the camps are becoming aged, and their memories — which are critical to a contemporary understanding of the trauma — may die along with them. The urgent need to sustain Holocaust memory coincides with a broader concern in contemporary culture with the preservation of historical memory. In *Twilight Memories: Marking Time in a Culture of Amnesia*, Andreas Huyssen argues that postmodern culture "is terminally ill with amnesia."[7] In a world capable of being instantaneously connected via the internet and various mass media, high-tech strategies of data storage and information retrieval have almost made "active remembrance," in the traditional forms of personal and collective memory, obsolete.[8] Videotape archives of survivors' testimonies have been established in various locations throughout the United States (the Fortunoff Video Archive for Holocaust Testimonies at Yale University being perhaps the best known). In this respect, postmodern culture offers a high-tech solution to a potential loss; saving these testimonies on tape for posterity enables the survivors' memories to become "rememories," in Morrison's sense, for others who have not experienced the trauma firsthand.

Simply making these tapes or having them on hand is not sufficient for the cultural work of Holocaust remembrance, however.

Like Morrison's *Paradise*, Huyssen emphasizes the need for memory to be active, not "frozen," and like Morrison's *Jazz*, Huyssen advocates memory as a collective and public performance, not just an individual and private act. The museum, for Huyssen, offers one kind of postmodern public space where the cultural work of remembering can be actively and collectively engaged. In fact, noting the proliferation of museums in recent decades, Huyssen argues that "museummania" characterizes contemporary Western and American culture because it is one instantiation of a profound desire to memorialize history, "to articulate memory in stone or other permanent matter."[9]

The Holocaust is the focus of well-known museums in Jerusalem (Vad Yashem), Los Angeles (the Beit HaShoah-Museum of Tolerance), and most recently Washington, D.C. (the United States Holocaust Memorial Museum), as well as many memorials elsewhere.[10] These sites might be one answer to the significant problem Huyssen raises: "How . . . are we to guarantee the survival of memory if our culture does not provide memorial spaces that help construct and nurture the collective memory of the Shoah?"[11] As we shall see, however, the function of museums does not easily jibe with the function of memorials. And the kind of sanctity required when approaching the topic of the Holocaust is not easily maintained in the postmodern, commodified space of the museum. This chapter turns first to the narrative of the Holocaust constructed in what is now the most-often visited national monument, the U.S. Holocaust Memorial Museum in Washington, D.C., and then to the poetry and essays of Irena Klepfisz, a child survivor. Bringing these two very different kinds of texts together suggests the possibility of using a language of fragments, absences, and silences to productively remember Holocaust history.

The Museum on the Mall

From the moment in 1979 when President Jimmy Carter approved the recommendation of the President's Commission on the Holocaust to build "a living monument" to the Holocaust under federal auspices to the April 1993 opening of the U.S. Memorial Holocaust Museum presided over by President Bill Clinton, controversy surrounded this project.[12] Many were skeptical that a museum memorializing the Holocaust could avoid rendering it as a Disneyesque spectacle or commodity. Others were critical of locating this kind of memorial/museum on the Mall amid such shrines to American glory as the Lincoln and Jefferson Memorials and the Washington Monument. The external architectural design, in fact, had to be altered to make the building "fit" into the Mall setting.[13] And there were serious debates over the contents and narrative of the permanent exhibit, one of the most contentious being the debate over whether to put human hair from the victims on display.

The controversies that the museum became embroiled in are related to the problem of finding adequate means to represent and to document the Holocaust. This problem of representation is connected not only to the uniqueness of the Jewish Holocaust, in which the full range of modern industrial efficiency was harnessed to carry out destruction on a massive scale,[14] but also to the challenges posed by the Holocaust deniers, those who argue that mass extermination did not occur in places like Auschwitz. How does (or, can) memory inform history? How can history be written if sufficient evidence cannot be found to substantiate certain claims? How can (or, should) a Holocaust historian maintain objectivity and impartiality? What kind of narrative can even begin to offer an adequate framework for telling the story of immense loss and trauma?

The phrase repeated by many survivors — "I could not believe what my eyes had seen" — suggests the degree to which the Holocaust exceeds the frames of human comprehension, let alone the tools of representation.[15] Despite this unavoidable problem, however, Holocaust history must be told, must be written. The question is not *whether*, but *how* to do this: Is it more effective to use the already inadequate tools of documentary history, or is it more appropriate to mark the silences, absences, limits of articulation of this unprecedented trauma? The U.S. Holocaust Memorial Museum embodies this fundamental dilemma in its sometimes harmonious, oftentimes conflicting roles as a museum and as a memorial. Most of the space on the second, third, and fourth floors is allocated to the permanent exhibit, whose major purpose is to preserve evidence, or traces, of the past. To function as a museum, this space must necessarily foreground archival and documentary projects — projects that have been called into serious question by many postmodern theorists. As a memorial, however, the building must resonate as a "sacred space,"[16] as a place to reflect upon the Holocaust as a historical tragedy that cannot and will not ever be registered, known, or articulated fully. To put this another way, while the role of a Holocaust *museum* is to represent the past as real, the role of a Holocaust *memorial* is to call attention to the failure of all attempts at representation.

A close look at the principles of organization and selection of the permanent exhibit can help to explore the tension between these divergent purposes. The exhibit is divided into three parts: "Nazi Assault 1933–1939," " 'Final Solution' 1940–1945," and "Last Chapter" (a look at rescue and resistance, liberator and survivor testimonies). As this sequence suggests, the museum relies on an emphatically clear and coherent historical narrative—a point reinforced by the museum guide given to all visitors, which carefully maps each floor of the museum and the permanent exhibit. Enabling visitors to gain an overarching understanding of Holocaust history by touring the permanent exhibit is certainly an important part of the museum's educational mission, but such a guiding principle can also lead to instances where the complexities of history are oversimplified or denied. For Edward T. Linenthal, who has written a detailed book on the development and design of the U.S. Holocaust Memorial Museum entitled *Preserving Memory*, such oversimplification occurs in the exhibit about the failure to bomb Auschwitz. Citing several reliable authorities who disagree with the interpretation presented in the museum that bombing Auschwitz was possible and would have saved the lives of Jewish prisoners, Linenthal argues that this is one instance in the museum where interpretation has been "elevated" to "historical truth."[17] Linenthal's discussion of this contentious issue suggests the degree to which the museum is invested in presenting an authoritative, unequivocal historical narrative. Like all the labels in the permanent exhibit, the labels and text accompanying the discussion of the failure to bomb Auschwitz adopt a professorial tone, and the labels and text are unsigned. This practice produces a facticity that masks the interpretive dimension of this part of the exhibit.[18]

In the careful selection of objects for the museum, one can discern another important principle that helped to shape the museum's mission and philosophy. The developers and planners were adamant that all the artifacts on display be authentic or genuine. Their commitment to this principle resulted in the astonishing recovery of pieces of Holocaust history: archivists for the museum, for example, went to Warsaw to talk with survivors and were shown a section of the original wall of the Warsaw Ghetto that public and official histories had forgotten. A section of this wall was cast, and the reproduction is on display in the museum. (Perhaps more important, a plaque commemorating the wall and its significance in history was placed at the original site in Warsaw.) The definition of "authentic," however, becomes rather ambiguous at times. By "authentic," the museum designers mean that the actual objects themselves are displayed *or* that a casting or reproduction of the actual object is on display. Because of their interest in providing as complete a chronological narrative of the Holocaust as possible, the designers had to resign themselves to this almost postmodern definition of authenticity. The result is that canisters of Zyklon B on display are accompanied by a sign reassuring museumgoers that the pellets of gas are "inactive,"[19] while the Polish Karlsruhe freight car on display is carefully described as being "one of several types used to transport Jews to the camps." The question is whether these differing degrees of authenticity have distinctive effects on visitors to the museum.

Huyssen argues that one important reason fueling contemporary museummania is that museum objects have an "aura" of the real for observers, an effect that has become increasingly valued in a fast-paced, mass media world of various simulations and simulacra.[20] There are certain objects in the Holocaust Museum that create such an aura. A mud-encrusted milk can on display, for instance, is one of three which Emanuel Ringelblum filled with documents concerning life in the ghetto and buried under the streets of Warsaw. This humble object becomes more than just a milk can: as an auratic object, it testifies to the heroism and foresight of people like Ringelblum and the resistance fighters of the ghetto. It also gives us occasion to pause and reflect on the conditions that surround the production of historical knowledge: what would the quality of our knowledge be if these milk cans had not been utilized, had not remained intact or been uncovered?[21] (In fact, one of the three milk cans has never been found.)

Whether an aura of the real can be evoked by blatant simulacra, no matter how authentic the casting, is another matter. The reproduction of the infamous "Arbeit Macht Frei" entrance gate to Auschwitz in the museum, for instance, appears to be so clean and obviously well preserved that it could almost be a movie prop. This entrance gate, in fact, is featured prominently on the first page of a brief satirical article on the museum that sports the title "Welcome to the Holocaust Theme Park."[22] The article insists that what visitors encounter in the museum is not the real, but the hyperreal. While we might be inclined to dismiss this argument as excessively critical or predictably postmodern, it does allow us to understand the ways in which the careful display of objects and the use of strategic spotlighting are exhibition techniques that the Holocaust museum shares with other museums. And because these exhibition techniques are the same, it is entirely possible that the carefully arranged and lit mound of shoes from Majdanek, for instance, or the cases of toothbrushes, scissors, and cutlery on display, may take on aesthetic qualities that empty these objects of their historical aura, thus preventing them from functioning as potent signifiers of enormous tragedy. Are such objects being enshrined through these techniques of display, or are they contextualized sufficiently to become metaphorically linked to unimaginable loss?

These objects, in fact, are accompanied by texts designed to enable them to "speak" appropriately. The utensils on display are framed by photographs of camp workers sorting the possessions of recently arrived Jews. The shoes are supplemented by lines from a poem written by Moses Schulstein, a Yiddish poet who lived from 1911 until 1981. Reproduced on the wall in monumental type, these lines read:

We are the shoes, we are the last witnesses.
We are shoes from grandchildren and grandfathers,
From Prague, Paris, and Amsterdam,
And because we are only made of fabric and leather
And not of blood and flesh, each one of us avoided the
    hellfire.[23]

Schulstein's poem not only tells the visitor why the shoes are important, it suggests a method of reading: by contemplating the shoes that remain, visitors grasp what is absent — the lives of millions of victims. In making this appeal, the poem suggests that the shoes cannot signify adequately on their own, a point Fredric Jameson raises in his analysis of postmodernism when he contrasts the viewer's experience of Van Gogh's painting *A Pair of Boots* to Andy Warhol's photographic negative *Diamond Dust Shoes*. Jameson argues that, in contrast to Van Gogh's painting, which evokes "the whole object world of agricultural misery, of stark rural poverty, and the whole rudimentary human world of backbreaking peasant toil, a world reduced to its most brutal and menaced, primitive and marginalized state," Warhol's *Diamond Dust Shoes* functions as "a random collection of dead objects hanging together on the canvas like so many turnips, as shorn of their earlier life world as the pile of shoes left over from Auschwitz." Clarifying this point, Jameson continues, "Andy Warhol's *Diamond Dust Shoes* evidently no longer speaks to us with any of the immediacy of Van Gogh's footgear; indeed, I am tempted to say that it does not really speak to us at all."[24] If the shoes from Majdanek displayed in the U.S. Holocaust Memorial Museum are akin to Warhol's shoes, as Jameson maintains, then the shoes do not speak by themselves, cannot signify in any kind of adequacy to the tremendous loss and devastation of human life. The designers of the museum, at some level perhaps recognizing this problem, have strategically placed Schulstein's poem above the shoes to guide the viewer's experience of them.

This analysis of the shoes rests upon a specular economy, however. What is moving about the mound of shoes may not be the sight of them, but the smell. As Vivian M. Patraka observes in her reading of the museum, "despite constantly blowing fans, the shoes smell from their own disintegration." The smell of leather disintegrating becomes an unexpected synecdoche for the devastation of the lives (no longer) attached to these shoes, and as Patraka asserts, the smell assists "our bodies in making memory" of this history.[25] What happens to museumgoers in this encounter with the mound of shoes is a complex interaction with the evidence on display, an interaction that emphasizes simultaneously the inadequacy of the representation and the effectiveness of such inadequacy.

In an essay entitled "Resonance and Wonder," Stephen Greenblatt draws a useful contrast between two principles for organizing museum exhibits. "Wonder," for Greenblatt, is the reaction evoked by a carefully managed display of unique works—it positions museumgoers as exalted *viewers*. By "resonance," Greenblatt indicates the power of a displayed object, often a "wounded artifact," to evoke a world beyond the boundaries of the exhibit and the museum, and to position museumgoers as engaged *readers*. "A resonant exhibition," Greenblatt elaborates, often pulls the viewer away from the celebration of isolated objects and toward a series of implied, only half-visible relationships and questions: How did the objects come to be displayed? What is at stake in categorizing them as "museum quality"? How were they originally used? What cultural and material conditions made possible their production? What were the feelings of those who originally held the objects, cherished them, collected them, possessed them? What is the meaning of the viewer's relationship to those same objects when they are displayed in a specific museum on a specific day?[26]

His example of a resonant exhibition is the State Jewish Museum in Prague, which includes artifacts from synagogues (silverwork, textiles, and Torah scrolls) as well as artwork from the Terezín concentration camp and a wall of names commemorating the Jews of Czechoslovakia who suffered at the hands of Nazis. The artifacts are not spectacular or monumental, they are not subjected to the kind of boutique lighting he sees as central to art museum exhibitions, and so the State Jewish Museum in Prague functions for Greenblatt not so much as a museum but as a memorial complex, a site that prompts visitors to recognize "barely acknowledged gaps, the caesurae, between words such as *state*, *Jewish*, and *museum*."[27]

The shoes from Majdanek in the U.S. museum are "wounded artifacts" in Greenblatt's sense: while they are "compelling not only as witnesses to the violence of history but as signs of use, marks of the human touch,"[28] they alone cannot make meaning; they require museumgoers to move beyond their role as viewers and to assume a role as readers. Such critical subjectivity is also fostered as visitors encounter a photograph of the mounds of hair at Auschwitz, a photograph that is set off in its own separate space adjacent to one of the main hallways. It is significant that what is on display is a photograph, not the hair itself,[29] for this display denies the logic of representative artifact found in most of the permanent exhibit. Viewing even the photograph of human hair requires visitors to enter a separate memorial space, a sacred space, in which to contemplate the (absent) object. If the "Arbeit Macht Frei" gate from Auschwitz suggests the dangers of "authentic," or transparent reproductions in the museum, the photograph of hair demonstrates the tremendous possibilities of self-conscious reproductions: this display in the museum suggests that the hair is too powerful an auratic object to be displayed in itself, and so viewing even a photograph of the hair produces a profoundly affecting experience.

Although the impulse to document and authenticate prevails in the exhibit space of the museum, other aspects of the building suggest the importance of emphasizing the limits of representation. The building was designed by architect James Ingo Freed, a German Jew who escaped to America in 1939 at the age of nine. Freed advocated a commitment to indirection and suggestiveness rather than direct or mimetic representation for the museum. "I did not want the building to be a 'theme park,' a replication of the Holocaust," Freed commented. "The Museum had to be something that partook of the flesh and blood of the Holocaust somehow, somewhere, *but not directly visible*" (emphasis added). Hence, his design for the museum includes what he calls "twists," "inversions," "typological" relations, and "metaphoric play." By not replicating or mimetically representing Holocaust locations, Freed's building becomes a "living" memorial—a memorial that does not maintain its own intentions or a single meaning, but resonates with meaning as visitors bring their own images and memories to it and allow them to evolve. "Meanings of memorials change radically," Freed insists, "and you have to accept that; otherwise you soon find that you've done something that is kitsch, that loses its power." The suggestiveness of the building is also crucial to its pedagogic function for Freed. Concerned that too direct a replication of a death camp would flatten or block the "visceral" and engaged response he wanted from observers, Freed used elements from the death camps—steel braces and red brick walls[30]—in the interior space visitors first encounter in the museum, the Hall of Witness, but these elements exist in a new context. Thus, the motifs from the death camps "never force themselves" on the observer; rather, as Freed describes it, they

linger like a suggestive stain in one's consciousness. And that suggestive stain has to linger there, and you have to slowly begin to be aware that this building is not made to be beautiful nor to suggest any specific, raw evil; it's designed to bring you to that crack in the building which says that it is not what it seems to be at first glance. The ambiguities were necessary because I intended to establish a dialogue about what happens to memory, what happens to invention, when time passes.[31]

A commitment to memory that is living, not frozen, hence a memory that is elastic and postmodern, is articulated in the contours of Freed's design.

The Hall of Witness. Photograph © Norman McGrath.

Freed's philosophy also works to disrupt productively the narrative flow of the museum. As Holocaust scholar James E. Young has pointed out, by making sense of the incomprehensible, Holocaust narratives can naturalize the horrific events: "Upon entering narrative, violent events necessarily reenter the continuum, are totalized by it, and thus seem to lose their 'violent' quality. . . . Once written, events assume the mantle of coherence that narrative necessarily imposes on them, and the trauma of their unassimilability is relieved."[32] Interestingly, the museum is designed in such a way that the coherent, legible narrative line of the permanent exhibit is physically interrupted in several places. Freed's design moves visitors on the third and fourth floors over glass bridges from the main exhibit area to the "tower" rooms (reminiscent of the crematoria smokestacks or guard towers of the camps). In addition, as visitors move from the fourth to the third to the second floors, each staircase has a resting area occupied by a monumental piece of abstract art. The emphasis on abstraction usefully interrupts the overarching narrative line and offers an invaluable counterpoint to the legible representation and comprehension articulated in the main exhibit spaces.[33] Neither Sol LeWitt's *Consequence*, a series of five squares painted directly on the wall "framed" in white and then surrounded by black wall space, nor Ellsworth Kelly's *Memorial*, four large white sculptured shapes attached to two facing walls, has an obvious, direct connection to anything in the exhibit or even to the Holocaust.[34] The viewer has to do the work, has to struggle to make connections; in so doing, the visitor can no longer function as a consumer of a particular historical narrative but has to become an active participant in interpreting and constructing Holocaust memory.

The concern about naturalizing the violence of the Holocaust was also evident in the discussions about the narrative resolution of the exhibit. Some felt that the exhibit should have a hopeful, triumphant ending, perhaps emphasizing acts of resistance and rescue to counter the previous images of victimization or pointing to the founding of Israel as a redemptive moment. Others felt that this kind of comforting resolution would do violence to the horror of the Holocaust and felt that the final mood should be more somber to promote reflection and remembrance. In the end, designers decided to include multiple resolutions to the exhibit—scenes of rescue and survival, of justice via the Nuremberg Trials, of exodus to what was then Palestine and to the United States. But the final exhibit is a film called *Testimony*, which consists of short video segments in which twenty survivors recount their Holocaust experiences. In Linenthal's view, "the voices in the episodic film help remind visitors that the individual reality of the Holocaust was much more chaotic than the museum's coherent narrative."[35] The video also works against sentimentalizing the Holocaust: filmed in contemporary surroundings, the survivors and their stories remind visitors that the Holocaust is not part of the past for them, it continues today to affect their lives in profound ways. As we become witnesses to these witnesses,[36] the obligation to remember takes on a pressing urgency.

This mood of contemplation and reflection is reinforced by the last public space visitors encounter. After leaving the second floor exhibits, traffic flows into Freed's Hall of Remembrance. A hexagonal-shaped "dome," this hall is occupied by absence. The walls have minimal adornment: names of the twenty most important camps are engraved on the walls, as are biblical verses; shelves on each wall hold hundreds of small remembrance candles; an eternal flame burns on one wall. But Freed wanted the predominant element of the Hall of Remembrance to be "the empty space in the middle, the polished floor with nothing on it": "This void becomes the core of remembrance. . . . It's the absence of people — the absence of six million. The absence is what we look at. We don't look at anything that's solid. The absence is all, I think, that you can have here."[37] Freed's commitment to suggestion and metaphoric play in the Hall of Remembrance (the six walls, for instance, alluding to the six million) acknowledges the limits of narrative coherence and direct representation by themselves to perform the crucial cultural work of Holocaust remembrance.

Underlying many of the decisions developers and designers made concerning the U.S. Holocaust Memorial Museum was the desire to avoid commodifying the Holocaust, to avoid creating a version of "Holokitsch." Early in the planning stages, a delegation visiting various camp sites and Holocaust memorials in Europe was appalled by what they witnessed at Auschwitz. One of the delegates described the scene this way: "Over the years Auschwitz has been transformed into a tourist mecca, with souvenir stands, shops, refreshment stands, parking lots for excursion buses, and vendors walking among the crowds selling postcards and snacks." A consultant to the delegation was similarly dismayed: "It wasn't enough to give them our parents and grandparents, our brothers and sisters. . . . We also had to leave them a billion dollar tourist industry."[38] Postmodern theory recognizes that there is no pure space outside the reach of capitalist commodification — not even a loca-

The Hall of Remembrance. Photograph © Norman McGrath.

tion like Auschwitz, which ought to be a sacred space, a place to contemplate and memorialize the nadir of Western culture in the twentieth century. Despite all of the ways in which the developers of the U.S. museum worked to prevent such commodification in their own building and exhibit space, the influence of the market and postmodern culture does not stop at the doors to the museum. Director Jeshajahu Weinberg, in fact, insisted that video monitors be included throughout the museum to tell the story of the Holocaust, saying that the museum could not afford to "be subtle"; its "visual historiography" would be a "crude method of expression." In response to concerns that his plans for the integration of audiovisual materials throughout the exhibit might result in a Disneylike atmosphere, Weinberg asserted, "Modern audiovisual technology will be indispensable: we must speak the language of 1990 and 2000."[39]

The use of video monitors or films in the museum is not the real threat, however. The problem beyond the museum's control, despite its somber subject matter and reverential atmosphere, is that visitors will function as tourists who engage the site superficially. One wonders if this sort of experience led to the response one visitor wrote in the museum's comment book: "I enjoyed this a lot."[40] Intended as a sacred space in which to carry on the work of memorializing Holocaust history, the museum on the Mall cannot completely detach itself from the desire for spectacle and entertainment value that visitors bring in the entry doors with them.

Irena Klepfisz: From Mourning to Remembrance

In its emphasis on a chronological and comprehensible narrative of Holocaust history, the U.S. Holocaust Memorial Museum both facilitates and undercuts a living memory of the Holocaust. Clearly other cultural forms are needed to nourish and sustain Holocaust history and memory. In contrast to the legible narrative requirements of museum exhibits, literary texts may be able to do the cultural work necessary to engage Holocaust memory, for literature, especially in the twentieth century, has honed its capacity to speak a language of fragments. The poetry of Irena Klepfisz, a child survivor, exemplifies this potential.

Irena Klepfisz was born on her father's twenty-eighth birthday, April 17, 1941, in the Warsaw Ghetto. She would know her father, Michał, only a short time. Near the end of her birth year, the Nazis began to make decisions about implementing "the Final Solution," and in July 1942, liquidation of the Warsaw Ghetto began. By October 1942, there were approximately 55,000 Jews left in the ghetto, compared to the estimated 445,000 who had lived there in early

1941.[41] Most of the Jews from the ghetto were shipped to Treblinka and killed there. Michał Klepfisz was forced onto one of these trains, but somehow managed to jump from the train and make his way back to Warsaw without being detected. The family otherwise evaded the major liquidation actions, and late in 1942 or early in 1943, Michał smuggled Rose, his wife, and Irena to the Aryan side of Warsaw. Mother and daughter survived the war by passing as Poles: Rose worked as a maid for a Polish family, while Irena was initially placed in a Catholic orphanage and later reunited with her mother. On April 20, 1943, the second day of the Warsaw Ghetto Uprising, Michał Klepfisz—a member of the Jewish Labor Bund resistance group, which was part of the Jewish Fighting Organization that planned the uprising—was killed during a skirmish with the Nazis in the brush factory district.[42] Rose and Irena remained in Poland for only one year after the end of the war. In 1946 they emigrated to Sweden, and in 1949 they came to the United States.

Irena Klepfisz has grappled, in both her essays and poems, with the implications of the history into which she was born. In fact, Adrienne Rich emphasizes this particular characteristic of Klepfisz's work in her discussion of the poet in *What Is Found There: Notebooks on Poetry and Politics*.[43] Rich describes Klepfisz as "unequivocally rooted in the matrix of history" and traces the impress of this history in the voice and poetics that Klepfisz employs. But what Rich finds particularly admirable about Klepfisz's writing is her ability to make Jewish history dynamic and meaningful for the exigencies of the 1990s. In Klepfisz's work "survivorhood isn't a stasis; the survivor isn't an artifact," Rich writes.[44] Indeed, Klepfisz's ideas about the significance of the Holocaust for herself, her own work, and the constitution of Jewish identity in America have evolved tremendously over the years.

In the early stages of her career, Klepfisz was skeptical that the Holocaust could be evoked in America without doing violence to the memory. In a 1982 essay significantly entitled "Resisting and Surviving America," Klepfisz discusses the many obstacles, both internal and external, that prevent Jews from strongly affirming their ethnic identity in America. One factor of great concern to Klepfisz is the commercialization and trivialization of the Holocaust:

I am, I repeat, convinced that people are turned off of the Holocaust because it has been commercialized, metaphored out of reality, glamorized, been severed from the historical fact. . . . This Holocaust is awarded Emmys, Oscars, Tonys, Best-Jewish-Book-of-the-Year awards. This phenomenon of co-opting is, of course, not atypical. It is very, very American. It is the process of mainstreaming whatever seems real and genuine, whatever seems threatening. It is a process of dilution, of wringing any reality or feeling out of true suffering or need or ideal. It is cheapness, vulgarity. (*DI* 64)[45]

In 1982, Klepfisz saw the Holocaust becoming simulacra in America, being tailored to fit the entertainment, mass media desires of the American public — precisely the kind of experience the designers of U.S. Holocaust Memorial Museum wanted to preclude.[46] During a 1983 trip to Poland with her mother to commemorate the fortieth anniversary of the Uprising, however, Klepfisz was disturbed to see that directly across from the *umschlagplatz* in Warsaw (the place where Jews boarded the trains that took them to Treblinka) a gas station stood. All that formally memorialized the location were a small wall, a plaque, and a candle (*DI* 93).[47] Evidently the struggle to maintain some locations as sacred spaces was not just an American phenomenon.

Klepfisz's trip to Poland in 1983 brought another perspective to the problems of Holocaust remembrance. While Holocaust memory in America might be in danger of being commodified and simplified, the opposite danger existed in Poland, of having few or no memorial spaces at all. During her visit, Klepfisz was outraged to find Jewish cemeteries in almost complete disrepair in Warsaw and Lodz.[48] At Treblinka, there were crosses to commemorate the Poles who died there, but no Jewish stars. The main monument at Treblinka had only Polish words on it — no Yiddish or Hebrew lettering. Because the Nazis set fire to Treblinka as they retreated, and because the memorials and monuments subsequently erected at the site were abstract and symbolic, Treblinka became an arduous task in grasping at historical interpretation for Klepfisz, her mother, and other visitors, not a means for preserving a traumatic history (*DI* 102–6). Because of these circumstances, Klepfisz began to reevaluate her national affiliations as a displaced Jew:

Returning to Poland in 1983, I was plunged back into a period of history in which Jews were powerless. Complicating my feelings even more was my acute awareness that the country to which I was returning was a Poland almost empty of any Jews. . . . Poland remains undzer heym, *our home, no matter how bitter the memories, how filled with disappointment and betrayal.* Amerike iz goles, *America is exile, a*

foreign land in which I speak a foreign tongue. But I will never live in Poland. I do
not want to, though I do not see an end to the mourning. (*DI* 88–89)

Exiled permanently from Poland, and despairing at its failure to
commemorate or remember the Holocaust, Klepfisz recognized
the necessity to write about the Holocaust in America, while trying
to avoid the commercialization of Holocaust history she saw so
clearly in American mass culture. Like the planners of the U.S.
museum, Klepfisz has had to struggle intensely with issues of representation and ethics in her treatment of the Holocaust.

Klepfisz's earliest poems are about her father, and though they
were written in 1971, they were not published until 1990, when her
selected poems and selected essays were collected and published as
companion volumes by Eighth Mountain Press. Their belated publication signals some reluctance on her part to include these poems
in her first two volumes of poetry—perhaps Klepfisz hesitated to
make public such personal history as a novice writer, or perhaps this
belated publication signals the difficult and traumatic process of
writing/representing the Holocaust.

In the poem "Searching for My Father's Body," Klepfisz mourns
the loss of the father she barely knew and the lack of a gravestone to
mark the spot where he is buried.[49] She tries to fill this double
absence through reading about Holocaust history, especially of the
Warsaw Ghetto Uprising, turning first to the index of a book to see
if her father's name is mentioned. The research is more difficult
than it seems initially, for the speaker of the poem quickly sees that
history is a matter of construction, not record: "It all depends on
who you knew, / or rather who knew of you, / that determines
history" (*FW* 29). Moreover, such reading makes her vulnerable to
pain. She tries to skim through books that have no index, but is not
always able to maintain her researcher's distance:

> Often caught by a particular sight
> I begin to read, despite myself,
> and learn a new name, another event,
> still another atrocity. I smell again
> the burning bodies, see the flames,
> wade through sewers in a last desperate effort,
> till some present distraction,
> like hunger or cold, draws

me back and I begin closing windows
and preparing dinner. (*FW* 30)

As in Morrison's concept of rememory, Klepfisz experiences the
pain and anguish of events that she has not personally experienced.
But unlike those who were killed, she has the possibility of putting
down the book, of stepping out of the agony, and returning to
ordinary life.

After dinner and some respite from her painful research, she
locates passages in three books that name her father, passages that
she weaves into the poem. Ironically, however, these textual memorials to her father do not satisfy the daughter-speaker after all. Two
of the excerpts tell of Michał's heroic death; his life, the daughter
realizes, remains unrecorded, leading to yet more unfulfilled longing: "I want more details / to fill up my emptiness" (*FW* 32). The
third excerpt tells of her father's work as a resistance fighter: when
all ways back into the ghetto from the Aryan side of Warsaw were
blocked, Michał would hide with friends, if possible, and if not, "*he
would go to sleep in the cemetery among the graves*" (*FW* 33). This passage
offers a small glimpse into his life and character, which the speaker
seizes on to move beyond the overwhelming specter of his death
and her endless mourning.

> And my father
> sleeps among the graves
> in Christian cemeteries
> grateful
> that there is a dry spell,
> that the contact will have a pistol,
> that he will be able to jump the wall,
> that perhaps tomorrow Marysha
> will find him a real place to sleep.
> It is here I see him most clearly
> as he sleeps leaning against a tombstone
> and dreams, never considering
> where he himself will one day be buried. (*FW* 34)

Rather than dwelling on his martyr's death, the daughter emphasizes the father's work in the underground, passing over to the
Aryan side and smuggling weapons back into the ghetto. She fo-

cuses on his ability to persevere despite the hostile surroundings (a *Christian* cemetery, the ghetto wall). Shifting into present tense for the closing stanza, the poet-daughter imagines her father alive, imagines a peaceful sleep for him. But this textual resurrection does not entirely end her grieving: his death is prefigured in the closing images of tombstones, and though the father sleeps peacefully at the end because he is not concerned with his own burial, the daughter-survivor cannot help but remember that his burial site will be forever unmarked.

The psychological wounds that survivors have to live with becomes the major theme of "The Widow and the Daughter," the second belated Holocaust poem published for the first time in 1990. The poem begins with an epigraph from the book *Doyres Bundistn* (Generations of Bundists) — "The widow Rose and small daughter Irena survived and now reside in New York" (*FW* 35) — signifying that like the hero/martyr Michał, they too have become part of history. The problem, however, is that they continue to live, and the poem questions whether they can ever move out from under the weight of history, the pain of their loss. At night in their New York apartment, the father's spirit returns to oppress them:

> And when the two crowded
> into the kitchen at night
> he would press himself between them
> pushing, thrusting, forcing them to remember,
> even though he had made his decision,
> had chosen his own way
> rather than listening to the pleas of her silence
>   (she once said: I never complained about his activities
>   and Michał said he was glad I was not like other wives
>   who wanted to draw their husbands back into safety)
> he would press himself between them —
> hero and betrayer
> legend and deserter —
> so when they sat down to eat
> they could taste his ashes. (*FW* 38)

In this poem, mourning for the father has turned to guilty anger — his decision to be a hero to the cause of resistance also meant that he had to "desert" and "betray" his own family. Because of his monumental death, his surviving wife and daughter will always live in his shadow, will always "taste his ashes."[50]

The raw emotion of Klepfisz's poem conveys a sense of the trauma that survivors continue to experience, and the ending of the poem refuses to allow even a scab to form on the open wound. This poem offers no post-Holocaust redemptive vision. In this respect it recalls the efforts of the planners of the U.S. Holocaust Memorial Museum to refuse a redemptive ending to the museum's historical narrative of the Holocaust so that visitors, who otherwise had no personal knowledge of the trauma, would remain disturbed and provoked by what they had seen in the museum. But for survivors, the Holocaust is not a museum exhibit that can be left behind and forgotten. Klepfisz has written of the continuing trauma survivors experience:

The Holocaust was not an event that ended in 1945 — at least not for the survivors. Not for me. It continued on and on because my mother and I were alone. Because my father's family no longer existed and I was its sole survivor. It continued on in the struggle of extreme poverty that we experienced in the early years in this country. It continued on and on, coloring every thought I had, every decision I made. It continued on in the Bronx, on ordinary streets, at the kitchen table. It continued on invisible. (*DI* 65–66)

In her poems from the 1970s, Klepfisz challenges herself to develop a poetics and voice that can bear witness to this ever-present distress.

In her first volume of poems, entitled *periods of stress,* self-published in 1975,[51] Klepfisz began to develop techniques to extend her poetic forms in ways that could voice Holocaust memory. Two innovations stand out: she uses lowercase letters extensively, omitting the capital letters that would begin a sentence; and she begins to allow large spaces to occupy her lines, spaces that do not just signal end-stops but abruptly halt the syntactic sequence. Through these techniques, Klepfisz's poems suggest that a fundamental inarticulateness is necessary in the face of such history, a tentativeness perhaps related to all the individual stories we can and will never know because of the very fact of genocide. This hesitation also has productive effects: in the Holocaust poems from this volume, Klepfisz stretches her own vision and allows herself to write in the first person about experiences she never had (detection and extermination, rape, gassing and burning) as well as including poems based on her personal history.

In "death camp," one of the most discomforting poems, the voice is of a young woman going to the gas chamber along with a rebitsin (rabbi's wife) whom she recognizes and remembers with bitterness. The precise cause of the speaker's anger is unspecified but revolves around some (inappropriate or perhaps accommodationist) advice the rebitsin gave her:

> when they turned   on the gas   i smelled
> it   first   coming at me   pressed myself
> hard to the wall   crying   rebitsin   rebitsin
> i am here with you   and the advice you gave me
> i screamed   into the wall   as the blood burst from
> my lungs   cracking   her nails in women's flesh
>   i watched
> her capsize   beneath me   my blood in her mouth
>   i screamed (*FW* 47)

These lines gasp for air as the speaker struggles against the gas to scream, to give voice to her torment. Readers too, as they work through this agonizing poem, must struggle like the speaker for breath, must struggle with the recognition that there is no hope. Indeed, Rich has remarked on this visceral effect: " 'death camp' is a poem of death so alive that its smoke remains in our nostrils."[52]

The poem continues in this way, refusing to allow much respite:

> when they dragged my body   into the oven   i burned
> slowly at first   i could smell my own flesh   and could
> hear   them grunt   with the weight of the rebitsin
> and they flung   her on top   of me   and i could smell
> her hair burning   against my stomach
>
> when i pressed through   the chimney
> it was sunny   and clear   my smoke
> was distinct   i rose quiet   left her
> beneath (*FW* 47)

There is a double irony at the end of this poem. By presenting a speaker whose voice continues on after the efforts to exterminate her, Klepfisz's poem suggests a kind of ironic triumph: despite Nazi efforts to erase Jews from the face of Europe, their voices remain

and continue to clamor for justice. There is also, however, a maca-
bre irony at the end: the rebitsin's body is placed on top of the
speaker's in the crematorium, but the speaker's smoke rises *above*
the rebitsin's. Readers cannot help but wonder why this speaker
displays such bitterness toward the rebitsin and not towards those
who have perfected the efficient machinery of the death camp.
Klepfisz's poem provokes precisely because the speaker wants to
blame the rebitsin rather than the Nazis, and in this way, it obliquely
conveys a terrible crisis of victimization: by focusing so concertedly
on the rebitsin, Klepfisz's speaker demonstrates the impossibility of
directing her screams, her calls for justice, to those in control, who
would not be (and historically were not) moved. Indeed, the poem
"death camp" dramatically explores the tensions between inarticulate speech and the articulate silences that Klepfisz identifies as
central to her poetics at this stage of her career: "I developed a way
of laying words out on a page and surrounding them with a lot of
empty space — the poems were sparse, the words far from each
other. They were as much about speaking as about silence. I was not
aware of this [at the time], but silence had become and remains a
central theme in my writing" (*DI* 168).

   The title of Klepfisz's volume, *periods of stress*, refers not only to
the distressing situations faced by Jews during World War II evidenced in poems like "death camp" in part one of the collection,
but also to various stresses of contemporary life portrayed in the
poems of part two, which examine paralyzing self-doubt, lesbians
trying to make their relationship work, and the difficulty of being
an artist in a dehumanizing world. Klepfisz's Holocaust poems are
carefully kept separate from these other poems so that parts one
and two of this volume are strikingly different in tone and theme.
Klepfisz explains in an essay that she was worried that her Holocaust
poems were more powerful than the other poems she had written,
and she "was very determined not to play into the commercialism
with which the Holocaust was becoming increasingly surrounded"
(*DI* 168). Wanting "to write about other things," Klepfisz began to
explore contentious contemporary subjects through her poetry in
the 1970s — feminism and lesbianism in particular. In her first volume of poems, however, these subjects would seem to have no direct relation to her Holocaust poetry, and so, Klepfisz explains,
periods of stress "reflected the strict divisions between my Jewish and
lesbian life" (*DI* 169).

This division would quickly and astonishingly be set aside, however, in Klepfisz's next volume of poetry: *Keeper of Accounts*, originally published in 1982.[53] *Keeper of Accounts* contains four interlinked parts, which together narrate the speaker-poet's successful struggle to bridge the gap between Poland and America, between the past and the present, and between her lesbian-feminist consciousness and her Jewish identity. Continuing to experiment with form, Klepfisz carries on her practice of making silence visible on the page, but she also turns to the long-poem form for much of the volume to articulate and work through the grievous divides mentioned above.

The first section of *Keeper of Accounts*, "From the Monkey House and Other Cages," consists of a long poem of the same title that focuses on two female monkeys in a zoo caged together. This poem is divided into two monologues; "Monkey I" speaks first, followed by "Monkey II." The poem dwells on their varying responses to the unchangeable fact of their being caged and, since they are female monkeys, to their being mated. At the beginning of the poem, Monkey I shares a cage with an older female monkey, who is weak, emaciated, and cold, but who holds her and tries to offer comfort. The older monkey tries to protect Monkey I when the zookeepers come to take her, but she is unsuccessful. The keepers take Monkey I, who is in heat, to perform invasive procedures with a "probe." The experience is traumatic, and Monkey I is forced to empty herself to endure the experience:

>   i did not move
> just sucked my breath
> with each new venture   into my deepest parts
> and then   with time
> i became   a dark dull color
> a gray rain   blending
> with the liquid   of her eyes. (*FW* 112)

The images and actions of these lines begin to exceed the original frame of reference for the poem: this is a poem not only about monkeys in a zoo, but also Jews in the camps. The allusion to cruel medical experimentation brings to mind the infamous Dr. Josef Mengele of Auschwitz, and Monkey I's survival strategy — of becoming "dark" and "dull" so that she can "blend" in — recalls the desire to efface oneself at roll call in the camps because to stand out in any way would mean being selected for extermination.

Klepfisz adds yet another dimension to this haunting poem when Monkey I is returned to her cage and finds that she is irrevocably alienated from the female monkey who formerly gave her comfort:

> i sat alone.   we were
> separate now   though
> she was still there
> in the cage   next to mine.
> her fur was stiff   her nostrils spread
> she eyed me   circled
> her back arched   ready for attack. (*FW* 113)

The loss of comfort and female intimacy becomes the focus of Monkey I's monologue. Soon after this moment of alienation, a male monkey is thrust into Monkey I's cage; the other female monkey reacts in a frenzy, perhaps as a futile attempt to warn Monkey I of what lies in store for her. Klepfisz describes the act of mating in an excruciatingly neutral tone:

> soon the trees budded   and i
> pinked   softened   and presented.
> he penetrated   withdrew
> penetrated   withdrew
> over   and over
> till i was dry
> and hard. (*FW* 116)

There is no desire, no pleasure, in this initiation into heterosexuality, only dull repetition. In fact, given the conditions of this sexual encounter—occurring in a cage, in accordance with the keepers' plans for mating—Klepfisz suggests not only the Nazi enthusiasm for racist eugenics but also the ways in which social norms bar and inhibit women's relationships with each other. Using the zoo setting and the images of cages, Klepfisz calls into question the ideological construction of heterosexuality as natural along lines similar to Adrienne Rich's analysis of "compulsory heterosexuality."[54]

Monkey I bears a child from this mating, and a family is formed, only to be torn apart as first the male and then the baby are removed from her cage. Left alone after this series of violent and traumatic manipulations, Monkey I ends her monologue thinking of the other female monkey:

> sometimes at night   i watch
> her asleep: the rigid bones
> the thinned out fur
>
> and i can see clearly
> the sky   the bars
> as we sat together
> in a spot of sun
> and she   eyes closed
> moved me
> moved me
> to the sound of the waters
> lapping
> in the small   stone pools
> outside. (*FW* 119)

The ending moment resonates with a vision of female connection amid these hostile surroundings and circumstances. In contrast to the repetitive and painful mating with the male monkey, Monkey I finds herself "moved" by the female monkey, recognizing sexual desire to be an important part of their former intimacy. This recognition offers the only solace and comfort possible in such conditions.

While Monkey I longs for connection at the end of her monologue, Monkey II emphasizes the need to remain apart from the other monkeys throughout most of her monologue. Admitting that "i have heard of tortures / yet remain / strangely safe," Monkey II keeps her distance and fervently hopes not to encounter the "probes" and "indignities" she nonetheless dreams about every night. These dreams are so vivid that she finds herself in torment every morning:

> waking   in early light
> alone   untouched
> i cry over my safety. (*FW* 121)

Like some who survived the Holocaust, she is terrorized by horrors she has not experienced and feels anxiously guilty about surviving. Her ability to keep herself apart from the other monkeys is disrupted when a female monkey who openly resists authority is placed in her cage. This female arrives "stunned and bruised," perhaps already having been beaten for her defiance. The only means of protest left to her is "refusing to eat," but eventually this method results in her becoming weak, then sick, then being "removed without resistance" from the cage (*FW* 123). When she returns to the cage, the female monkey seems to have adopted a victimist point of view: "we create / the responses around us," she tells Monkey II (*FW* 123). No longer able to resist those in authority, she redirects her rage toward Monkey II, biting and clawing her. She is removed from the cage again, and when she returns she is passive, perhaps tamed, but only for awhile. Eventually, she cannot bear this caged existence and begins to protest by "bang[ing] her head / against the wall," continuing until she draws blood, sheds tufts of fur, and falls into unconsciousness. Monkey II's reaction to this suicide is not like the almost supercilious disgust she has expressed toward previous monkeys; rather, she feels the loss acutely, finding herself mourning and remembering that "there had been much between us / in gesture" (*FW* 127). Like Monkey I, Monkey II affirms her bond with another woman, a bond so significant it alters her dreams:

> dizzy
> with messages   i would lie
> down   dream of different
> enclosures. (*FW* 128)

Because of this encounter, Monkey II is able to look beyond the bars of her cage and dream of a world outside of the zoo / camp.

Though I have described the long poem "From the Monkey House and Other Cages" as consisting of two monologues, the poem is, in fact, dialogic in effect. Monkey I and Monkey II have experiences that are sometimes shared, sometimes unique, so they arrive at perspectives on their experiences that sometimes concur, sometimes conflict. Klepfisz's poem, however, refuses to judge one reaction or position as being better than another. This is crucial, for if we read the monkeys as camp prisoners, their significant differences suggest the need to accept and understand a diversity of

responses to the death camp experience and the terror of genocide. But by giving them the voices of monkeys at a zoo, Klepfisz
insists on one common reference point: both bear witness to the
traumatic ways in which "others" are constructed as alien to the
social order, dehumanized, and then cruelly violated.

In *Testimony: Crises of Witnessing in Literature, Psychoanalysis, and
History*, Shoshana Felman and Dori Laub argue that the Holocaust
marks a crisis of knowledge so acute that history becomes an inadequate witness to the trauma. They turn instead to literature and to
film, as indirect and belated narratives, in order to locate ways of
registering the profoundly traumatic repercussions of the Holocaust.[55] Operating along lines similar to Felman and Laub's perspective, Klepfisz's long poem, "From the Monkey House and Other
Cages," obliquely, and thus powerfully, invokes the Holocaust. This
strategy of indirectly referencing the Holocaust pervades the entire
volume, even when cages or camps or Klepfisz's personal history is
not mentioned explicitly.

The title of the second section of poems is "Different Enclosures," echoing the final line of Monkey II's monologue. The poems
in this second section take up the issue of women's work, testifying
to the ways in which pink-collar (clerical) workers are underpaid
and patronized, as well as to the economics of women writers like
Klepfisz, forced to do clerical work and other tasks to support themselves while regretting the loss of time and attention to give what is
most important to them.[56] On the surface, this subject matter seems
feminist, not specifically Jewish. But Klepfisz links class consciousness directly to Jewish identity in her essays. First of all, because her
father and mother were active in the Jewish Labor Bund, a socialist
revolutionary movement among working-class Eastern European
Jews, Irena and her mother settled in an enclave of bundists when
they emigrated to New York a few years after the end of World War II;
this environment instilled in Klepfisz the importance of class analysis and political activism.[57] At the same time, Klepfisz became aware
of how working-class characteristics could elicit open hostility: she
tells of being a student at the City College of New York, where she
was required to take a speech test for admission purposes and, like
many other students, was then required to take four semesters of
speech, in part, as she describes it, as a means of "divesting us of our
working-class Jewish Bronx and Brooklyn accents" (*DI* 151). Another (post)traumatic effect of the Holocaust was to force Jews into

exile, as well as into severe poverty, since most survivors lost everything in the war; thus the ripple effects of the Holocaust were felt in
their new lives taking shape in America. The poems of "Different
Enclosures" bear witness to these forms of post-Holocaust trauma.

The Holocaust similarly becomes an absent presence in the third
section of poems from *Keeper of Accounts*, entitled "Urban Flowers,"
in which the speaker-poet visits the Brooklyn Botanical Gardens
and meditates upon the flowers found in her urban surroundings.
It quickly becomes obvious that the word flowers is wrenched from
any typical associations in this poetry. The speaker of these poems is
drawn not to roses or lilies or orchids, or to other conventionally
sensuous and beautiful flowers celebrated in traditional pastoral or
love literature. Instead, she is fascinated by cacti and lithops (which
significantly are also called "living stone"); she takes note of the
labyrinthine roots of narcissus bulbs rather than the flowers, and to
an abutilon, or indoor maple, that "burst[s] forth with orange flowers" despite the "savage hues of our captivity" (*FW* 165). These
plants do not articulate an aesthetics of decorous beauty or orna-
ment; they articulate an aesthetics of "bare essentials," of how to
survive being uprooted and transplanted into "inhospitable soil"
(*FW* 164). Like the *lebn geblibene* (the Yiddish term for survivors,
literally the ones remaining alive), these plants are survivors that
sometimes bloom despite their alien and hostile surroundings.

In the fourth and final section of *Keeper of Accounts,* resonantly
entitled "Inhospitable Soil," the poet-speaker learns to endure and
then grow in the American soil into which she has been transplanted during the aftermath of World War II. This section begins
with an epigraph from Klepfisz's good friend and fellow lesbian-
feminist writer Melanie Kaye/Kantrowitz:

i can't go back
where i came from was
burned off the map

i'm a jew
anywhere is someone else's land (*FW* 167)[58]

The pervasive sense of exile and otherness alluded to here inhabits
the three long poems that comprise this section.

In "Glimpses of the Outside," the speaker rents a home in Cherry Plain, where in her daily life an awareness of how she has been shaped by the Holocaust comes into focus. A small piece of information claims her attention:

> Cherry Plain was once called South Berlin   before
> the war   and then they probably became self-conscious.
>   (*FW* 169)

The change of name marks a convenient forgetting of history for the inhabitants of this town, but this luxury is not available to the speaker of the poem. Even the activity of gardening is laden with history: transplanting wildflowers to the ground around the house, she discovers that some plants (like those who survived the Shoah only to commit suicide afterwards) cannot endure being transplanted to new soil, no matter how careful she is. Why not?

>   I consider
> the possibilities: individual will   personality   simple
> biochemical make-up. Whatever. (*FW* 171)

The speaker speculates, refusing to decide upon a single specific factor. She then recalls an incident from childhood, when she trapped fireflies in a bottle and they died despite her efforts to treat them gently:

>   I do not understand
> that not even the dusty grass   hurriedly pressed through
> the narrow bottleneck   will keep them alive   that
> inevitably   in such confinement (is it a lack of air
> or simply a lack of space for flight?)   their light will
> dim and die. (*FW* 171)

Some experiences, this memory suggests, are so traumatic for the participants that there is no way of living past them, of working through them.

Even if one does survive a torturous past, the trauma remains and can make someone vulnerable to becoming implicated in other tragic histories. This occurs in Klepfisz's poem when the speaker drives through an idyllic valley and notices a disquieting sign:

"Indian Massacre Road"   a sign indistinguishable
from any other in lettering and color   posted modestly
at an obscure crossing (*FW* 172)

From her perspective, this road sign signifies how easily collective
amnesia can take hold in America; it is

but a barely noticeable
vestige   of one history forgotten and unattended. (*FW* 172)

Like the specter of Native American genocide, which as we have seen
for Erdrich is a part of history that is not over, that haunts contemporary America, the Holocaust continues to frame the speaker's
present experiences and responses. This point is made dramatically
clear when a young male plumber, who has come to inspect the
worn-out pump for the well, tells the speaker that he will try to repair
it for her: " 'I'll take anything on,' " he says, perhaps intending to
reassure her, " 'as long as it's white' " (*FW* 172). The reference to
color stands out, for there is no immediate antecedent for this
allusion to the pump's whiteness. Perhaps unwittingly, certainly
quite naturally and casually, the young man has voiced an allegiance
to whiteness that can only summon up the Holocaust and Nazi
racism for the speaker.

This harrowing moment leads into a visit from the speaker's
mother, a survivor who, even in America, presumably a safe place
for Jews, continues to survey everyone around her to assess

who are
the safe ones   and who are not. (*FW* 173)

Telling the mother's story, the speaker recognizes that her mother
will forever be shaped by the strategies she developed to survive the
Holocaust. She also recognizes that her own responses and perspectives are similarly formed. Putting her mother on the train that
will take her back home at the end of the visit, the speaker relives a
prior traumatic moment evoked by what should be a normal act of
separation:

Departures
swell old   undefined fears in me   the fear of permanent

separations. Old   long-forgotten departures   which
remain active in me   like instinct. The fear of being
lost and never found   of losing all trace   all connections
severed   the thread broken. (When after two years   she
came to get me from the orphanage   I cried when I caught
sight of her   and raised my arms to her. I was barely
three   but I had not forgotten.) Of endless   futile
searches for relatives long vanished   or even worse
alive   but not traceable. (*FW* 176)

Separation anxiety is a psychoanalytic commonplace used to describe a painful but normal individuation process for children.
Given the historical circumstances of mother and daughter in this
poem, however, there is no possibility of resolving this basic human
anxiety.

Anxiety about separations, in fact, haunts the speaker's relationships with people other than her mother. In the last part of
"Glimpses from the Outside," the speaker mourns the death of a
close friend, Marcia Tillotson, to whom the poem is dedicated. The
death of this friend seems almost too much to bear because of the
loss and exile that the speaker continues to experience. But at
the very moment when the poem reaches its most despairing point,
the speaker decides to plant flowers in the inhospitable soil of
Cherry Plain:

                                            I plant bulbs
like a skeptic   never fully believing   these drab
lifeless lumps   will bloom next year   in full exotic color.
Nothing   I think   staring at the sixty-year-old ash
should be taken for granted. I push my trowel   deeper
sift out the slivers of glass   the heavy nails   place
the bulbs in their designated places   then cover them
with soil   flattening the surface with my hand. (*FW* 182)

This action shows a willingness to face the sharp, painful layers of
history signified by the images of nails and shards of glass (the latter
perhaps resonating with the historical memory of *Kristallnacht*),
and to act as though the trauma can be worked through. In the face
of an almost inconceivable tragic history, the poem finally and elo-

quently insists that one survives by continuing to struggle, by continuing — somehow — to believe in life.

The significance of the speaker's recognition at the end of "Glimpses of the Outside" is witnessed in the long poems that follow it: "*Bashert*" — the title is a Yiddish word that Klepfisz translates as "inevitable, (pre)destined" — and "Solitary Acts." The speaker faces her history directly, narrating moments of her mother's, her father's, and her close friend Elza's Holocaust experiences in "*Bashert*," and narrating moments from her aunt Gina's life and work in the resistance movement in "Solitary Acts."[59] It is difficult to tell these stories; in fact, the speaker of "Bashert" recalls an incident from April 17, 1955, when she was asked to light a remembrance candle for children who died in the Holocaust and she found herself "numb with terror":

I fear these people with blue numbers on their arms, people who are disfigured and scarred, who have missing limbs and uneasy walks, people whose histories repel me. Here in this auditorium, they abandon all inhibitions, they transform themselves into pure sound, the sound of irretrievable loss, of wild pain and sorrow. Then they become all flesh, wringing their hands and covering their swollen eyes and flushed faces. They call out to me and I feel myself dissolving. (*FW* 195)

It is impossible to bear witness to this collective anguish, the speaker fears, without collapsing under the weight of the tragedy. And elsewhere in "*Bashert*," the speaker wonders, "Are there moments in history which cannot be escaped or transcended, but which act like time warps permanently trapping all those who are touched by them? . . . Or can history be tricked and cheated?" (*FW* 192). She resolves in "*Bashert*" and "Solitary Acts" to cheat history by becoming a witness to history, by finding the words and the forms that can communicate the "pure sound" and "irretrievable loss" of those who survived and those who died.

To do this, she must build bridges between her personal Holocaust history and her life in America. The speaker of "Bashert" revisits moments from her own past to make these connections. Thinking about a walk she took through the inner city of Chicago in 1964, the speaker glimpses another tragedy in the making: "I begin to see the incessant grinding down of lines for stamps, for jobs, for a bed to sleep in, of a death stretched imperceptibly over a lifetime. I begin to understand the ingenuity of it. The invisibility. The Holocaust without smoke" (*FW* 193). Remembering the black and Puerto Rican students she taught English to in Brooklyn in 1971, the speaker recognizes their desire for the tools of language and grammar, for jobs, and for acceptance as directly linked to her own desire for a place of belonging. Making these connections gives her the courage to revisit and rewrite a jagged moment of history. The speaker alludes to a traumatic moment from Elza's life that she has previously narrated: as a young girl in Poland passing as a Christian, Elza is sent to a shop to buy a notebook and is given the wrong change; when she points out the error to the shopkeeper, he responds quite threateningly with these words, " 'Very accurate. Just like a Jew. Perhaps you are a little Jewess?' " (*FW* 192). In these circumstances, of course, Elza can do nothing but deny the accusation. Haunted by her Holocaust experiences, the speaker recalls, Elza eventually begins to blame Jews for their own victimization. Recalling the ominous words of the Polish shopkeeper later in the poem, however, the speaker gives the response Elza could not: she proclaims herself a Jew in spite of all the pressures in America to assimilate and in spite of all the anti-Semitic stereotypes of Jews as money-mongers. "Like these, my despised ancestors / I have become a keeper of accounts," the speaker announces, not just once but twice (*FW* 199, 200). The phrase "keeper of accounts" alludes to the stereotypical association of Jews and money (Jews as usurers, for instance), but the speaker reclaims this term in a positive sense: like her ancestors, she will keep scrupulous accounts—not of monetary transactions, but of history and Holocaust memory. She vows to become, in Susan Stanford Friedman's words, "a poet-historian."[60] By remembering her Jewish, woman-centered, activist legacy and communicating it to others, she can intervene in a world that remains violently anti-Semitic.[61]

She begins her work as a historian by telling the story of her Aunt Gina in the last long poem of the volume, entitled "Solitary Acts." The need to keep scrupulous account of history is dramatized in Gina's story, who died in Poland during the war and was buried under a Christian name. Knowing the necessity for disguised naming and coded communication, recognizing the implications of genocide for documentation, the speaker wonders if it is even possible to write Holocaust history:

You are to me   everything
that remains   outside my grasp
everything   in this world
that is destroyed   with no one
there to rescue the fragments
to hear the words.
So much of history   seems
a gaping absence   at best a shadow
longing   for some greater
definition   which will never come
for what is burned   becomes air
and ashes   nothing more. (*FW* 203)

The speaker acutely grasps the difficulty of writing a history of the Holocaust — a history that must be built from absences and silences, from air and ashes. Thinking further about her Aunt Gina's life, though, the speaker realizes that focusing on loss or mourning the destruction is not the answer. She resolves, somehow, "to rescue the fragments":

So I cling   to the knowledge of your
distant grave   for it alone
reminds me   prods me   to shape that shadow. (*FW* 203)

As the speaker recognizes a moral imperative to face and tell this traumatic history, she becomes, like her aunt, a resistance worker: as a keeper of accounts, she will revise the historical accounts to honor those who survived and those who died; she will participate in the project of Holocaust remembrance so that it never happens again. And once she commits herself to this task, the speaker is amazed to discover that she has begun to feel hopeful: "I need to hope. And do," she explains to Gina (*FW* 209).

In *Unclaimed Experience: Trauma, Narrative, and History*, Cathy Caruth outlines a relationship between trauma and history that illuminates Klepfisz's commitment to history at the end of *Keeper of Accounts*. Caruth writes: "For history to be a history of trauma means that it is referential precisely to the extent that it is not fully perceived as it occurs; or to put it somewhat differently, that a history can be grasped only in the very inaccessibility of its occurrence."[62]

This inaccessibility in Klepfisz's case is amplified by the fact that she was a child in the 1940s and therefore only indirectly aware of the ravages of the Holocaust. In Caruth's formulation, there is a useful gap between the occurrence of an event and the perception of that event as a trauma, a belatedness that creates the possibility of history. Klepfisz's career follows such a trajectory: a child of the ghetto who survives, who after the fact becomes aware of the terrible time into which she was born, and who subsequently vows to become a keeper of accounts, a historian. Klepfisz's poetry bears witness to the Holocaust through the indirect referentiality that Caruth theorizes is the core of history as trauma, a history that "arise[s] where *immediate understanding* may not."[63]

Always looking to history to identify these gaps, Klepfisz's perspective on the project of Holocaust remembrance has developed in new directions since the publication of *Keeper of Accounts*. During her 1983 trip to Poland, Klepfisz became acutely aware that Nazism destroyed an entire culture and history along with the lives of Jews during World War II:

> Though I had been raised in almost a *khurbn kultur*, a Holocaust culture, I was totally unprepared for the experience. In Poland I saw the *shadows* of Jewish-Polish culture and was able to infer from them the magnitude of what had taken place. It was like stepping into a negative rather than a photograph. I was overcome by the sudden realization of the scale of the loss. . . . I knew that I would never take Yiddish culture for granted, never abandon it again. (*DI* 158)

Identifying a new wound of this traumatic history, Klepfisz experienced firsthand what Holocaust historian Lucy S. Dawidowicz has described as an irreparable tragedy: "The annihilation of the 6 million European Jews brought an end with irrevocable finality to the thousand-year-old culture and civilization of Ashkenazic Jewry, destroying the continuity of Jewish history."[64]

To bear witness to this destruction in her most recent poems and essays, Klepfisz makes use of Yiddish words and phrases, interspersed with English. Her halting Yiddish not only suggests the loss of culture, language, and homeland resulting from the Holocaust, however; it also seeks to assuage this loss. By using Yiddish, Klepfisz attempts to undo some of the damage, to inspire a renewed interest in *Yidishkayt* in America.[65] For Klepfisz, Yiddish signifies an important political and feminist orientation. As opposed to the religious, and often Zionist, implications of Hebrew, Yiddish is associated for Klepfisz with the socialist and secularist philosophy of the Jewish Labor Bund. This connection became especially important as Klepfisz grew alarmed that Holocaust memory was being injudiciously employed to justify Israeli policies toward Palestinians; rooting one's identity in *Yidishkayt* became a way for her to affirm herself as a Jew in America, while opposing Israeli imperialism.[66] Yiddish is also a gender-inflected language, as Rich observes in her analysis of Klepfisz: Yiddish poetry "was largely written by men yet [written] in the language called *mame-loshn* or 'mother tongue': vivid, emotionally vibrant, vernacular, as opposed to Hebrew, the language of scholarship and religious study, reserved for men only. Yiddish was a people's language, a women's language, the language of the Ashkenazic Jewish diaspora."[67] By using this language in her most recent poems, Klepfisz has found a means to articulate her complicated gender, sexual, ethnic, historical, and personal identities. More importantly, she has found a way to move beyond mourning the unfathomable loss that the term "Holocaust" evokes, to remembering the collective spirit and rich culture of Jewish people.

In the 1990 essay "*Khaloymes* / Dreams in Progress: Culture, Politics, and Jewish Identity," Klepfisz warns against using the Holocaust as a foundation for Jewish American identity. She writes,

As someone touched directly by the events of the war, I am committed to its memorialization, to understanding its implications historically and psychologically. But being conscious of the complex Jewish life before the Holocaust, I am disturbed to see U.S. Jews whose concept of Jewish history is limited to the years 1939–1945 and whose sense of Jewish authenticity derives solely from those years. These Jews place the Holocaust at the center of their Jewishness, rely on their parents' experience to legitimize themselves, look to Jewish victimization and anti-Semites to define and shape their identity. To be born a child of survivors is to be a *real* Jew. One need not be or do anything else. (*DI* 204–5)[68]

Klepfisz's remarks indicate her commitment to remembering Holocaust history, even as they suggest the limits of such history as an end in itself. The Holocaust must be remembered, but not in a way that would freeze this period of time, simplify the lessons it might teach, or underwrite a narrative of Jewish identity linked solely to persecution and martyrdom.

Klepfisz's strong sense of the proper use and potential abuse of Holocaust history resonates with Pierre Nora's theoretical understanding of the relationship between history and memory in the contemporary world, a relationship in which history continually threatens to annihilate memory in order to remain a "universal authority." Nora coins the term *lieux de mémoire* to describe the vital relationship between history and memory that he sees as crucial to the late twentieth century: for Nora, *lieux de mémoire* are informed by critical, self-conscious history, but they ultimately "escape from history" to mobilize the will to remember.[69] Klepfisz's essays and poems are *lieux de mémoire*, in Nora's sense. For Klepfisz, recounting Holocaust history offers one starting point for remembering the incredibly rich, complicated, and long history of Jews as a people. Moving from mourning and loss to cultural renewal, Klepfisz's poetry becomes an important model for facing a traumatic history without commodifying the Holocaust and telling this history so that people will want to remember — the events themselves, and so much more.

Chapter Five
Joy Kogawa and the Peculiar "Logic" of Internment

Cathy Caruth's *Unclaimed Experience* reminds us that a history of traumatic wounds is necessarily a belated narrative, necessarily a complicated reconstruction and indirect referencing of the original wound and the subsequent recognition of it. Given the circumstances of the Holocaust (examined in the previous chapter) and the policies that led to the internment of American and Canadian citizens of Japanese ancestry (the subject of this chapter), it is no wonder that the articulation of these wounds and traumas in narrative form took decades to come to fruition. But there is an important difference in American public consciousness of these historical moments. The U.S. Holocaust Memorial Museum has consolidated, to some degree, public memory and historical consciousness of this terrible epoch of the twentieth century, while internment in the United States and Canada has remained on the fringes of collective memory, despite the successful movements for redress and reparations in both countries in the 1980s. In 1992, fifty years after the issuing of Executive Order 9066, which created the conditions for internment, Manzanar (in California), one of the ten so-called relocation centers in which Japanese American citizens were held in the 1940s, was designated a national historic site, and in 1993, Rohwer (in Arkansas) became a national historic landmark. Such designations are only a necessary first step on the long road to establishing a collective memory of what is a terrible mark on the institutions of democracy in both the United States and Canada.[1]

Although there were sympathetic Anglos in both the United

States and Canada in the 1940s who actively opposed the internment of Japanese American citizens and aliens, their vigorous protests were drowned out by the racism and war-driven anxieties of the public and the politicians. The acclaimed photographer Ansel Adams went to Manzanar in the fall of 1943 to take photographs that are both exquisite and damning. Although these photos were originally published in 1944, in a book significantly entitled *Born Free and Equal*, the work became so controversial that public burnings were organized to destroy copies of the book en masse.[2] A despairing Adams would later decline to renew the copyright on the book and photos; instead, he donated the negatives and prints of Manzanar to the Library of Congress "in hopes that the full story would eventually — perhaps at a more objective time — reach most of the American people."[3] Dorothea Lange, working for the War Relocation Authority, also went to Manzanar to make a photographic record of the camp. Her images, taken in 1942, suggest unabashed sympathy for the internees and created tensions between herself and her immediate supervisors.[4] Her well-known photograph of a dust storm at Manzanar is beautifully composed and politically scathing: its symmetrical composition captures the camp against its breathtaking Sierra Nevada backdrop and poses the American flag furling in the wind in the center foreground of the image. The dust that swirls in the air is not only an important element testifying to the uncomfortable and wretched conditions of the camp when such storms would arise, but it also shows the flag besmirched by dust, a way of signifying the lapse of democratic principles that led to internment.

Because to denounce the camps was necessarily also to question the status of the United States and Canada as democratic nations and to call into question one's own patriotism and loyalty, little public, official, or cultural support was available for those who wished to voice their opposition. Even the internees themselves, and their children and grandchildren, have found it difficult to speak of the experience. Some argue that silence on the subject of internment has to do with Japanese temperament and philosophy, citing the Japanese phrase *shikataga-nai*, which is usually translated as "it cannot be helped." Why rail about something that cannot be helped? Would not the best strategy be simply to endure and focus on what you can control or change? Other scholars have pointed out that

Dust storm at Manzanar, July 1942. Photograph by Dorothea Lange.

the Issei (first-generation Japanese) and Nisei (second-generation) often did not want to share their painful histories, partially out of shame, and so many children of internees have grown up knowing nothing of their own parents' traumatic experiences.[5] The silence continues to haunt families today. Janice D. Tanaka's 1999 film, entitled *When You're Smiling*, explores Sansei (third generation) memories of internment and resettlement. In the film, a Japanese American woman talks about her sister, Amy, who saw slides of the camps one day in a class at the University of California, Santa Cruz, and recognized their grandmother and aunt in some of the images. Amy realized with a shock that she had never heard of this part of her family's history. After class, she asked the professor how to get her own copies of the images; she obtained them and gave them as

Christmas presents to her relatives, hoping to surprise them. They were not pleased.[6] For Japanese Americans and Japanese Canadians, there has been a crisis in witnessing similar to what Dori Laub has identified as a terrible crisis for Holocaust survivors.

In Rea Tajiri's 1991 film, *History and Memory*, an autobiographical and innovative look at the experience of internment, the daughter-speaker of the film remarks, "I began searching for a history, my own history. Because I had known all along that the stories I had heard were not true, and parts had been left out."[7] Her family was interned at Poston, Arizona, despite the fact that her father fought for the United States in World War II. The film reports a stupefying moment: while they were interned, their house was stolen — someone hiked it up on jacks one day, and the next day they backed a truck under it, lowered the house, and drove away with it. Although Rea Tajiri did not experience the camps herself, she points to the ways in which a traumatic history can come to haunt others, as the daughter-speaker of the film says, "I remember having this feeling growing up that I was haunted by something. That I was living within a family full of ghosts. There was this place that they knew about — I had never been there, yet I had a memory for it. I could remember a time of great sadness before I was born. We had been moved, uprooted. We had lived with a lot of pain. I had no idea where these memories came from. Yet I knew the place."

Despite the flourishing of multicultural, ethnic literature in America since the 1960s, internment — like other traumatic histories — is a subject that is not easily located in popular literature, anthologies, or other texts. There are some moving poems by contemporary writers such as Mitsuye Yamada, David Mura, Janice Mirikitani, James Mitsui, and Lawson Inada, while Hisaye Yamamoto has written poignant short stories about internment and the difficulties of postinternment life. But the reception of such works has often been less than enthusiastic. Miné Okubo's *Citizen 13660*, a visual and verbal account of her experience first at the Tanforan Assembly Center in California and then at Topaz in Utah, was published in 1946, right after World War II, but went out of print. It was republished in 1983 by the University of Washington Press, a press that has been instrumental in keeping in print two other works that focus on internment in America: John Okada's *No-No Boy* (originally published in 1957; republished in 1976 and 1986) and Monica Sone's *Nisei Daughter* (originally published in 1953, republished in

1979). Perhaps one of the most often cited autobiographical works on internment is Jeanne Wakatsuki Houston and James D. Houston's *Farewell to Manzanar*, which did not appear until 1973, nearly thirty years after internment had ended.[8]

The collective amnesia surrounding internment and other antidemocratic policies affecting people of Japanese heritage during the 1940s has been broached in recent decades by events in the social-political sphere such as the Asian American movement and the redress and reparations movements that took hold in the late 1970s. In the cultural arena, perhaps the most important event has been the 1981 publication of Joy Kogawa's *Obasan*, the most widely studied novel of internment to date.[9] Like Irena Klepfisz's Holocaust poetry, which connects personal and family experiences to a monumental historical rupture, Kogawa's novel occupies an interesting space between history and fiction. Her family was interned at Slocan in British Columbia, Canada, so personal history (autobiography) informs her novel, but Kogawa also drew on materials from the Public Archives of Canada, in particular using the letters of Muriel Kitagawa to her brother Wes as a source for the section of the novel that renders Aunt Emily's journal. The novel also includes a historical document: a memo protesting attempts to deport people of Japanese ancestry, which was sent to the House and Senate of Canada in April 1946.

The same year that *Obasan* was published, 1981, Ann Gomer Sunahara's *The Politics of Racism: The Uprooting of Japanese Canadians During the Second World War* appeared. Like Kogawa, Sunahara drew upon Muriel Kitagawa's letters for her historical analysis.[10] It is perhaps not merely accidental that Sunahara's and Kogawa's books appeared in the same year: Canada has a "thirty-year rule" that disallows access to certain government documents for this length of time, and so the silence and amnesia surrounding internment in Canada was in part institutionally or structurally produced.[11] But because of the wealth of information on internment that has been made available in recent years, it has also become possible to recognize the degree to which the process and policies of internment constituted a breach in democratic principles so extreme that silence and forgetting were inevitable results. It is worth examining the historical record in detail to understand why *Obasan* was such a breakthrough novel and how the novel has come to play a significant role in creating historical memories of internment.

History and Hysteria

As many historians have observed, the attack on Pearl Harbor on December 7, 1941, unleashed an anti-Japanese frenzy in both the United States and Canada, but the troubling actions that followed such hysteria often remain in the shadows. To appreciate the profound trauma these actions inflicted on the lives of Japanese Canadians and Americans, we must examine the historical record closely and critically, for what began presumably as a matter of "national security" quickly escalated into an unconscionable and staggering set of policies targeting one group on the basis of race. As the following discussion of the "logic" of internment suggests, an uncritical reliance on policy, procedure, and reason can produce terrifying results.

Within months of the attack on Pearl Harbor, the United States and Canada prepared to move all people of Japanese heritage, whether they were citizens or aliens, out of the West Coast regions. The orders passed in both countries that eventually made internment possible, however, were phrased neutrally. Executive Order 9066, issued by President Roosevelt on February 19, 1942, said nothing directly regarding people of Japanese origin; rather, it authorized the Secretary of War to designate "military areas" from which *all persons* who did not have permission to enter and remain would be excluded in the interests of national security. Like Executive Order 9066, the Order in Council (PC 1486) passed under the War Measures Act in Canada on February 24, 1942, authorized the Minister of Justice to exclude or remove "any or all persons" from any designated "protected area" in Canada.[12] Sunahara points out that Canada and the United States had agreed to set similar policies for the Japanese population in both countries, so both orders strategically "were broad enough to be used against anyone — citizen or alien, white or non-white, as individuals or as a group."[13] But in both countries, a chain of events had already been set into motion that made it possible for these ostensibly broad orders to be used primarily to abrogate the civil rights of Japanese American and Japanese Canadian citizens.

Between the bombing of Pearl Harbor and before the passing of Executive Order 9066 and PC 1486, "enemy aliens" in both countries had already been made subject to certain orders and restrictions. They were not to have in their possession any firearms, short-wave radios, cameras, or other items that might be used for espionage or fifth-column enterprises; they were ordered to register with the authorities; and they were eventually required to follow a strict curfew and were prohibited from entering or remaining in protected military zones. In the United States, these protected areas quickly expanded so that by February 4, 1942, they included most of the West Coast. In Canada, Order in Council PC 365 was passed on January 16, 1942, requiring all "male enemy aliens" of military age to leave the protected military zones along the British Columbia coast by April 1, 1942. What Executive Order 9066 and Order in Council PC 1486 did, in contrast to these previous regulations, was to expand the rules of military necessity to *citizens*, thus making it possible to subject Japanese American and Japanese Canadian citizens to the same regulations that were required of (mostly Japanese) "aliens." Indeed, these orders in both countries were quickly followed by notices that affected "all persons of Japanese racial origin" (the phrasing in Canada) or "all persons of Japanese ancestry" (the phrasing in the United States). Two days after Order in Council PC 1486 was passed, a notice signed by Louis S. St. Laurent, Minister of Justice, extended the restrictions and removal orders for all enemy aliens to "all persons of Japanese racial origins."[14] One month after President Roosevelt signed Executive Order 9066, U.S. Army Lieutenant General DeWitt issued Public Proclamation No. 3, which extended military regulations to "all alien Japanese, all alien Germans, all alien Italians, *and all persons of Japanese ancestry.*" On that same day, March 24, 1942, DeWitt issued Civilian Exclusion Order No. 1, which required "all persons of Japanese ancestry, including aliens and nonaliens," to evacuate Bainbridge Island, Washington, on or before noon of March 30, 1942. This exclusion order was to be the test case for the evacuation of all people of Japanese ancestry from the West Coast.[15]

Both the United States and Canada had initially planned to exclude Japanese aliens and citizens from their coastal regions and allow them to resettle where they liked in the interior regions. Both countries soon realized, however, that anti-Japanese feeling was so strong among whites that the "evacuees" would need to be "resettled" and "protected" in specific relocation centers, or camps. Even before the outbreak of World War II, vehemently anti-Japanese organizations, fueled by a mixture of racism and capitalism, existed in both countries: members of the White Canada Association and the

Native Sons of the Golden West (in California), to name just two groups, felt that Japanese immigration was threatening their sense of racial balance (despite the strict quotas that had been passed in both countries), and they resented the economic successes of the Japanese. These organizations used rhetoric that advanced their own nativist claims, referring to Japanese aliens and Japanese American citizens alike as "foreigners" and "immigrants" in order to argue that "natives" (meaning themselves, of course) had a greater claim than "immigrants" to the land, resources, and so on. This appeal to nativism could only be sustained with the aid of national and personal amnesia, as these groups of white supremacists conveniently forgot their own past histories as immigrants.[16] Rather than challenging this amnesia, a number of politicians in both countries began to exploit anti-Japanese sentiments for their own reelection purposes. Ironically, when authorities in the United States and Canada were granted the power to search premises belonging to Japanese aliens without any reasonable cause, these searches demonstrated to the general public that they had something to fear from the Japanese who lived and worked among them (as did the later decision to exclude them from all coastal regions).

The process of carrying out internment produced other traumatic repercussions. Because they were allowed to bring with them to the camps only what they could carry, the internees experienced severe financial and material losses as well as dispossession. The day after the bombing of Pearl Harbor, Canadian authorities began to impound all boats owned by "Japanese" fishermen in the interests of national security; one month later, also in the interests of national security, Order in Council PC 288 was passed requiring these boats to be sold to non-Japanese fishermen. This forced sale meant that the boats were often purchased at prices well below their actual value. Evacuees under full-scale internment plans in both countries were given so little time between the call to report to an assembly center and the date they were required to be there that they often sold cars, businesses, houses at an incredible loss. Mrs. Tetsu Saito and her family owned the Ruth Hotel in Los Angeles when they were ordered to evacuate in 1942. Although the hotel was valued at $6,000 (they had paid off the mortgage in full), they were offered only $300 for it and were forced to accept this ridiculously low figure to get anything at all for the hotel before they were removed to Manzanar.[17] Other internees tried to put their property under someone else's guardianship, rather than selling it outright, but they too experienced hard losses. Evacuees from the Fraser Valley in British Columbia were forced to sell the land they had painstakingly worked and made fertile over decades to a government agency instituting a Veterans' Land Act program designed to reward this land to returning Anglo-Canadian soldiers of World War II.[18] And on January 23, 1943, the Canadian government passed Order in Council PC 469, which ordered all property of internees to be sold and the money used to pay for housing, food, and other provisions of camp life: in other words, Japanese Canadians were to be impoverished to pay for their own incarceration.

Life in the assembly centers, where decisions were made about which camp each family would be sent to, also was harsh. Some of the assembly centers were hastily converted horse stables at race tracks, reeking of manure and teeming with maggots. To get to the camps, Japanese Canadian and Japanese American evacuees were placed onto trains with covered windows, so they would not be able to see where they were going.[19] In the United States once they arrived at their destination, they soon realized that what had been described to them as "relocation centers" were in fact concentration camps, for they were surrounded by barbed wire and under the watchful eye of armed guards.[20] Quarters were excruciatingly small; privacy was nonexistent; every moment of daily life became subject to camp rules and camp routines.

Not only were the policies leading to the internment and dispossession of citizens patently unjust, but the injustice continued in the courts and in subsequent attempts to "repatriate" as many "Japanese" as possible when the war was over. There were three important court challenges in the United States to the curfew and exclusion orders once they were extended to all persons of Japanese ancestry: *Hirabayashi v. United States*, *Korematsu v. United States*, and *Ex parte Endo*.[21] Gordon Hirabayashi refused to report to an assembly center at the appointed time; he was convicted of violating the curfew restrictions and for failing to comply with the exclusion orders. Fred Korematsu also refused to report to an assembly center and, in fact, had minor plastic surgery so that he could remain with his Caucasian fiancee; he was charged with and convicted of failing to comply with the exclusion orders. Both Hirabayashi and Korematsu continued to appeal their convictions until they reached the U.S. Supreme Court, arguing in part that the curfew and exclusion orders were unconstitutional because they disciminated on the basis of race. The Supreme Court rejected those arguments in both cases, ruling unanimously that the Hirabayashi conviction should stand and rendering a split decision in the Korematsu case with the majority voting to uphold the evacuation orders.

Similar to unfortunate Supreme Court rulings in the past—rulings that deemed segregation constitutional or vacated the rights of American Indians at critical moments—these decisions by the highest court in the land were highly politicized and unduly influenced by wartime doctrines. More than fifty years later, we now know that Supreme Court Justices William O. Douglas and Frank Murphy had serious reservations about upholding the Hirabayashi conviction, but were pressured by their fellow justices into concurring with the majority.[22] The court thus unanimously—and egregiously—ruled that wartime measures and military necessity justified the curfew restrictions and that "there was no unconstitutional deprivation of rights."[23] Chief Justice Stone, who wrote the majority opinion, justified racial discrimination in this way: "We cannot close our eyes to the fact, demonstrated by experience, that in time of war residents having ethnic affiliations with an invading enemy may be a greater source of danger than those of a different ancestry." But Justice Murphy, who originally wrote a dissenting opinion that strangely enough was later submitted as a concurring opinion in the Hirabayashi case, argued: "Today is the first time, so far as I am aware, that we have sustained a substantial restriction of the personal liberty of citizens of the United States based upon the accident of race or ancestry. . . . It bears a melancholy resemblance to the treatment accorded to members of the Jewish race in Germany and in other parts of Europe."[24]

There was serious dissent among the justices as the Supreme Court considered the Korematsu case, in part because the court considered the effects and consequences of exclusion, and not just the curfew restrictions as it had in the Hirabayashi case. Nonetheless, arguments based on military necessity won the day, and the justices voted 6–3 in favor of upholding Korematsu's conviction. Clearly, as these cases suggest, Japanese Americans who looked to the courts to uphold their constitutional rights must have felt utterly discouraged and disheartened. There seemed to be no way to gain official or public support for their rights as citizens.[25]

The third case brought before the Supreme Court involved the detainment of Mitsuye Endo, a Japanese American citizen who was interned first at Tule Lake, then moved to Topaz. Endo had been issued a permit to leave Topaz, having passed the loyalty test required, but because of rampant racism outside the camps she could not find a community that would accept her.[26] The authorities decided to continue to detain her at Topaz, despite having issued a permit allowing her to leave. Endo then petitioned federal courts for a writ of habeas corpus and was turned down. When her case reached the Supreme Court, the justices quickly and unanimously decided that Endo was being detained illegally, but the announcement of the court's decision was delayed. The ruling in the Endo case would have called into question the internment of all loyal citizens once it was made public, and so the Supreme Court held off announcing their decision until the Roosevelt administration was prepared to call an end to internment altogether.[27] Endo won her appeal, but the victory was muted coming in the wake of the government's own announcement that the camps would be closed.

The twists and turns of Endo's case also make visible the emphasis placed upon ascertaining individual loyalty as a means to ending internment. As General DeWitt's infamous observation, "A Jap is a Jap," suggests, Japanese Americans were placed in the unprecedented position of being assumed to be disloyal and having to prove their loyalty. The difficulty of doing so given the public and official anti-Japanese climate was tremendous. Arguing for the necessity of internment in February 1942, for instance, a paranoid DeWitt countered his critics' observations that no act of espionage or fifth-column activity had occurred or even been detected on the West Coast, by claiming that "the very fact that no sabotage has taken place to date is a disturbing and confirming indication that such action will be taken."[28] How can loyalty be claimed (let alone proven) given this peculiar kind of logic?

As the dubious constitutionality of interning American citizens started to prick consciences belatedly and as the cost of interning so many people became evident, officials began looking for a way to start dismantling the program. They decided to allow "loyal" citizens to apply for a "leave clearance" by completing a loyalty questionnaire. This set of questions would also serve another purpose: the United States desperately needed additional troops for the war effort, and authorities wanted to use the questionnaire to screen and recruit Nisei for military service.[29] The questionnaire administered in 1943 was ill conceived and badly handled. Questions 27 and 28, in particular, created havoc for many respondents. The former asked if the individual was willing to serve in the U.S. Armed Forces; as Roger Daniels suggests, it must have bewildered female respondents as well as aged Issei and noncitizens who tried to answer it.[30] The latter proved to be so problematic that the question was eventually rewritten. The original wording asked respondents whether they could "swear unqualified allegiance to the United States" and "forswear any form of allegiance or obedience to the Japanese emperor." It was subsequently revised, as follows:

No. 28. Will you swear to abide by the laws of the United States and to take no action which would in any way interfere with the war effort of the United States?

Unfortunately, many of the questionnaires with the original phrasing had already been administered before the wording was changed, and respondents who had already answered were not recontacted. The question as it appeared initially was in effect unanswerable for Japanese immigrants who had been in this country for decades but had not been allowed to become citizens (because of previous legislation that disallowed naturalization for Asians). For individuals who were no longer "Japanese," but who had not been allowed to become "American," there was no way to answer question 28 without becoming exiled. Even for the Nisei, who were citizens of the United States, deciding how to answer question 28 as originally phrased was difficult: did answering "yes" mean that an individual was admitting he or she had previously been in allegiance with Japan and would now forswear this allegiance? Contributing to the problems with this questionnaire is the fact that camp officials never informed the respondents that they could simply refuse to answer these questions. Many wrote "No-No" to questions 27 and 28 (hence the title of Okada's novel) — some out of confusion and bewilderment, others out of utter discouragement produced by internment and various injustices. Some tried to qualify their answers to questions 27 and 28. The government, despite a growing awareness of the problems with the questionnaire, used the 6,700 "no" responses and the 2,000 qualified responses to question 28 to declare these individuals "disloyal."[31]

There was tremendous motivation to identify as disloyal as many internees as possible in the United States (and in Canada, as we will see below), because it was becoming increasingly essential to come up with a way to justify the detention of citizens in concentration camps. Branding these citizens "disloyal" was one means of justification, but even more perniciously, it led to efforts to deport all so-called "disloyal" individuals. In 1944, Congress passed Public Law 405, otherwise called the Denaturalization Act, which made it possible for Japanese Americans to "voluntarily" (and rather easily) renounce their citizenship. Michi Weglyn points out that this piece of legislation was particularly reprehensible, for it was "a procedure generally not allowed in civilized countries due to the well-known reaction of war hysteria."[32] Many Japanese Americans had lost hope altogether in the United States and in democracy during their internment experiences, and some of them, out of bitterness, did decide to renounce their citizenship voluntarily. But many of the renunciations were a product of duress, poor communication, and coercion. Evidence of duress was most apparent at Tule Lake, where certain internees who had decided to renounce their citizenship put enormous pressure on others to also renounce and become "truly" Japanese.[33]

When many of the renunciants became fully aware of what they had done, they tried to cancel their applications for renunciation. But the government made it extremely difficult for them to do so, creating the absurd possibility that Nisei renunciants who had been born in the United States would be "repatriated" to Japan. The effect of this conundrum was to create a new class of ex-citizens (actually, they became people without a country since only a small portion of the Nisei held dual citizenship), termed "native American aliens" (note the lowercase n). Appalled at the coercive conditions under which the Nisei had renounced their citizenship, San Francisco attorney Wayne M. Collins decided to challenge the renunciation process and the "repatriation" (deportation) orders that were subsequently handed down. He could find no other attorney willing (or brave enough) to help him challenge the United States government on behalf of these individuals. Even "the national office of the ACLU categorically forbade intervention on behalf of [the] renunciants," but the Northern California branch of the ACLU, headed by Ernest Besig, decided to ignore this directive and did give some aid to Collins. Collins became the sole legal counsel for thousands of renunciants and continued to battle these issues in court until 1959, when Attorney General William P. Rogers admitted the United States had made a terrible mistake and announced that the government would restore citizenship to 4,978 Nisei.[34] This was a terribly belated, but significant victory for the Nisei.

The situation regarding deportation efforts was similar in Canada, where internees were asked in early 1945 to complete a repatriation survey. In effect, this survey presented them with two hard choices: "repatriation" to Japan (a country many of them had never seen before) at some unspecified future point in time, or immediate resettlement in Canada east of the Rocky Mountains. The option most of them wanted — to return to their former communities in British Columbia — was conspicuously absent, and in fact, Japanese Canadians were not allowed to return permanently to the British Columbia coast until 1949. Faced with these choices, many opted for repatriation because of the way the government stacked the deck. Those who chose repatriation were given relief money to support them and were told they could live and work in British Columbia until their deportation (by choosing "Japan," in other words, many of them were really choosing British Columbia and hoping things would change before they were deported). In contrast, internees who chose resettlement had to accept a government-designated destination (a sizable number were assigned to sugar beet farms in Alberta and Manitoba) and were offered a "placement allowance" that was a substantially lesser amount than the relief money given to repatriates. Combined with administrative errors, tension in the camps, confusion and anger, many Japanese Canadians, like their American counterparts, renounced their citizenship. Sunahara reports, "By August 1945, 6,884 Japanese Canadians over sixteen years of age had signed for repatriation. With their 3,503 dependents, they represented almost 43 percent of the Japanese population of Canada."[35]

As in the United States, widespread abuses regarding the deportation of citizens started to become public knowledge, but Canadian officials, like those in America, were determined to pursue deportation at all costs. On December 15, 1945, Orders in Council PC 7355–57 were passed, allowing the repatriation program to proceed. But the political tide in Canada turned more quickly on this issue than in America: a Canadian Supreme Court ruling in February 1946, while upholding the government's authority to deport the (6,884) renunciants, blocked the deportation of their (3,503)

Manzanar, July 1997. Photograph © AP/Wide World Photos.

dependents. This split decision was a catalyst in the unraveling of the deportation program.

Historical accounts of this era often conclude by noting that the hysteria of the war years began to dissipate rather quickly once the Allied victory was declared and that the most egregious policies were halted by the end of the decade. From a policy standpoint, this redemptive ending is almost tenable. But we might question if the less visible effects of these pernicious policies could be so easily set aside. Indeed, the effects continued to haunt the postwar years, culminating in the United States in the creation of the Commission on Wartime Relocation and Internment of Civilians, which was charged with the responsibility of studying the circumstances surrounding internment. In 1983, the Commission came to the conclusion that internment was thoroughly unjustified. The Commission's report was immediately protested by various parties who claimed that Japanese Americans were indeed a threat to national security during World War II. To rebut such claims, the Commission added a sentence to the final version of the report, stating unequivocally that no Japanese Americans were ever proven to engage in sabotage or espionage or even collusion with Japan during World War II.[36] Despite the Commission's comprehensive investigation, internment apologists continue today to debate its conclusions. Even now, when Manzanar has had national historic site status for almost a decade, the camp remains controversial: National Parks Service superintendent Ross Hopkins, who is in charge of Manzanar, has an unlisted phone number because of the death threats and arson attempts that have been made. Many protestors feel that the camp as a national historic site impugns proper American patriotism and national honor.[37]

Even though the facts of internment are available today to anyone who wishes to know them, internment continues to haunt not only the lives of contemporary Japanese Americans and Canadians but also the national body more broadly. It is a deep wound, and deep wounds leave permanent scars. To explore this dimension of history, however, is ultimately beyond the bounds of history as a discipline, and so we need to turn to novels like *Obasan* to frame and investigate these issues.

Obasan: A History of Trauma

In 1993, in *Reading Asian American Literature*, Sau-ling Wong observed that, "despite the enormity of Japanese American internment, there is as yet no single book-length treatment of it comparable in range and intensity to Joy Kogawa's novel on Japanese Canadian relocation, *Obasan*. And no one quite knows why."[38] The historical narrative outlined above offers one possible response to Wong's query: the public hysteria and oppressive policies, the silencing of oppositional voices, along with the consolidation of military, executive, and judicial authority in the 1940s produced a peculiar and perverse "logic" that defied (and continues to exceed) clean or precise lines of analysis and comprehension. Given the profound physical and psychological wounds inflicted on Canadian and American citizens of Japanese ancestry in the 1940s, it is perhaps more surprising, to return to Wong's observation, that a novel like *Obasan* exists at all than that others like it have not yet appeared.

As many scholars and reviewers have acknowledged, the historical dimensions of *Obasan* are significant. Kogawa's novel fulfills an important cultural role in bringing to public consciousness the cruel history of Japanese Canadians (and indirectly, Japanese Americans) in the 1940s. Reading *Obasan* alongside Sunahara's historical study, in fact, demonstrates the degree to which the novel seeks to document or record internment and its ravages. Kogawa's novel alludes to and dramatizes such injustices as the confiscation of all boats owned by Japanese Canadian fishermen, the curfew and exclusion orders, the unsanitary and demeaning conditions of Hastings Park, the wanton seizure of property, the forced selling of Fraser Valley farms, the reduction of individuals to numbers (Uncle's is 00556), the fracturing of families under Canadian internment regulations, the poverty of the camps that continued under the coercive dispersal policy, and the threat of deportation and the absurdities of "repatriation." Throughout the novel, we also find mentioned some of the important public figures of the time: Prime Minister Mackenzie King; Tom Shoyama, editor of the *New Canadian*; Mr. Morii, the sometimes unscrupulous liaison between Japanese Canadians and the authorities; Minister of Justice St. Laurent; the infamous anti-Asian alderman from Vancouver, Halford Wilson; T. B. Pickersgill, the commissioner of Japanese placement, who was in charge of administering the repatriation survey and deportation policies; as well as other officials.

While Kogawa and Sunahara discuss some of the same topics and figures of history, however, the narrative forms they employ are quite different. As is typical of historical writing, Sunahara follows a predominantly chronological order; her prose style is clear and explicit. Kogawa's narrative, in contrast, is circular; her prose style is lyrical and suggestive, even enigmatic at times.[39] Like Sunahara, Kogawa is committed to speaking the unspoken, in bringing to light a terrible epoch of history, and like Sunahara's book, Kogawa's novel is informed by documentary research (using some of the same documents, in fact). But because she is writing fiction, Kogawa is able to create a narrative form that both communicates and complicates the details of history. Scholar Erika Gottlieb has described the structure of the novel as "puzzles arranged in a concentric pattern" to capture its intricate form.[40] Indeed, the following discussion of *Obasan* emphasizes that through its complicated chronology and circular form, the novel is able to render not just history, but history as trauma.

The novel opens in 1972. The adult Naomi Nakane and her Uncle (Isamu) are taking a walk to the coulee, a walk they have taken together many times before, but not until the end of the novel is the significance of this walk revealed to Naomi and the reader. The second chapter takes place one month later: Naomi, who is a schoolteacher, is called out of her class to take a phone call, a call that informs her that Uncle has died suddenly. She leaves immediately to be with Obasan (the Japanese word for aunt—or woman, as Gayle K. Fujita notes), whom she finds at the kitchen table as chapter 3 begins.[41] From this point onward, the narrative dwells more on the past than on the present moment: Naomi recollects her childhood in Vancouver; her mother's journey to Japan and continuing absence; the years she spent in a ghost-town camp at Slocan with Obasan, Uncle, and her brother, Stephen; and the years of poverty and hard labor after the war was over, while working on a sugar beet farm in Granton, Alberta. The rush of memories becomes so intense that the present-time action of the novel—which really covers only a couple of days, from Uncle's death to the day after his funeral—takes more than thirty chapters to complete.

Through this lengthy exploration of memory, the novel suggests how difficult it is to come to terms with a tragic past. Especially for Naomi, the main character and narrator, such recollection is troubling and difficult; there are issues from her childhood that have never been resolved, issues that, as an adult, she continues to try to evade. Readers soon understand the desire for such evasion. Piecing together fragments of memory, Naomi not only recalls moments of comfort and happiness, she also remembers terrifying dream images, sexual abuse by a neighbor in Vancouver, the splintering of her family, her unfulfilled longing for her mother, and her increasing estrangement from her brother as he internalizes the racism of Anglo-Canadian culture.[42] While the novel points to personal circumstances that make Naomi reluctant to revisit the past, it also becomes clear that she does not want to face the pain of history. She, quite simply, does not want to read Aunt Emily's journals and papers relating to the injustices of the internment period. "Crimes of history," Naomi thinks to herself, "can stay in history." Out loud to Aunt Emily, Naomi says, " 'Life is so short . . . the past so long. Shouldn't we turn the page and move on?' " (50, 51). Her aunt, a writer and activist, does not agree: " 'The past is the future,' Aunt Emily shot back" (51). The word choice "shot" is significant here in

pointing to Naomi's fear of being wounded by the kind of knowledge Aunt Emily represents. A few pages later, she reflects, "If it is
not seen, it does not horrify. What is past recall is past pain" (54). If
Naomi could, she would seal herself off from the knowledge of the
past that will surely bring her pain. But because of Uncle's death,
which unleashes memories of other deaths and losses, Naomi must
begin to reckon with the return of what has been repressed.

In this respect, Kogawa's novel explores territory similar to Caruth's *Unclaimed Experience*. Caruth's analysis of trauma as wound
is particularly helpful for understanding Naomi's distress. Noting
Freud's view of trauma as a wound of the mind, Caruth insists that
trauma involves a double wound: the wound of the original catastrophe and the wound of its recollection. As Caruth carefully points
out, however, the originating wound is unspeakable, even unrecog-
nizable, at the moment it is experienced: it is "not available to
consciousness until it imposes itself again, repeatedly, in the night-
mares and repetitive actions of the survivor." Caruth thus argues
that "trauma seems to be much more than a pathology, or the simple illness of a wounded psyche: it is always the story of a wound that
cries out, that addresses us in the attempt to tell us of a reality or
truth that is not otherwise available."[43] Without trauma, in other
words, the wound would be unspoken or unrecognized. Naomi,
near the end of the novel, remembers a dream that strikingly echoes
Caruth's theory of trauma: "In my dreams, a small child sits with a
wound on her knee. The wound on her knee is on the back of her
skull, large and moist. A double wound. The child is forever unable
to speak. The child forever fears to tell. I apply a thick bandage but
nothing can soak up the seepage" (291). Appearing on both her
knee and her head, the wound in this dream links body and mind. It
also involves the crisis of articulation that Caruth outlines. The
trauma of this dream is double, indeed, resulting not only from the
seriousness of the wound, a wound so vast no bandage can soak up
all the blood, but from an inability to tell, an inability to speak of the
wound.

Naomi's wound is double in another sense: it involves both personal loss and has larger, historical dimensions. Uncle's death at
the beginning of *Obasan* initiates a crisis that triggers the memory
of long forgotten wounds for Naomi, particularly concerning the
painful, unexplained absence of her mother. Not until near the end
of the novel is the reader able to see that Naomi's and Uncle's first

walk to the coulee in 1954 came immediately after Uncle and Obasan learned what had happened to Naomi and Stephen's mother in
Japan. The mother, however, has asked Uncle and Obasan not to
tell the children about her suffering to spare them pain (one of the
refrains of this scene and the novel overall is "kodomo no tame,"
meaning "for the sake of the children"). And so, not until the family gathers together after Uncle has died in 1972 do Naomi and
Stephen learn that their mother was horribly disfigured by the
atomic bomb dropped on Nagasaki in 1945 and that she eventually
died in Japan. Until 1972 Naomi and Stephen remain in a crisis
of not knowing why their mother never returned from Japan or
whether she was dead or alive. The considerable pain that the
mother's silence and absence must have caused them is not spoken
directly; it is a wound that cries out indirectly in Naomi's night-
mares, silences, and numbness.

To come to terms with her mother's absence and silence —
involuntary at first, then chosen — Naomi must not only be willing
to face her own loss, she must also open herself up to the painful
historical record preserved in Aunt Emily's journal and papers.
Her mother went to Japan, along with Grandma Kato (her own
mother), in September 1941, and they were trapped there after the
bombing of Pearl Harbor in December 1941. The grandmother
cannot return to Canada after the war because she is a Japanese
citizen; though she has not lived in Japan for years and though
almost all of her extended family lives in Canada, Canadian officials
refuse to give her permission after the war is over to rejoin her
family. Stephen and Naomi's mother initially cannot return to Canada after the war because, despite being born in Canada, she is
regarded by Canadian officials as Japanese. She also wants to bring a
child with her — her orphaned niece named Chieko, whom she has
adopted. Eventually the Canadian authorities recognize her right
to return to Canada, but they refuse to allow her to bring the child.
The mother then decides not to return to Canada, perhaps because
of the child, perhaps because of the devastating physical wounds
she has suffered. Given these exigencies, however, it is clear that the
mother's physical absence is not a sign of any lack of love for Naomi
and Stephen, something that Naomi fears throughout the novel.
But to understand the mother's puzzling absence, one must know
the history of Canadian attempts to expatriate Japanese Canadian
citizens after the end of the war. This historical explanation is so

crucial that the novel has a double ending: one is the narrative resolution of Naomi's story; the other is a historical document (mentioned previously), an excerpt from a memo sent by the Co-operative Committee on Japanese Canadians to the House and Senate of Canada in April 1946, protesting Canadian deportation and expatriation policies.[44]

Obasan thus encourages readers to become sensitive to the ways the exigencies of history shape and constrain individual lives. It also prompts readers to listen for what is unspoken and unspeakable in such dire circumstances. The novel emphasizes the necessity for this kind of subtle reading strategy from its very beginning. The opening page of each chapter has unusual typography: blocks of extra empty space separate the lines of type, signifying the historical silences and absences that haunt the novel. The urgency of learning to read both words and blank space, speech and silence, is also apparent in the lyrical prose poem that precedes the first chapter of *Obasan*:

There is a silence that cannot speak.
There is a silence that will not speak.
Beneath the grass the speaking dreams and beneath the dreams is a sensate sea. The speech that frees comes forth from that amniotic deep. To attend its voice, I can hear it say, is to embrace its absence. But I fail the task. The word is stone. . . .
Unless the stone bursts with telling, unless the seed flowers with speech, there is in my life no living word. The sound I hear is only sound. White sound. Words, when they fall, are pockmarks on the earth. They are hailstones seeking an underground stream.
If I could follow the stream down and down to the hidden voice, would I come at last to the freeing word? I ask the night sky but the silence is steadfast. There is no reply. (n.p.)

Reading this passage evokes significant philosophical questions: Does silence necessarily mean absence of meaning? Is it possible paradoxically to speak through silence? And if it is, how does one learn to "read" silence as the "living word"? The image of amniotic fluid in this passage suggests that these difficult queries are precipitated by Naomi's absent and silent mother,[45] but the unfolding of the novel also suggests that these issues are linked to the internment period, when words failed utterly to halt the injustices and so silence became a way, perhaps the only way, to survive. King-Kok Cheung's eloquent reading of the novel demonstrates the degree to which "attentive silence" functions as the living word in *Obasan*.[46] My focus is slightly different: how does one distinguish between the "silence that *cannot* speak" and the "silence that *will not* speak"? This is the dilemma that chafes Naomi throughout the novel.

Naomi, having been raised by Obasan and Uncle (who are characterized by traditional Japanese reticence throughout the novel), is understandably more comfortable with silence than with words. The silence of the adult Naomi, however, is continually and vigorously challenged by Aunt Emily. Scholars of the novel have paid great attention to this central tension, and there are lively debates about which aunt and which position the novel endorses—Aunt Emily's words or Obasan's silence. But the paradoxes of the opening prose poem—where words may be stones, where silences can speak— direct readers to scrutinize such an easy opposition. Naomi's description of Emily and Obasan early in the novel is often read as setting the stage for the ongoing debate about words and silence that runs throughout the novel, but her precise language is actually ambiguous. "How different my two aunts are," Naomi reflects. "One lives in sound, the other in stone. Obasan's language remains deeply underground but Aunt Emily, BA, MA is a word warrior" (39). Notice that the contrast Naomi describes is figured not as "sound" and "silence," which would be the proper binary, but as "sound" and "stone." Obviously there is more at stake here than a neat opposition between words and silence. To fully understand this tension, we need to analyze Naomi's evaluation of her two aunts at greater length.

Aunt Emily is not only a word warrior, she is the voice of history in the novel. Her journal—begun as a series of letters to her sister to inform her of what happens to the Nakane and Kato families while she is trapped in Japan during the war—records the step by step development of the internment program. She is also the preserver of documents: letters from officials informing family members of certain policies and regulations, her own letters of inquiry and protest, newspaper clippings, and the like. "'It matters to get the facts straight,'" Aunt Emily tells Naomi. "'Reconciliation can't begin without mutual recognition of facts. . . . What's right is right. What's wrong is wrong. Health starts somewhere'" (219). This insistence on facts signifies Aunt Emily's investment in a concept of history aligned with documentation, a concept of history linked to a particular kind of articulation: Aunt Emily relies on written words and explicit language to identify and rectify egregious wrongs.

Early in the novel, Naomi resists Aunt Emily's pushiness perhaps for the wrong reasons. When Aunt Emily exclaims impatiently to Naomi, " 'You have to remember. . . . You are your history. If you cut any of it off you're an amputee. Don't deny the past. Remember everything. If you're bitter, be bitter. Cry it out! Scream! Denial is gangrene' " (60), she uses the images of physical wounds and illnesses to make Naomi aware of the costs of repression. Naomi acknowledges this position as valid when she begins to remember the beautiful house in Vancouver her family lived in until internment, a sweet memory that necessarily leads to the recognition of irreparable loss since the house was seized as part of the dispossession policies accompanying internment.[47] Later in the novel, however, Naomi resists Aunt Emily's insistence on marshaling historical facts for somewhat different reasons:

And I am tired, I suppose, because I want to get away from all this. From the past and all these papers, from the present, from the memories, from the deaths, from Aunt Emily and her heap of words. I want to break loose from the heavy identity, the evidence of rejection, the unexpressed passion, the misunderstood politeness. I am tired of living between deaths and funerals, weighted with decorum, unable to shout or sing or dance, unable to scream or swear, unable to laugh, unable to breathe out loud. (218)

At this point in the novel, Naomi has read Aunt Emily's journal and many of the documents she has preserved. Similar to Klepfisz's reckoning with Holocaust history, Kogawa's Naomi feels the weight of a terrible history and wonders if scrupulous documentation of hardship and injustice can do anything other than to serve as a depressing reminder of death and loss. Because she has become intimately familiar with this history, Naomi has earned the right to be wary of words, to be wary of historical facts — especially when they do not tell the whole story, as in the newspaper clipping Aunt Emily has saved that talks about "Grinning and Happy" Japanese sugar beet workers (231–32, 236). Toward the end of the novel, Naomi is in a position to question whether Aunt Emily's insistence on words and concrete historical knowledge can in any meaningful or significant sense heal the wounds of history her own family has experienced.

The aggravation Aunt Emily causes Naomi, as the above analysis suggests, stems not only from differences in personality—Aunt Emily's verbal effusiveness versus Naomi's silence and reticence — but also from their different viewpoints about the usefulness of historical knowledge. This is important to keep in mind because, early in the novel when she is being prodded by Aunt Emily's insistence on history and memory, Naomi tries to use Obasan's silence to sanction amnesia: "Didn't Obasan once say, 'It is better to forget'?" (54). Naomi's attempt to attach forgetting to silence, however, is significantly undercut. As the rest of the novel demonstrates, Obasan and Uncle do remain silent at crucial moments, but silence for them is a survival strategy, not a willful evasion of knowledge, as Naomi would like it to be. The complexity of Obasan's silence is clearly evident in a brief incident that Naomi recalls as part of their move from the camp at Slocan to the sugar beet farm in Granton. In a restaurant where they have stopped to eat, Naomi remembers "two unshaven men": "Throughout the meal, one keeps beckoning to me with his crooked finger and he winks and holds out a five-dollar bill. Whenever I glance around he is there staring, his stubbly red-blotched face hanging down, and as he breathes, his whole chest and shoulders heave. The man beside him grins and nods, pointing to the money" (227–28). Only a child, Naomi is puzzled by this behavior. Because of the sexual abuse she experienced in Vancouver, Naomi perhaps recognizes the gesture as a proposition, but the sordidness of the five dollars seems to escape her. In any case, she calls Obasan's attention to it: "I poke Obasan's arm and she shakes her head so slightly it is almost as if there is no movement. Her lips have barely changed but there is a tightness to them. She has the same wary expression as we leave the restaurant" (228). Clearly, Obasan has observed what is going on before Naomi pokes her, but she knows how ineffective protest or words can be in such a situation.[48] This incident suggests, moreover, that Obasan's silence is not the sign of evasion or forgetfulness, as Naomi tries to maintain. Unlike Naomi at the beginning of the novel, Obasan and Uncle have full knowledge of the cruelties of internment, racism, and poverty—and the pain of knowing that in the face of such injustice silence was perhaps their only refuge.

It is essential to question Naomi's initial linking of Obasan to amnesia and Aunt Emily to history to recognize Obasan's significant role in the novel as a preserver of history. While Aunt Emily is the voice of history in the novel, Obasan articulates the silences and wounds of history that cannot speak directly. Here we should recall an important distinction between Aunt Emily's and Obasan's wartime experiences. Emily gets clearance to go to Toronto, where she is able to join together with other Japanese Canadians and sympathetic Anglos, and thus, in contrast to Obasan, she has no personal experience of the narrow life passed in the camps or of the grueling hardships involved in sugar beet farming.[49] Obasan, because she has experienced and survived the oppressive conditions of internment and dispersal, is linked to the silence that cannot speak (to return to the terms of the novel's opening prose poem). Such wounds of history, as Caruth's work on trauma suggests, can be referenced only obliquely, not directly. Obasan, in this regard, is aligned with members of the family who have been wounded by internment. These wounds are recorded literally on their bodies: Grandma and Grandpa Nakane do not survive Hastings Park and internment; Naomi and Stephen's father contracts tuberculosis and becomes so ill that he never leaves the camp hospital, even after internment has ended, and he eventually dies there; Stephen has a broken leg that does not heal correctly, so he spends much of his time in the camp at Slocan burdened by another cast; Naomi almost drowns and spends a couple of weeks recuperating in the hospital. These numerous physical ailments testify obliquely to a fundamental and debilitating kind of dis-ease.

Obasan's "attentive silence," as Cheung describes it, is necessary along with Aunt Emily's verbal protest, to re-collect the past in the novel. While Aunt Emily gathers and saves documents, pamphlets, and her own journal, Obasan preserves objects from the past. Naomi significantly observes Obasan's penchant for accumulating objects: "She has preserved on shelves, in cupboards, under beds — a box of marbles, half-filled coloring books, a red, white, and blue rubber ball. The items are endless. Every short stub pencil, every cornflakes box stuffed with paper bags and old letters is of her ordering. They rest in the corners like parts of her body, hair cells, skin tissues, tiny specks of memory" (18). But rather than seeing this accumulation as a record of the past, Naomi initially is more inclined to attribute it to bad housekeeping, as her inspection of Obasan's refrigerator suggests: "The refrigerator is packed with boxes of food bits, a slice of celery, a square of spinach, half a hard-boiled egg. . . . There are some indescribable items in the dark recesses of the fridge that never see the light of day. But you realize when you open the door that they're there, lurking, too old for mold and past putrefaction" (54).

Like the house proper, the attic too is packed with objects or fragments of the past. Looking at "the tools Grandfather Nakane brought when he came to this country — chisels, a hammer, a mallet, a thin pointed saw, the handle extending from the blade like that of a kitchen knife," Naomi "can feel the outline of the plane with a wooden handle which he worked by pulling it toward him" (28). Such objects not only preserve memories, but they allow Naomi to rememory (in Morrison's sense) something she perhaps never witnessed.[50] The attic also contains Uncle's ID card with his required registration number (#00556), stacks of magazines and newspapers, and a trunk holding scraps of fabric and clothing from their previous — almost unimaginable — lives in Vancouver before internment. The rummage through the attic, though, is not an easy stroll down memory lane. Naomi brushes against a spider web at one point, and the sensation of being caught precipitates a sudden flash of memory: "Like threads of old spiderwebs, still sticky and hovering, the past waits for us to submit, or depart. When I least expect it, a memory comes skittering out of the dark, spinning and netting the air, ready to snap me up and ensnare me in old and complex puzzles. Just a glimpse of a worn-out patchwork quilt and the old question comes thudding out of the night again like a giant moth. Why did my mother not return?" (30–31).

When she remains silent about what happened to Naomi and Stephen's mother even when pressed by the adult Naomi (a terrible silence since it causes severe anguish), Obasan is associated with the silence that *will not* speak. But most often in the novel, Obasan is associated with the silence that *cannot* speak. Hence her commitment to preserving the past in the form of objects, food, and clothing. Because these forms of historical knowledge are nonverbal, they require a method of reading that operates via suggestiveness and indirection, that understands silence as a powerful means of articulation. Naomi becomes a sensitive reader of silences and aporias when, as the narrative unfolds, she returns to the squashed red, white, and blue ball that Obasan has saved. Originally a gift from Uncle Dan to Naomi, this ball is attached to a painful moment of childhood: hiding under a cot in her father's study in their Vancouver house, Naomi finds the ball as she eavesdrops on a desperate conversation between Aunt Emily and her father — a conversation that reveals some members of the family are already in Hastings Park and her father is now required to report to a work camp. The adult Naomi is able to appreciate Obasan's preservationist fervor for the recovery of this memory: "The ball I found under the cot that day was never lost again. Obasan keeps it in a box with Stephen's toy cars on the bottom shelf in the bathroom. The rubber is cracked and scored with a black lacy design, and the colors are dull, but it still bounces a little" (92). A few chapters later, the ball once again figures into a significant recovered memory. Naomi recalls how sullen and troubled Stephen was on the train to Slocan, and in a gesture of comfort and generosity, she gave him her ball. By preserving this ball and other objects, Obasan functions like Aunt Emily in making possible a critical and necessary re-collection of the past for Naomi.[51]

To comprehend Obasan's role, Naomi must recognize that some aspects of the past cannot be articulated directly, but require ellipsis and indirection. In other words, she comes to understand the connection between trauma and history that Caruth has emphasized and underscored. "For history to be a history of trauma," Caruth writes, "means that it is referential precisely to the extent that it is not fully perceived as it occurs; or to put it somewhat differently, that a history can be grasped only in the very inaccessibility of its occurrence."[52] As noted earlier, Caruth suggests that there are wounds so profound, so traumatic, that the historical narrative which attempts to articulate them must necessarily be oblique and indirect precisely in order to be referential. Caruth's formulation thus offers a significant intervention into the crisis of historical referentiality in a postmodern epoch. Unwilling to endorse radical relativism or naïve historical positivism, Caruth holds on to referentiality while problematizing its transparency.

It is essential to keep Caruth's careful theoretical intervention in mind while considering *Obasan* as a postmodern historical novel. In a 1989 essay Donald C. Goellnicht argues that *Obasan* corresponds to Linda Hutcheon's idea of the postmodern novel as historiographic metafiction. That is, in Goellnicht's view, the major function of *Obasan* is not to render history but "to demonstrate that history is relative," a story constructed by ideology and language.[53] Arnold Davidson has incisively located the contradictory moment of Goellnicht's argument: while claiming that history is relative, Goellnicht "proceeds to present quite unproblematically much of the history in question."[54] In a 1996 issue of *Canadian Literature*, Rachelle Kanefsky notes this contradiction in order to argue staunchly against Goellnicht's reading of *Obasan* and postmodern theory in general. For Kanefsky, the significant value of *Obasan* (and its sequel, *Itsuka*) lies in its rejection of postmodern relativism, in its emphasis on "historical reality."[55] Caruth's theory enables us to see this debate between postmodern and humanist readings of Kogawa's novel, between radical relativism and reference/truth/reality, as overly antagonistic and polarized.

Caruth's idea of history as trauma, involving a displaced yet referential link to a terrible wound, suggests that *Obasan* can be both referential and deconstructive, can function as a historical text and as a critical examination of historiography. This is clearly evident in the two extended historical narratives incorporated in the novel. The first is Aunt Emily's own journal. Her letters to her sister record the insidious erosion of civil rights for Japanese Canadians; they also record the limits of Aunt Emily's ability to understand these events. Aunt Emily attempts to explain the troubling developments at first with the platitude "War breeds utter insanity" (99–100). Soon, however, she points to an unsettling comparison: "Mind you, you can't compare this sort of thing to anything that happens in Germany. That country is openly totalitarian. But Canada is supposed to be a democracy" (103). The words "supposed to be" open up a terrifying prospect — Is Canada in 1942 a democracy anymore? Is it becoming a nation where racism will be legalized? A few weeks later, after visiting Hastings Park, where she sees constables vigilant about maintaining the segregation of men and women and a sign explaining their actions — " 'to prevent further propagation of the species' " (116) — and where she sees a traumatized and broken down Grandma Nakane, Aunt Emily writes to her sister: "Nesan, maybe it's better where you are, even if they think you're an enemy" (117). Aunt Emily's ability to comprehend the tide of events eventually results in an unprecedented declaration, an end to all her attempts to explain and make sense of the events unfolding around her. "I asked too much of God," she writes in her journal (126). Placed in the midst of an inconceivable breakdown in legal justice and democratic principles, she lays blame on herself for what has happened — a misplaced blame, to be sure, but the only "logical" explanation available to her under these conditions.

Despite her firm commitment to recording events as they happen, Aunt Emily loses direction, is thrown into a crisis so deep that it becomes impossible for her to continue to narrate a linear history of events in which she is a direct participant. Reading Aunt Emily's journal, Naomi, as a discerning reader, pays attention not just to the events that are recorded but to Aunt Emily's growing dismay. Naomi sees that, "in the face of growing bewilderment and distress, Aunt Emily roamed the landscape like an aircraft in a fog, looking for a place to land — a safe and sane strip of justice and reason" (95). But one of the lessons of history for Naomi is that this period of history defies reasonable explanations: "The tension everywhere was not clear to me then and is not much clearer today. Time has solved few mysteries. Wars and rumors of war, racial hatreds and fears are with us still" (93). Later in the novel, Naomi confesses, "I suppose I do need to be educated. I've never understood how these things happen. There's something called an order-in-council that sails like a giant hawk across a chicken yard, and after the first shock there's a flapping squawking lunge for safety. One swoop and the first thousand are on ships sailing for disaster. I can remember the chickens in Slocan, their necks and tiny heads thrust low, diving for shelter, one time that a hawk came circling down" (225). Naomi recognizes here that knowing the concrete particulars of history — the orders in council, for instance — is not enough to explain the disaster of internment and dispersal. She (like Kogawa's novel) has to turn to an indirect reference — to an extended simile involving hawks and chickens — to register the shock and fear associated with this history.

The importance of heeding both events/facts and trauma/subjective reactions is underscored later in the novel when Naomi finally hears Grandma Kato's letter describing what happened to their relatives in Japan in 1945. The B-29 bombings of Tokyo on March 9, 1945, kill Grandma Kato's mother, as well as her sister and her sister's husband. But this loss is only a prelude to the devastation wrought by the atomic bomb dropped on Nagasaki on August 9, 1945, which the letter describes in excruciating detail. Though the events happened in 1945, the letter Grandma Kato writes is dated 1949 — testifying to the capacity of a terrible wound to result in a trauma that comes to crisis years after the fact. Trauma is also registered in the narrative form of the letter: "Grandma's letter becomes increasingly chaotic, the details interspersed without chronological consistency. She and my mother, she writes, were unable to talk of all the things that happened. The horror would surely die sooner, they felt, if they refused to speak. But the silence and the constancy of the nightmare had become unbearable for Grandma and she hoped that by sharing them with her husband, she could be helped to extricate herself from the grip of the past" (282–83).

This devastating letter, written by Grandma Kato to help alleviate her own distress, has important therapeutic effects for Naomi. It, first of all, gives Naomi the concrete information about her mother that she has craved for years. It also makes quite clear what the costs of silence are. The grandmother and mother initially cannot speak of the disaster, later they will not, but their silence does not enable them to forget. Immediately after she hears this letter, Naomi addresses her mother (in spirit) and locates willful silence as a primary cause for their estrangement: "Gentle Mother, we were lost together in our silences. Our wordlessness was our mutual destruction" (291). But Naomi does not stop at this moment of mourning. Piecing together the traumatic story of her mother's life, Naomi is able to recognize the love signified by her mother's silence and absence: "I am thinking that for a child there is no presence without flesh. But perhaps it is because I am no longer a child I can know your presence though you are not here. The letters tonight are skeletons. Bones only. But the earth still stirs with dormant blooms. Love flows through the roots of the trees by our graves" (292). While this moment marks the resolution of Naomi's personal quest as a daughter, it also indicates the importance of the reading strategy that the adult Naomi has learned, a reading strategy that pays careful attention to articulate silences and absences.

This method has important implications for the way the novel functions as history. Caruth argues that a central component of trauma is the way in which the wound cries out to others: "We could say that the traumatic nature of history means that events are only historical to the extent that they implicate others," and so "history, like trauma, is never simply one's own. . . . History is precisely the way we are implicated in each other's traumas."[56] Caruth's remarks remind us that history is not a personal, completely subjective narrative, but a narrative that needs to implicate others if it is to be recognized as history. In *Obasan*, Naomi initially focuses only on her own pain and suffering, but Grandma Kato's letter implicates

Naomi in her mother's and grandmother's traumas, enabling Naomi to come to an empowering understanding of history. Through Naomi's story, Kogawa's novel traces a traumatic history that seeks to implicate readers in the story of internment and dispersal, dispossession and deportation that so severely affected Japanese Canadians. Emphasizing history as trauma, *Obasan* acknowledges that history is not only a matter of knowledge but a matter of belief. In its connection to archival sources and to autobiography, Kogawa's novel is clearly interested in conveying information about internment that evades official narratives and contemporary formations of collective memory. But facts alone are not sufficient to carry out this cultural and national project, as Kogawa has observed in an interview: "Documents and facts are intended to direct our prejudiced hearts but rarely provide direction by themselves. I have boxes and boxes of documents but what I need is vision and vision comes from relationship. Facts bereft of love direct us nowhere."[57] To influence "our prejudiced hearts," the facts need to be believed, they need to be made meaningful and compelling.

Kogawa's emphasis on facts *and* love touches upon the problem of creating counterhistories. David Palumbo-Liu, in an essay probing the dilemmas and possibilities of using ethnic memories to counter dominant versions of history, wonders whether counterhistories like *Obasan* can become anything more than "a problematic *minor* narrative." His reading of the novel's double ending ultimately leads to a pessimistic answer to this question: "The last page of the novel does not end with [Naomi's moment of] reconciliation and forgiveness. . . . Instead, Kogawa ends her novel by citing a passage from history that attests to the utter failure to revise history."[58] Kogawa's emphasis on "love" and "relationship" as the way to move "our prejudiced hearts" offers a way to address the important issue Palumbo-Liu raises. As a traumatic history, *Obasan* conveys the intense suffering caused by the policies and injustices of the 1940s to move the reader toward compassion and understanding, for through such empathetic recognition the facts can be seen as history. Both compassion and facts are necessary, as the double ending of the novel suggests. The last chapter about Naomi is marked by rebirth imagery, as she becomes reconnected to her mother in spirit and decides to revisit the coulee where she and Uncle used to walk. But the last chapter of the novel is a historical document, the memorandum mentioned above. The reader who is moved by Naomi's traumatic story, the novel suggests, is now ready to become implicated in Canada's (and by extension, the United States') traumatic history, is perhaps now ready to take in the staggering, often stupefying details of that history.

By ending with a little-known memorandum from 1946 vigorously opposing the orders in council and other prejudicial policies of the time, *Obasan* reminds readers of the severity of the injustices that Japanese Canadians encountered during the 1940s and implicitly calls attention to the failure of any efforts in subsequent years to address the injustices. When the novel was published in 1981, amnesia and denial continued to surround internment history. But this is not the end to the story: Kogawa's novel has made possible a different ending to this history of injustice. On September 22, 1988, the Mulroney government announced a compensation settlement for Japanese Canadians, and parts of *Obasan* were read aloud in the Canadian House of Commons.[59] *Obasan*'s success in moving readers toward a sympathetic, impassioned understanding of history is clearly witnessed in its positive effects on the call for redress and reparations for Japanese Canadians. The ability of Kogawa's novel to shape the course of recent events in the national-political arena suggests that contemporary historical literature by women can play a significant role in restoring collective memory, and that ultimately such acts of historical recovery are needed for personal, collective, and national healing to occur.

Epilogue
History and Healing

The preceding chapters have emphasized history as wound, history as trauma, in order to call attention to an important dimension of contemporary women's writing: the need for these texts to bear a double burden—and to function as both history and literature. The narrative sequence we have traced through Louise Erdrich's novels of Native America, through Toni Morrison's reconstruction of African American history, through Irena Klepfisz's Holocaust poems, and through Joy Kogawa's haunting novel of internment involves facing the past, identifying gaps and silences, and coming to terms with a deeply painful legacy. These literary texts, however, are not only about history; they are also about healing the wounds of history. It may very well be that this dual emphasis distinguishes historical literature written by women. Even when these authors do not identify themselves as feminist, their work remains committed to intervening in injustices; even while they accept the contingencies of writing history in postmodern conditions, they insist on their ability to correct the historical record, to write a counterhistory that can address and work through the wounded histories of their people. It is this activist emphasis that aligns these writers and their texts with the goals of feminism.

The final movement of Erdrich's and Morrison's interlinked historical novels, or of Klepfisz's and Kogawa's haunted histories, does not lead to unmitigated despair and hopelessness, but instead emphasizes the usefulness of reckoning with history and memory. Indeed, both Erdrich and Morrison write linked novels not only to face their people's tragic histories, but to transform the historical narratives in order to create the conditions for a livable life today and a promising future tomorrow. Similarly, Klepfisz's development as a poet involves coming to understand how reckoning with Holocaust history can lead to a revitalized memory of the long, rich tradition of Jewish culture. Kogawa's novel *Obasan*, perhaps the strongest example of how writing a traumatic history of injustice can lead to healing, helped to raise public consciousness and built momentum leading to an official apology and recompense for Japanese Canadian internees (policies followed in the United States a few years later). It is crucial to recognize how history may lead to healing in order to avoid constructing victimist narratives where American Indians once again lose or where African Americans never recover from slavery.

Many other contemporary women writers, especially minority women, have felt the imperative to face a wounded past and to struggle toward healing themselves and their people. In fact, the movement from history to healing runs throughout contemporary women's literature, as the following discussion of several diverse texts suggests. This epilogue focuses on history and healing to examine how it is possible to move beyond a wounded history, not through willful forgetting or amnesia, but by working through the trauma ethically and successfully. Doing so involves a crucial move away from individual isolation and despair. These texts demonstrate that, under the right conditions, sharing traumatic histories with others can heal the community, can inspire collective resistance and survival.

Scars May Be Signs of Healing

In Linda Hogan's recent novel *Solar Storms*, there is a line of women who are scarred indelibly.[1] Hailing from a group of native peoples called the Elk Islanders, Loretta Wing and her daughter Hannah smell sweet, like almonds—they are so impoverished that they eat the cyanide-poisoned carcasses of deer white settlers have left out to rid the land of its wolf population. Loretta has "dark circles and lines" on her face, traces of the pain and suffering she has barely lived through (37). Some of the people are frightened of her, for they sense that "something terrible"—a "bad spirit" or "bad medicine"—lives within her, but a few see that her wounds come from forces beyond her, "from watching the desperate people of her tribe die," from being raped by white men as a girl (39). Telling

Loretta's story to Angel Wing (Loretta's granddaughter), Agnes Iron (Angel's other grandmother) emphasizes how a traumatic past can come to haunt a person: "That was how one day she became the one who hurt others. It was passed down. . . . But Loretta wasn't the original sin. It was just that something inside her had up and walked away and left the rest behind. There was no love left in her. There was no belief. Not a bit of conscience. There wasn't anything left in her" (39). Completely engulfed by a painful history, Loretta remains empty of any human or humane feeling throughout her life; worse yet, she passes on this terrifying emptiness to her daughter, Hannah.

Abandoned by her mother, Hannah is ten years old when she washes up on shore and immediately reminds the people of the terrible spirit that lived inside her mother. Described as having "a bad spirit, a heart of ice," and being afflicted by the old-time disease of "soul loss," Hannah appears to be incapable of love and connection (98). In contrast to most of the people, who steer clear of Hannah, Bush (a surrogate mother figure in the novel) attempts to befriend the girl and care for her. Determined to wash the sweet almond smell of cyanide from Hannah's body one day, Bush makes a horrific discovery: "Beneath all the layers of clothes, her skin was a garment of scars. There were burns and incisions. Like someone had written on her. The signatures of torturers" (99). Like her mother, and certainly because of her mother, Hannah has been overwritten with pain, torture, and wounds so deep her only recourse is to wear multiple layers of clothes both waking and sleeping as a kind of insulation or protection. Bush comes to understand that there is a traumatic connection between Hannah's wounds and tribal history:

I saw it in time, her life going backward to where time and history and genocide gather and move like a cloud above the spilled oceans of blood. That little girl's body was the place where all this met. . . . She was the sum total of ledger books and laws. Some of her ancestors walked out of death, out of a massacre. Some of them came from the long trail of dying, people sent from their world, and she was also the child of those starving and poisoned people on Elk Island. (101)

A tribal elder concurs with Bush's perspective on Hannah: " 'I can see them. All of them. She is the house, the meeting place' " (101). Permanently scarred by the genocidal history of native peoples in

North America, Hannah is beyond saving. The Catholic priest calls her "a miracle in reverse" and says he has no power to help her (100). The native peoples are terrified by her, perhaps because she embodies their own wounded histories. A tribal elder remembers that there used to be a kind of medicine for the unfathomable soul sickness that haunts Hannah: " 'They used to call back lost or stolen souls. . . . They beckoned spirits out from an innocent body.' What was needed was a ceremony, he said, the words of which were so beautiful that they called birds out of the sky, but the song itself would break the singer's life. No one still alive was strong enough to sing it" (101).

There is no one character in the novel capable of singing the powerfully beautiful song the elder calls for. But Hogan's novel, in its intensely rhythmic and lyrical prose, constitutes such a song. To explore the possibility of singing a song that can cure a wounded history, the novel focuses on Hannah's daughter Angel, who has been repeatedly bitten by her mother, causing her face to be painfully wounded. Seventeen years old when the novel opens, Angel does not remember her mother, how she got her scars, or why she has grown up in Oklahoma among foster families far removed from her own relatives and tribe. She returns at the beginning of the novel to the boundary waters area between the United States and Canada to lay claim to her family and to find out about her mother, and so the question that drives the novel is whether or not Angel is condemned to repeat her grandmother Loretta's and her mother's life stories, or whether there is a way to heal this torturous, painful history. Angel's story is thus allegorical; it is symbolic of how to face and work through the most traumatic moments in Native American history.

A key moment in this development is when Angel is able to take a good, long look at her face in the mirror. Early in the novel, she smashes a mirror when she tries to look at herself and her scars directly. But as she locates herself in relation to a loving group of female relatives (Agnes, her paternal grandmother; Dora, her paternal great-grandmother; and Bush, who serves as a surrogate mother), she is able to face herself and to confront her wounds. Bush tells her at a crucial moment: "Some people see scars and it is wounding they remember. To me they are proof of the fact that there is healing" (125). There is indeed healing for Angel as the novel unfolds, and she is not condemned to repeat the fate of her mother, her grandmother Loretta, or even her half-sister, Henriet, who cuts herself with scissors, razor blades, knives, or anything else that will scar her. Because Angel is able to break this cycle of pain and mutilation, the novel holds out hope for native peoples who are likewise suffering from a legacy of historical wounds and scars. For it is not only Angel's return to her family that aids her healing; it is her growing identification as a tribal member that is crucial to her strength and rebirth. In the company of her female relatives, their friends and community, Angel learns the old stories, and she discovers that she is a plant dreamer (someone who has visions of medicinal plants). She finds a native language and narrative possibilities to give shape to herself, to the new tribal self she is becoming.

Since Angel's rebirth involves her native identity, her awakening and growth parallel the line of development for native peoples in the novel. Along with Angel's story, the novel tells the story of how the government has planned to build dams, reroute rivers, and ruin tribal lands in order to produce cheap electricity. The last half of the novel traces Angel's, Bush's, Agnes's, and Dora-Rouge's journey to the remote tribal territory where the scarring of the land is taking place. During their arduous journey, the women confront despair, moments of intense pain, and the death of Agnes. Yet the three women who survive do complete the journey, and they join the native community in planning ways to protest the dams and to block the construction. Their local activism comes a few years after the takeover of Wounded Knee in 1973, and along with the recurring references to AIM (the American Indian Movement), *Solar Storms* charts an affirmative ending not only for Angel, but for Indian activism and for preserving tribal cohesion and indigenous beliefs in the contemporary world. In this way, Hogan's novel emphasizes that wounded histories can be healed, that scars are not just signs of wounds but are also signs of healing.

Breaking the Silence Is the First Step

Janice Mirikitani was born in 1942, the year Japanese Americans were evacuated from the West Coast and moved to internment camps. Many of the poems she has written and published over the years attempt to break the silence of internment and its aftermath and to imagine the inner life of her father and mother, who evidently chose not to talk about such things. In "For My Father," the speaker-daughter is angry at the father and exclaims, "Father, / I wanted to scream / at your silence" (67).[2] But as the poem continues, she is able to see her father's wounds and his vulnerability; even though he remains silent, she recognizes that the fresh strawberries he grows to sell to the white Americans who can afford to buy them (while his own family cannot) are watered with his own tears. Similarly, the speaker-daughter of "Desert Flowers" addresses the mother to let her know that "Your tears, mama, / have nourished us" (30). The body of the poem, however, focuses on the incredible irony of her mother's postwar work: she makes boutonnieres for the American Legion. As she works, she wounds her fingers trying to wind thin wire around flower stems to hold tiny banners that read, " 'america for americans' " (29). Crafting these poems decades after internment was abandoned as a policy, decades after World War II ended, Mirikitani returns to the wounds of history in order to come to terms with this legacy.

"Breaking Silence," a poem dedicated to her mother, offers an important strategy for healing these wounds: testimony as cure. Printed in two columns, the poem presents the daughter's memories of and perspectives on her mother on the left side, while the right column includes excerpts from her mother's 1981 testimony before the Commission on Wartime Relocation and Internment of Japanese American Civilians. When the poem opens, images of paralysis and deep injury immediately claim the reader's attention: the mother's ear is only a "glass cave," her tongue "crippled," her eyelashes "mute" and "wet" (56). But as the mother begins to testify, the act of breaking the silence begins to heals her wounds, strengthening both herself and her daughter. The daughter remembers a vibrant pre-internment mother—a mother who once smelled like the flowers she grew so abundantly, a mother who once could work the earth so wondrously that it "birth[ed] / fields of flowers, / mustard greens and tomatoes / throbbing like the sea." But the life of this mother was irrevocably altered by the events of 1942, when

Our bodies were loud
with yellow screaming flesh
needing to be silenced
behind barbed wire. (57)

The mother's testimony before the commission breaks that silence. More important, the mother lays blame where it belongs: "I was coerced, " "we were singled out," our property "was stolen or destroyed." She speaks up, even when she is told her time for speaking has run out:

Mr. Commissioner . . .
So when you tell me I must limit testimony,
when you tell me my time is up,
I tell you this:
Pride has kept my lips
pinned by nails
my rage coffined.
But I exhume my past
to claim this time.
My youth is buried in Rohwer,
Obachan's ghost visits Amache Gate.
My niece haunts Tule Lake.
Words are better than tears,
so I spill them.
I kill this,
the silence . . . (58)

In so testifying, the mother exposes how the brief time she is allowed for her remarks cannot do justice to the anguish internment caused her family, a family separated and shipped to three different camps, and so devastated that the mother uses death-in-life images to articulate the trauma. Testifying before the commission, the mother returns to these haunting moments of the past, not only to speak of the loss but to claim her anger, to claim her pride; it is this double legacy that allows her testimony to serve a significant healing function. From this moment on, the poem builds to an epiphany: "There are miracles that happen, / she said, / and everything is made visible." Making everything visible means, of course, that the traumatic past must be confronted directly, but it also involves the possibility of working through and beyond the internalized racism stemming from the war years and their aftermath, to "recognize ourselves at last" as beautiful, as "unafraid," as "a rainforest of color and noise" (59).

This kind of empowerment is also fiercely earned in Mirikitani's ten-part poem "Prisons of Silence," which is written from the perspective of a young woman in an internment camp who has learned a hard lesson: "The strongest prisons are built / with walls of silence" (60, 61). Keenly aware that in "a country of betrayal" it is impossible to contest unjust policies that allow private property to be confiscated, that require loyalty oaths to be sworn, that lock Japanese American citizens behind barbed wire, the speaker realizes that she cannot even speak out against the vicious white Americans who scream "Filthy Jap!" and "Go home, Jap!" at her and at her people (61). The most severe loss, however, comes when her husband enlists to fight for the United States in the hopes of freeing himself and eventually his wife. He is killed, and his young widow becomes a figure of death in life, living in a tomb.

Like "Breaking Silence," "Prisons of Silence" turns to testimony as a means to heal the wounds. Prompted by the ghost of her dead husband, the female speaker of the poem claims her own rage, and at that moment,

We heal our tongues.

We listen to ourselves

   Korematsu, Hirabayashi, Yasui.

We ignite the syllables of our names.

We give testimony. (64)

And this makes all the difference: breaking the silence, not just in private but by giving public testimony, draws the wounded people together and transforms collective memory. And so the poem ends by focusing on "we" — who have come together by facing this terrible history, who can now call for justice and reparations, who can now "soar / from these walls of silence" (65).

The Voices of the Ancestors Still Clamor to Be Heard

Luci Tapahonso's poem "In 1864" offers an important lesson about historical rememory: if a people is resilient, facing history will uncover not only the ghosts of the past but also the sweet moments.[3] Tapahonso brings the past and the present, the wounds and the beauty, into exquisite balance and harmony in her poem.

"In 1864" begins with an epigraph explaining why the date is a moment in Navajo history that cannot and should not be forgotten:

> In 1864, 8,354 Navajos were forced to walk from Dinetah to Bosque Redondo in southern New Mexico, a distance of three hundred miles. They were held for four years until the U.S. government declared the assimilation attempt a failure. More than 2,500 died of smallpox and other illnesses, depression, severe weather conditions, and starvation. The survivors returned to Dinetah in June of 1868.

The tone is matter of fact, for this is a history we have heard before, a wounded history that many native peoples across the Americas share. The poem proper is set in contemporary times, and thus it asks implicitly, What is the relation of 1864 to Navajo people today? The opening lines seem to bear no inflection of this history, as readers are introduced to a young daughter sleeping, dreaming of "mountains, / the wide blue sky above, and friends laughing." The daughter is in a car, on a trip with her mother and perhaps other siblings or relatives. By the end of the poem, this daughter will be crying as she hears the stories her mother tells and becomes connected to the history of her people. The first is a contemporary story that tells of a Navajo man, an electrician, who is working on a project "installing power lines on the western plains of New Mexico." As he works, he sees that the landscape corresponds to the descriptions of the land in the "old stories" he has heard, he begins to hear "cries and moans carried by the wind," and he starts to hum songs from his childhood. After a few days, he can no longer work on this project because he continually hears the voices of his ancestors clamoring in pain, ancestors no doubt who experienced the "long walk" of 1864. Hearing these voices changes the man's life; he returns to his family, to his children, and perhaps will tell them of what he has heard.

The second story relates what happened in 1864 to their family. The mother tells her daughter what her own aunt has told her, and she begins the story by recalling the way her aunt always started: " 'You are here / because of what happened to your great-grandmother long ago.' " This beginning tells us that the story is important enough to be told and retold orally, first by the great-grandmother who experienced the long walk in 1864, then through the aunt's memorable retelling of the story, on to the present moment of the poem when the mother draws her daughter into connection with this history. The history is traumatic: the story tells of efforts to force the Navajo to be rounded up and removed to Bosque Redondo by burning their fields, killing their sheep, attacking the people. On the long walk, people who cannot keep the pace — old ones, pregnant women — are shot and killed. The Rio Grande crossing is terrifying; many people die because they cannot swim. This part of the story carries the injunction, "We must not ever forget their screams and the last we saw of them — / hands, a leg, or strands of hair floating." The ethical act required here — never to forget this traumatic moment — involves the daughter and, by extension, all Navajo today (and Tapahonso's readers as well), in a commitment to carry and accept the weight of this history and the anguish that goes with it. Who would, given the burden of history as trauma, willingly want to do so?

But just as the epigraph to the poem ends with the astonishing return of the surviving Navajo to their rightful homelands in 1868, so too does the mother's recounting of the story emphasize survival and resilience:

All the way
we told each other, "We will be strong, as long as we are
together."
I think that was what kept us alive. We believed in ourselves
and the old stories that the holy people had given us.

The old stories — both the holy stories of priests and stories of the long walk — offer a kind of healing as they testify to and inculcate the adamant strength and belief necessary for the people's survival. Because these stories continue to be told, the Navajo today remain strong as a people, united and strengthened by sharing this traumatic history. The voices of the ancestors continue to clamor, and this makes healing possible.

The poem ends by returning to the present tense, as the mother notices her daughter is crying and unable to speak. So she tells her another important lesson of history, that sometimes good things can emerge from the most terrible moments. The mother adds to the story of the Navajo at Bosque Redondo and informs her daughter that during this confinement, the people began to make fry-bread (which would become a tradition), learned to love strong coffee, and began to sew what is now known as traditional dress: "long, tiered calico skirts" and "fine velvet shirts for the men." The poem thus ends not with painful history but with an uplifting vision of the people:

> They decorated their dark velvet
> blouses with silver dimes, nickels, and quarters.
> They had no use for money then.
> It is always something to see — silver flashing in the sun
> against dark velvet and black, black hair.

Only by knowing the history of the long walk, only by listening to the voices of the ancestors, can the daughter (and readers) come to appreciate the final image the mother conveys, an image of dancing and motion and life using present tense verbs to underscore that it continues, beautifully, today.

Not Only Deconstruction, but (Re)Construction

History informs *Borderlands / La Frontera: The New Mestiza*, Gloria Anzaldúa's collection of essays and poems that has made "border-lands" a well-known metaphor for a hybrid transcultural space that cannot be articulated on conventional geographic or national-symbolic maps of either the United States or Mexico.[4] In her poems Anzaldúa writes of a Chicano family that kills its pet deer rather than face the game warden's accusation of illegal hunting ("Cer-vicide"), of an Anglo farm owner who calls in immigration authori-ties to have his undocumented workers arrested and deported right before payday so he will not have to pay them (*"El sonavabitche"*), and of a greedy Anglo land claimant who rapes a Chicana in front of her husband, then smothers her, and orders his cohorts to lynch the husband ("We Call Them Greasers"). These poems are difficult to read, not because of their form or line lengths or language, but because they communicate deep wounds. Anzaldúa's original plan for the collection was to have a series of poems prefaced by a ten-page introduction,[5] but ten pages became nearly one hundred pages as she worked on the volume and felt compelled to explain Chicana/o identity, history, language, and culture to her readers.

One of the strong emphases in *Borderlands / La Frontera* is the need to deconstruct official records to recover the history of the land and the people that has been overwritten by the history of the United States and its cultural and political dominance. In the first essay of the volume, "The Homeland, Aztlán: *El otro México*," Anzaldúa demonstrates the power of critical deconstructions: she dislodges a hegemonic view of American history by presenting her own revisionist history of the border between the United States and Mexico. She includes historical information about the migration of indigenous peoples into the Americas from the Bering Straits; she recounts a history of cross-cultural contact and domination that began when Cortés invaded Mexico in the sixteenth century, which leads into her history of the dispossession of Mexicans and Chicanos as Spanish colonialism yielded to Anglo-American conquest. Anzaldúa provides additional facts that shape her critical perspective on United States history: she notes that U.S. forces invaded Mexico in 1846, and she mentions specifically the signing of the Treaty of Guadalupe-Hidalgo in 1848, which, by making Texas part of the United States, forcibly separated indigenous peoples into two different nations. The presentation of this historical material is crucial for the criticism of the border that follows. Anzaldúa's deconstructive strategies and revisionist history call into question the obsession with fixed borders that leads the border patrol and immigration authorities to commit such absurd and unnatural acts as "returning" Pedro—a Spanish-speaking, fifth-generation American—to Mexico, a land he had hardly seen before.

Moreover, Anzaldúa notably uses her reading of history to suggest that the current border dividing the two countries is not a fixed, unchanging line, but a temporary and arbitrary political arrangement. Her reading of history suggests a postnationalist future in which borderlands, not borders, will predominate,[6] a future when indigenous peoples will no longer be split at the root:

> 1,950 mile-long open wound
> > dividing a *pueblo*, a culture,
> > > running down the length of my body,
> > > > staking fence rods in my flesh,
> > > > > splits me   splits me
> > > > > > *me raja   me raja*

> This is my home
> this thin edge of
>   barbwire.
>
> But the skin of the earth is seamless.
> The sea cannot be fenced,
> *el mar* does not stop at borders.
> To show the white man what she thought of his arrogance,
> *Yemaya* blew that wire fence down.
>
> This land was Mexican once,
>   was Indian always
>   and is.
>   And   will be again. (2–3)

The present moment is painful in these lines of poetry (included in the first essay). Calling the border a "wound" and personalizing it as a wound not only to the "skin" of the earth but to her own "flesh," Anzaldúa powerfully conveys her critique of the border as a kind of violent inscription. The word "*pueblo*" is italicized in the above stanza to summon its rich meanings as a Spanish word associated with "the people" and with a strong community: it calls forth a time in the past when indigenous people moved freely across this divide. But Anzaldúa also works to heal this wound by ending the poem with her confident vision of a future time when indigenous people will reclaim and repossess the land.

Given the complex history of the border told in the first essay, readers cannot help but feel the keen irony of Anzaldúa's personal experience of English-only education. "I remember being caught speaking Spanish at recess," Anzaldúa recounts, "that was good for three licks on the knuckles with a sharp ruler. I remember being sent to the corner of the classroom for 'talking back' to the Anglo teacher when all I was trying to do was tell her how to pronounce my name. [']If you want to be American, speak American,' " the teacher says. " 'If you don't like it, go back to Mexico where you belong' " (53). In *Borderlands / La Frontera*, Anzaldúa's response to this bigotry and linguistic terrorism is not despair or self-defeat, however; instead, she claims many languages as her own and lists them, almost defiantly:

1. Standard English
2. Working class and slang English
3. Standard Spanish
4. Standard Mexican Spanish
5. North Mexican Spanish dialect
6. Chicano Spanish (Texas, New Mexico, Arizona and California have regional variations)
7. Tex-Mex
8. *Pachuco* (called *caló*) (55)

Anzaldúa gives particular attention to Chicano Spanish, for it has been dismissed not only by Anglos but by Chicanos themselves. "Chicano Spanish is a border tongue which developed naturally," Anzaldúa insists (55). Seeing it as a natural development, of course, is directly related to one's knowledge of history and the border, and so Anzaldúa goes on to explain that "change, *evolución, enriquecimiento de palabras nuevas por invención o adopción* have created variants of Chicano Spanish, *un nuevo lenguaje. Un lenguaje que corresponde a un modo de vivir.* Chicano Spanish is not incorrect, it is a living language" (55). Knowing history makes it possible to move beyond the disabling view that Chicano Spanish is a deficient form of Spanish and to claim Chicano Spanish as a unique and beautiful borderlands language.

In the essay that ends part one of *Borderlands / La Frontera*, "*La conciencia de la mestiza /* Towards a New Consciousness," Anzaldúa describes the lethal "ignorance" of the "dominant white culture," an ignorance that results in a "whitewash[ed]" and "distort[ed]" view of Chicano history, and she points out that "a misinformed people is a subjugated people" (86). She insists that the only way to achieve a revolutionary consciousness of *mestiza* identity, language, geography, and community is via historical knowledge. "Before the Chicano and the undocumented worker and the Mexican from the other side can come together, before the Chicano can have unity with Native Americans and other groups," Anzaldúa explains, "we need to know the history of their struggle and they need to know ours. Our mothers, our sisters and brothers, the guys who hang out on street corners, the children in the playgrounds, each of us must know our Indian lineage, our afro-*mestisaje*, our history of resistance" (86). For Anzaldúa, knowing one's history and communicating it with others significantly involves a movement away from individual isolation and painful silence and towards collective memory and resistance.

Historical knowledge, however, is not gained simply by recovering the past, Anzaldúa points out; it involves a continual deconstruction and (re)construction of the historical knowledges/narratives already in place. Describing *"El camino de la mestiza /* The Mestiza Way" in the last essay of *Borderlands / La Frontera,* Anzaldúa depicts the *mestiza* as a historian who researches the past but then selects the details that will be useful for the people to contemplate in their present situation. "Her first step is to take inventory," Anzaldúa writes, and to ask, "Just what did she inherit from her ancestors? This weight on her back—which is the baggage from the Indian mother, which the baggage from the Spanish father, which the baggage from the Anglo?" (82). The *mestiza* historian does not stop at this point, however; she critically analyzes what her inventory of ancestors and the past has brought to light. *"Pero es difícil* differentiating between *lo heredado, lo adquirido, lo impuesto,"* Anzaldúa observes. So the *mestiza* "puts history through a sieve, winnows out the lies, looks at the forces that we as a race, as women, have been a part of" (82). Healing the wounds of history, for Anzaldúa, involves not only deconstructing the official story and constructing missing knowledges, but also reconstructing history in such a way that the people will have a useful story to tell themselves—to renew collective memory and to imagine a promising future.

Anzaldúa's strategy of narrative and historical reconstruction opens up the larger impetus behind contemporary women's historical literature: to use literature to tell the other side of history and to refashion the narrative so that the history comes out right this time. These are not histories of conquest and death any longer. They become histories of survival and resilience in the powerful fictional and lyrical worlds of writers like Kingston, Erdrich, Morrison, Klepfisz, Kogawa, Hogan, Mirikitani, Tapahonso, Anzaldúa—and many others.

Notes

Chapter 1. History as Wound

1. Fredric Jameson, *The Political Unconscious: Narrative as a Socially Symbolic Act* (Ithaca: Cornell University Press, 1981), 102.

2. Maxine Hong Kingston, *China Men* (New York: Knopf, 1980) and *The Woman Warrior* (New York: Knopf, 1976). All references to *China Men* will be cited parenthetically in the text. Kingston has said that she worked on the material for these books together, but that because of history, the stories of her female relatives were so different from the stories of her male relatives that she needed two different books, two different narrative forms and genres, to tell them. See Kingston, "Eccentric Memories: A Conversation with Maxine Hong Kingston," interview by Paula Rabinowitz, *Michigan Quarterly Review* 26 (1987): 179–80.

3. Maxine Hong Kingston, "Talk with Mrs. Kingston," interview by Timothy Pfaff, *New York Times Book Review*, 15 June 1980, 25.

4. Toni Morrison, "Living Memory: A Meeting with Toni Morrison," interview by Paul Gilroy, in *Small Acts: Thoughts on the Politics of Black Cultures*, by Paul Gilroy (London: Serpent's Tail, 1993), 179.

5. A special section of the *Journal of American History*, vol. 82 (Dec. 1995), includes several essays that analyze this controversy; see especially Richard H. Kohn, "History and the Culture Wars: The Case of the Smithsonian Institution's *Enola Gay* Exhibition," 1036–63, for a careful consideration of the exhibit as originally planned; and Edward T. Linenthal, "Struggling with History and Memory," 1094–1101, for a cogent analysis of why the exhibit proved so controversial.

6. I borrow the term "history wars" from the title of a collection of essays edited by Edward T. Linenthal and Tom Engelhardt; see *History Wars: The Enola Gay and Other Battles for the American Past* (New York: Metropolitan Books-Henry Holt, 1996). Another important battle over American history occurred in the late 1980s as public school history curricula were scrutinized and revised in New York state and California. This movement broad-

ened and culminated in the October 1994 publication of a document titled *National Standards for United States History: Exploring the American Experience*; see Edward Berenson's review essay, "The Use and Abuse of History," *American Quarterly* 48 (1996): 507–15, for a judicious assessment of curricula revisions.

7. Black History Month grew out of Negro History Week, which was established in February 1926 by the African American historian Carter G. Woodson. Expanded in 1976 to a month-long observance, this celebration of the achievements of African Americans was initially designed to encompass the birthday of Frederick Douglass on February 14.

The first International Women's Day was March 8, 1911. In 1981, Rep. Barbara Mikulski (D-MD) and Sen. Orrin Hatch (R-UT) cosponsored a joint congressional resolution proclaiming the week of March 8 National Women's History Week. In 1986, the National Women's History Project (founded in 1979 by Molly MacGregor) helped expand the celebration to the entire month of March.

8. Adrienne Rich, "Resisting Amnesia: History and Personal Life," *Blood, Bread, and Poetry: Selected Prose, 1979–1985* (New York: Norton, 1986), 145.

9. Ibid., 137, 148.

10. Adrienne Rich, *What Is Found There: Notebooks on Poetry and Politics* (New York: Norton, 1993), 140.

11. Ibid., 139, 122.

12. Shoshana Felman and Dori Laub, *Testimony: Crises of Witnessing in Literature, Psychoanalysis, and History* (New York: Routledge, 1992), xviii.

13. Avery F. Gordon has argued that sociology as a discipline must avail itself of literary fictions for reasons similar to Felman and Laub's: "In the twentieth century, literature has not been restrained by the norms of a professionalized social science, and thus it often teaches us, through imaginative design, what we need to know but cannot quite get access to with our given rules of method and modes of apprehension"; see *Ghostly Matters: Haunting and the Sociological Imagination* (Minneapolis: University of Minnesota Press, 1997), 25.

14. Roland Barthes, "Historical Discourse," in *Introduction to Structuralism*, ed. Michael Lane (New York: Basic Books, 1970), 153.

15. Jacques Derrida, *Of Grammatology*, trans. Gayatri C. Spivak (Baltimore: Johns Hopkins University Press, 1976), 158.

16. Hayden White, *Metahistory: The Historical Imagination in Nineteenth-Century Europe* (Baltimore: Johns Hopkins University Press, 1973).

17. As these comments suggest, I follow Jean-François Lyotard's view of postmodernism as the collapse of metanarratives and the proliferation of local narratives, articulated first in *The Postmodern Condition: A Report on Knowledge*, trans. Geoff Bennington and Brian Massumi (Minneapolis: University of Minnesota Press, 1984), but developed further in *The Differend: Phrases in Dispute*, trans. Georges Van Den Abbeele (Minneapolis: University of Minnesota Press, 1988) to locate Auschwitz and the Holocaust as a historic cataclysm that ruptures all belief that a wholly adequate language, narrative form, or historical account can be arrived at. Lyotard usefully relates postmodernism to the incommensurable conditions of World War II;

to his insistence on the Holocaust as rupture, I would add the bombing of Hiroshima and Nagasaki. The influence of Lyotard on my thinking about postmodernism will become clear in the chapters that follow.

18. Walter Benjamin, *Illuminations: Essays and Reflections*, ed. Hannah Arendt, trans. Harry Zohn (New York: Schocken Books, 1968), 256.

19. Linda Hutcheon, *The Politics of Postmodernism* (New York: Routledge, 1989).

20. David Cowart, *History and the Contemporary Novel* (Carbondale: Southern Illinois University Press, 1989); David W. Price, *History Made, History Imagined: Contemporary Literature, Poiesis, and the Past* (Urbana: University of Illinois Press, 1999).

21. Stacey Olster, *Reminiscence and Re-Creation in Contemporary American Fiction* (Cambridge: Cambridge University Press, 1989), 137.

22. Elisabeth Wesseling, *Writing History as a Prophet: Postmodernist Innovations of the Historical Novel* (Amsterdam: John Benjamins Publishing, 1991); see especially chap. 7.

23. In the introduction to *History Made, History Imagined*, Price implies that he will approach the novels he discusses as history: "The novelists examined here . . . often employ the poetic imagination as a means of questioning history, which, in turn, produces a countermemory or counternarrative to the popular and uncritically accepted referent that we take to be the historical past. They produce speculative novels of poietic history in that they expand the referential field of the past so as to provide the grounds upon which to construct a critique of that same past and, at the same time, imagine new possibilities for the future" (3–4). In his subsequent chapters, however, Price emphasizes the philosophies of history developed by Giambattista Vico and Friedrich Nietzsche as a context for reading the novels as history, and thus his study ultimately addresses ideas about history and the value of history rather than history per se.

24. David Palumbo-Liu, "The Ethnic as Post-': Reading *Reading the Literatures of Asian America*," *American Literary History* 7 (1995): 167–68.

25. Rafael Pérez-Torres, *Movements in Chicano Poetry: Against Myths, Against Margins* (Cambridge: Cambridge University Press, 1995), 168.

26. Lois Parkinson Zamora, *The Usable Past: The Imagination of History in Recent Fiction of the Americas* (Cambridge: Cambridge University Press, 1997), 41.

27. Fredric Jameson, *Postmodernism, or, the Cultural Logic of Late Capitalism* (Durham: Duke University Press, 1991), 25.

28. Jameson himself, in the conclusion to *Postmodernism*, wonders whether oppositional movements should be viewed as completely commodified within the framework of multinational capitalism: "Are the 'new social movements' consequences and aftereffects of late capitalism? Are they new units generated by the system itself in its interminable inner self-differentiation and self-reproduction? Or are they very precisely new 'agents of history' who spring into being in resistance to the system as forms of opposition to it, forcing it against the direction of its own internal logic into new reforms and internal modfications?" Immediately after posing this possibility, however, Jameson turns to his characteristic pessimism: "But this

is precisely a false opposition, about which it would be just as satisfactory to say that both positions are right; the crucial issue is the theoretical dilemma, replicated in both, of some seeming explanatory choice between the alternatives of agency and system. In reality, however there is no such choice"; see Jameson, *Postmodernism*, 326.

29. Benjamin, *Illuminations*, 255.

30. Cathy Caruth, "Introduction: The Insistence of Reference," in *Critical Encounters: Reference and Responsibility in Deconstructive Writing*, ed. Caruth and Deborah Esch (New Brunswick: Rutgers University Press, 1995), 2. So important is this distinction that Caruth reiterates it: "deconstruction does not deny reference, but denies that reference can be modeled on the laws of perception or of understanding" (2).

31. Caruth, *Unclaimed Experience: Trauma, Narrative, and History* (Baltimore: Johns Hopkins University Press, 1996), 11.

32. Carolyn Forché, Introduction to *Against Forgetting: Twentieth-Century Poetry of Witness*, ed. Forché (New York: Norton, 1993), 31. Forché's anthology is organized according to historical events, beginning with poems witnessing the Armenian genocide (1909–1918) and continuing through poems that witness the present-day struggle for civil and human rights in South Africa and China.

33. Forché, Introduction to *Against Forgetting*, 32. Forché argues that the convenient opposition "personal" and "political" is not appropriate to describe the effects of these poems. She sets up the term "social" as a mediating space of resistance: "the social is a place of resistance and struggle, where books are published, poems read, and protest disseminated"; see Introduction to *Against Forgetting*, 31. As I see it, Forché's use of the term "social" is a way to describe and insist upon the significant influence literature can have on the way a society or culture thinks about history, an influence that is not as direct (or as compromised) as the word "political" suggests.

34. Andreas Huyssen, *Twilight Memories: Marking Time in a Culture of Amnesia* (New York: Routledge, 1995), 1, 9.

35. Huyssen, *Twilight Memories*, 35. Huyssen points to the collapse of the modernist avant-garde as one of the major factors leading to a transformed museum space in postmodern culture. The demise of the avant-garde destabilizes "the old quality argument, often advanced by traditionalist critics in order to marginalize the art and culture of minority groups or peripheral territories. This kind of argument is losing ground in an age that does not offer any clear consensus as to what actually belongs in a museum. Indeed, the quality argument collapses once the documentation of everyday life and of regional cultures, the collecting of industrial and technological artifacts, furniture, toys, clothes, and so forth becomes an ever more legitimate museal project, as it has in recent years"; see *Twilight Memories*, 22.

36. Huyssen, *Twilight Memories*, 255, 258.

37. Jameson, *The Political Unconscious*, 9.

38. Benjamin, *Illuminations*, 255.

Chapter 2. "Haunted America"

1. Drex Brooks, *Sweet Medicine: Sites of Indian Massacres, Battlefields, and Treaties* (Albuquerque: University of New Mexico Press, 1995).

2. Patricia Nelson Limerick, "Haunted America," in *Sweet Medicine: Sites of Indian Massacres, Battlefields, and Treaties,* by Drex Brooks (Albuquerque: University of New Mexico Press, 1995), 119–63.

3. Limerick, "Haunted America," 121.

4. Leslie Marmon Silko, "Here's an Odd Artifact for the Fairy-Tale Shelf," review of *The Beet Queen,* by Louise Erdrich, *Studies in American Indian Literatures,* n.s., 10, no. 4 (1986): 179.

5. Few mainstream reviewers of Erdrich's first two novels made an effort to situate Erdrich's work historically, culturally, or geographically beyond mentioning that her major characters were Chippewa. Narratives of Indians as victims abound in the reviews, and ignorance leads to some rather crude characterizations of June in *Love Medicine* as, for instance, "a woman who has been having a fling in town" (D. J. R Bruckner, review of *Love Medicine,* by Louise Erdrich, *New York Times,* 20 Dec. 1984, C21). The early reviewers of *Love Medicine* also assumed, despite Albertine's commentary to the contrary, that June was actually trying to walk home from Williston, North Dakota, to the reservation — a distance of approximately 235 miles — when she dies in the blizzard at the beginning of the novel. It may be that Silko's criticisms are misdirected toward Erdrich's language and could be more productively addressed to the ignorance on the part of mainstream readers and reviewers, which might make it necessary to narrate historical and political subtexts more directly. Susan Pérez Castillo analyzes the Silko-Erdrich controversy at greater length than I do here; see "Postmodernism, Native American Literature, and the Real: The Silko-Erdrich Controversy," *Massachusetts Review* 32 (1991): 285–94. In contrast to Silko's reading of *The Beet Queen,* Julie Maristuen-Rodakowski argues that Chippewa history is significant in Erdrich's first two novels ("The Turtle Mountain Reservation in North Dakota: Its History as Depicted in Louise Erdrich's *Love Medicine* and *The Beet Queen,*" *American Indian Culture and Research Journal* 12, no. 3 [1988]: 33–48), and Dennis M. Walsh and Ann Braley look at latent "Indianness" in *The Beet Queen* ("The Indianness of Louise Erdrich's *The Beet Queen*: Latency As Presence," *American Indian and Culture Research Journal* 18, no. 3 [1994]: 1–17). See James Stripes's essay for a more general analysis of history in Erdrich's work: "The Problem(s) of (Anishinaabe) History in the Fiction of Louise Erdrich: Voices and Contexts," *Wicazo Sa Review* 7, no. 2 (1991): 26–33.

6. Deborah Stead, "Unlocking the Tale," *New York Times Book Review,* 2 Oct. 1988, 41.

7. Hayden White, *Tropics of Discourse: Essays in Cultural Criticism* (Baltimore: Johns Hopkins University Press, 1978), 40. White's use of "men" in this comment instead of a gender-neutral "we" or "historians" is unfortunate.

8. The degree to which photography at the turn of the century helped to

market this image as a reality is fascinating. Christopher Lyman analyzes the photographs of Edward S. Curtis to prove that Curtis did not simply record Indians in their familiar surroundings in his photographs, but that he retouched the images in the darkroom so that they would convey his view of what traditional Indians should look like. In the case of his famous photograph titled "The Vanishing Indian — Navajo," Curtis deliberately darkened the print to give the impression that Indians were indeed disappearing; see Lyman, *The Vanishing Race and Other Illusions: Photographs of Indians by Edward S. Curtis* (Washington, D.C.: Smithsonian, 1982). R. David Edmunds analyzes the trope of the vanishing Indian in the writing of academic Native American history; see "Native Americans, New Voices: American Indian History, 1895–1995," *American Historical Review* 100 (1995): 717–40.

9. Hayden White, *Metahistory: The Historical Imagination in Nineteenth Century Europe* (Baltimore: Johns Hopkins University Press, 1973).

10. Hayden White, "Getting Out of History," *Diacritics* 12, no. 3 (1982): 2–13.

11. Louise Erdrich, *Tracks* (New York: Henry Holt, 1988) and *The Bingo Palace* (New York: Henry Holt, 1994). All quotations from Erdrich's novels will be cited parenthetically in the text using the following abbreviations: *T* for *Tracks*, *BP* for *The Bingo Palace*.

12. For several reasons, I refer to the history of the Turtle Mountain Chippewa in dealing with Erdrich's sense of history: it is the band of which she is a member and whose history she learned as she was growing up — evidenced in the acknowledgments sections of both *Tracks* and *Love Medicine* as well as various interviews; it is the only band of Chippewa that was allotted land in North Dakota, the setting for Erdrich's novels; and the dating of the novels corresponds loosely to the historical events concerning this band. Erdrich's concern for the injustices caused by allotment extends beyond Turtle Mountain, however; see the article she and Michael Dorris coauthored on the problem of property rights at the White Earth Chippewa Reservation in Minnesota, "Who Owns the Earth?" *New York Times Magazine*, 4 Sept. 1988, 32–36+.

13. I have followed Gerald Vizenor's distinction between "Chippewa" and "Anishinaabe" in this chapter: he points out that "Chippewa" is a term whites gave to the tribe to be used in treaties, whereas "Anishinaabe" (plural "Anishinaabeg") is the older, oral tribal name; see *The People Named the Chippewa: Narrative Histories* (Minneapolis: University of Minnesota Press, 1984), 13–21. Applied to Erdrich's novels, this distinction is important, for only Nanapush in *Tracks* calls the people "Anishinabe." Erdrich uses a spelling of "Anishinabe(g)" with only one *a*, and although most scholars of Native America today prefer the term "Ojibwa" to Chippewa, Erdrich's characters almost always use the latter; in this chapter I have followed her practices.

14. Stephen Janus, the superintendent of the Turtle Mountain Chippewa in 1912 — the year in which *Tracks* opens — was noted for using words like "able-bodied" and "expert" to describe the people and their transition to

agricultural capitalism. His inflated, romantic view of life for the Turtle Mountain Chippewa is a sharp contrast to the opening of *Tracks*. See Gregory S. Camp, "Working Out Their Own Salvation: The Allotment of Land in Severalty and the Turtle Mountain Chippewa Band, 1870–1920," *American Indian Culture and Research Journal* 14, no. 2 (1990): 31–32.

15. Carl Waldman reports that disease wiped out 25 to 50 percent of Native American peoples in contrast to an estimated 10 percent death rate from Indian-white warfare. The threat of tribal extinction due to disease is exemplified by the Mandans, a Dakota tribe which "declined from 1,600 to 131 during the smallpox epidemic of 1837"; see Waldman, *Atlas of the North American Indian* (New York: Facts on File Publications, 1985), 166.

16. David Lowenthal has written, "No historical account can recover the totality of any past events, because their content is virtually infinite. The most detailed historical narrative incorporates only a minute fraction of even the relevant past; the sheer pastness of the past precludes its total reconstruction"; see *The Past Is a Foreign Country* (Cambridge: Cambridge University Press, 1985), 214–15.

17. Simone Weil, *The Need for Roots: Prelude to a Declaration of Duties Toward Mankind* (New York: G. P. Putman's Sons, 1952), 224–25.

18. The issue of (re)constructing American history from an Indian perspective as it relates to the politics of documentation is discussed in several essays in *The American Indian and the Problem of History*, ed. Calvin Martin (New York: Oxford University Press, 1987); see, in particular, the essays by Michael Dorris and Haunani-Kay Trask. Peter Nabokov's edited volume *Native American Testimony: A Chronicle of Indian-White Relations from Prophecy to the Present, 1492–1992* (New York: Viking-Penguin, 1991) might be characterized as an attempt to avoid the problems of documentary history for Native Americans. Nabokov calls the work a "chronicle" perhaps to distinguish it from history, but the volume includes a mostly chronological series of testimonies from native peoples about key historical events, periods, and transitions.

19. Not all reservation lands throughout the United States were allotted. The stated motive behind allotment — to open up "surplus land" to settlement by whites — was a determining factor only in those areas of the country where the reservation lands were arable. Thus, "most of the land cessions in this period occurred in the areas of greatest White interest: the Chippewa areas of Wisconsin and Minnesota, the Sioux country of North and South Dakota, and the Indian lands in central and western Oklahoma Territory"; see Wilcomb E. Washburn, ed., *History of Indian-White Relations*, vol. 4 of *Handbook of North American Indians*, ed. William C. Sturtevant (Washington, D.C.: Smithsonian, 1988), 66. Perhaps the history of allotment explains why Erdrich's Chippewa characters, who are from lands that were subjected to allotment, are afflicted by a homelessness and rootlessness not shared by Leslie Marmon Silko's Laguna Pueblo characters in *Ceremony* and *Storyteller*, who remain on land held by the tribe historically.

20. Mary Jane Schneider, *North Dakota Indians* (Dubuque: Kendall-Hunt, 1986), 85.

21. I am grateful to Donald Parman for his assistance with these details.

22. See Stanley N. Murray, "The Turtle Mountain Chippewa, 1882–1905," *North Dakota History* 51, no. 1 (1984): 16, 29.

23. Catherine Rainwater has written an important essay analyzing how conflicting narratives and cultural codes in Erdrich's novels produce a kind of alienation for the reader that can lead to "epistemological insight"; see "Reading between Worlds: Narrativity in the Fiction of Louise Erdrich," *American Literature* 62 (1990): 405–22.

24. Two recent collections of essays that focus on Native American women's history are attempting to fill some of these gaps: see Nancy Shoemaker's *Negotiators of Change: Historical Perspectives on Native American Women* (New York: Routledge, 1995) and Laura F. Klein and Lillian A. Ackerman's *Women and Power in Native North America* (Norman: University of Oklahoma Press, 1995).

25. I have extended Robert Silberman's description of June in *Love Medicine* to characterize Fleur here; see "Opening the Text: *Love Medicine* and the Return of the Native American Woman," in *Narrative Chance: Postmodern Discourse on Native American Indian Literatures*, ed. Gerald Vizenor (Albuquerque: University of New Mexico Press, 1989), 104. Two of Erdrich's other novels also revolve around the disappearance of a key mother figure: June, walking in blizzard conditions, dies at the beginning of *Love Medicine* (1984, rev. ed. New York: Harper, 1993); Adelaide abandons her children by flying off in a plane at the beginning of *The Beet Queen* (New York: Henry Holt, 1986). Erdrich seems particularly sensitive to the social dislocations these mothers experience that cause the family to fracture; see Hertha Wong's "Adoptive Mothers and Thrown-Away Children in the Novels of Louise Erdrich," in *Narrating Mothers: Theorizing Maternal Subjectivities*, ed. Brenda O. Daly and Maureen T. Reddy (Knoxville: University of Tennessee Press, 1991), 174–92. Moreover, the absence of these women from the narrative (Fleur in addition to June and Adelaide) is analogous to the omission of women from history.

26. Pauline's desire to be "wholly white" is understandable in light of the discrimination that the Catholic Church practiced in nineteenth-century North Dakota. Valerie Sherer Mathes points out that Native American women were not allowed to join religious orders until the latter part of the century when separate sisterhoods for Native American women were founded. One of the religious figures important in this movement was Father Francis Craft, who was part Mohawk and who successfully established a community of Native American sisters on the Fort Berthold Reservation. Unfortunately, he forbade the women to eat meat and "because this was the mainstay of the Plains tribes' diets, their health slowly began to deteriorate." By 1894, the sisters were only five in number, the others having died of tuberculosis or having left the order. See Mathes, "American Indian Women and the Catholic Church," *North Dakota History* 47, no. 4 (1980): 22, 24.

27. bell hooks, *Black Looks: Race and Representation* (Boston: South End Press, 1992), 191.

28. Susan Stanford Friedman's "Identity Politics, Syncretism, Catholi-

cism, and Anishinabe Religion in Louise Erdrich's *Tracks,*" *Religion and Literature* 26, no. 1 (1994): 107–33, offers a particularly insightful reading of Pauline's struggle for identity and her allegiance to Catholicism.

29. This passage also suggests that Pauline's denial of her tribal identity is never completely achieved: she still hears the "low voices" and "shadows" of the Pillagers that other people will become deaf and blind to.

30. Despite their differing orthographies, these names are consonant. The name Naanabozho has been transcribed variously as Manabozho, Nanabush, Wenebojo, Nehnehbush, to cite a few. See Gerald Vizenor's "Trickster Discourse," in *Narrative Chance: Postmodern Discourse on Native American Indian Literatures,* ed. Vizenor (Albuquerque: University of New Mexico Press, 1989), 187–211, for an influential analysis of the trickster as postmodern.

31. Although his confident anthropological analysis is off-putting, see Victor Barnouw's *Wisconsin Chippewa Myths and Tales* (Madison: University of Wisconsin Press, 1977) for a transcription of Wenebojo stories organized to provide a full narrative of the trickster's attributes and actions.

32. Wong argues that Nanapush, in fact, is the character "who 'mothers' most consistently throughout the novel"; see "Adoptive Mothers," 185.

33. Stead, "Unlocking the Tale."

34. Raymond DeMallie, *The Sixth Grandfather: Black Elk's Teachings Given to John G. Neihardt* (Lincoln: University of Nebraska Press, 1984), 232. I have quoted Black Elk's words as they appear in DeMallie's text (rather than the popular paperback version) because DeMallie works directly from transcripts of John Neihardt's 1931 and 1944 interviews with Black Elk. Although I agree with DeMallie's general assessment that Neihardt's telling of Black Elk's life matches the spirit, but not the letter, of Black Elk's words, in the chapter on the heyoka ceremony, Neihardt is the author of the famous, rather romantic description of the purpose of the heyoka ceremony — "You have noticed that the truth comes into this world with two faces. One is sad with suffering, and the other laughs; but it is the same face, laughing or weeping"; see Black Elk and John Neihardt, *Black Elk Speaks* (Lincoln: University of Nebraska Press, 1979), 188–89. To approximate Black Elk's description I have used DeMallie as the source here.

35. Louise Erdrich and Michael Dorris, "Louise Erdrich and Michael Dorris," interview by Bill Moyers, in *Conversations with Louise Erdrich and Michael Dorris,* ed. Allan Chavkin and Nancy Fehl Chavkin (Jackson: University Press of Mississippi, 1994), 144. Erdrich has commented elsewhere that humor is an aspect of her fiction often underappreciated by mainstream critics. In a 1986 interview conducted by Hertha Wong, Erdrich notes that literary critics tended to characterize *Love Medicine,* her first novel, as "devastating," but tribal people saw it as "funny"; see "An Interview with Louise Erdrich and Michael Dorris," interview by Hertha Wong, in *Conversations with Louise Erdrich and Michael Dorris,* 49. One of the few literary critics other than Kenneth Lincoln to emphasize Erdrich's humor is William Gleason; see "'Her Laugh an Ace': The Function of Humor in Louise Erdrich's *Love Medicine,*" *American Indian Culture and Research Journal* 11, no. 3 (1987): 51–73.

36. Kenneth Lincoln, *Indi'n Humor: Bicultural Play in Native America* (New York: Oxford University Press, 1993), 54–55.

37. Gerald Vizenor suggests that the tragic Indian is a construction of photographic practices: because of the slow shutter speeds of Curtis's cameras, his Indian subjects were required to remain unsmiling and face the camera stoically, prepared to sit as still as possible while the image was exposed; see Vizenor, *Crossbloods: Bone Courts, Bingo, and Other Reports* (Minneapolis: University of Minnesota Press, 1990), 48.

38. Kimberly M. Blaeser has written a compelling essay on Native American texts that use humor "to unmask and disarm history." She also uses the phrase "Righting History" and is interested in the ways in which "trickster reversals" can transform history into "healing story"; see Blaeser, "The New 'Frontier' of Native American Literature: Dis-Arming History with Tribal Humor," in *Native Perspectives on Literature and History*, ed. Alan R. Velie (Norman: University of Oklahoma Press, 1994), 37–50. While Blaeser's and my approach have much in common, our selection of literary texts to illustrate this transformation is very different. Blaeser works with imaginative historical texts, or texts that give playful, fictitious histories, such as Vizenor's *The Heirs of Columbus*; in contrast, by focusing on Erdrich's novels, I explore alternative representations of events that actually happened.

39. Lincoln, *Indi'n Humor*, 25, 35.

40. See in particular Gerald Vizenor's "Casino Coups," in *Manifest Manners: Postindian Warriors of Survivance*, by Vizenor (Hanover, N.H.: Wesleyan University Press-University Press of New England, 1994), 138–48; and Vizenor's *Crossbloods*, especially pages x-xiii, 18–24. The violent confrontation over gaming at the Mohawk reserve Akwesasne is detailed in Rick Hornung's book: *One Nation Under the Gun* (New York: Pantheon, 1991). Whether or not contemporary gaming on Indian lands has any connection to traditional games and traditional stories is a tangled question. The earliest games of bingo in America used a large bowl to hold the markers with letters on them; perhaps this equipment is not so distant from the bowls that the Chippewa traditionally used to carry out various "dice" games; see Stewart Culin, *Games of Chance*, vol. 1 of *Games of the North American Indians* (1907; rpt., Lincoln: University of Nebraska Press, 1992), especially pages 44–49, 61–68. But seriousness and ceremonialism distinguished these dice games and the moccasin game Vizenor mentions from "mere" gaming, as is apparent in many of the ethnographic accounts in Culin. Even if this sense of ceremony is missing from contemporary Indian casinos, it is present to some degree in Erdrich's handling of bingo in the novel since Lipsha receives his bingo guidance from his mother's spirit. The combination of chance and skill, of fate and choice, of life and death apparent in traditional Indian games is also represented in traditional Chippewa stories of the Great Gambler: see Gerald Vizenor's *Summer in the Spring: Anishinaabe Lyric Poems and Stories*, rev. ed. (Norman: University of Oklahoma Press, 1993), 124–31, for the legends, as well as his novel *The Heirs of Columbus* (Hanover, N.H.: Wesleyan University Press-University Press of New England, 1991) for another retelling. Erdrich never directly invokes the story of the Great Gambler in *The Bingo Palace* or elsewhere, but it is clear from

the acknowledgments to the novel that a love of card games is part of her Chippewa inheritance since it is associated with her Turtle Mountain grandfather, Pat Gourneau. In fact, the poem "Turtle Mountain Reservation" in *Jacklight* (New York: Henry Holt, 1984), 82–85, is dedicated to Gourneau and portrays a grandfather figure who still uses words from the old language ("a word / that belongs to a world / no one else can remember") and yet enjoys playing bingo. See John Purdy's "Against All Odds: Games of Chance in the Novels of Louise Erdrich," in *The Chippewa Landscape of Louise Erdrich*, ed. Allan Chavkin (Tuscaloosa: University of Alabama Press, 1999), 8–35, for an extended discussion of gaming as a theme in Erdrich's novels.

41. Vizenor, "Casino Coups," 148.

42. Hélène Cixous, "The Laugh of the Medusa," trans. Keith Cohen and Paula Cohen, *Signs* 1 (1976): 875, 878, 885.

43. Wong's essay on Erdrich offers a compelling investigation of the (non)applicability of feminist criticism in relation to Native American women; see "Adoptive Mothers." In *Indi'n Humor*, Lincoln argues that the humor of Erdrich's novels is Indi'n *and* feminist.

44. Catherine Rainwater persuasively discusses this card playing scene to analyze the ways in which *The Bingo Palace* "snares" readers, conjoining us in a "subtle, counter-colonial" design; see *Dreams of Fiery Stars: The Transformations of Native American Fiction* (Philadelphia: University of Pennsylvania Press, 1999), especially pages 26–32.

45. In his well-known study *The Trickster: A Study in American Indian Mythology* (London: Routledge and Kegan Paul, 1956), Paul Radin writes, "Laughter, humour and irony permeate everything Trickster does" (x) — a description that pertains to Fleur's role in the novel at this particular moment. But unlike the traditional trickster, which Radin describes as being noted for tricks and exploits that oftentimes get beyond his control, Fleur is not laughed at: she is always the one who laughs in *The Bingo Palace*.

46. *California v. Cabazon Band of Mission Indians*, 480 US 202 (1987).

47. *Indian Gaming Regulatory Act, U.S. Code*, vol. 25, sec. 2701 (1988).

48. Some native peoples who are critical of bingo and casinos point out that the requirement to negotiate compacts with the state in effect limits tribal sovereignty. They, therefore, argue that the IGRA does as much to harm tribal sovereignty as to support it, and they are opposed to casinos established on reservations because of this dilemma.

49. *Indian Gaming Regulatory Act*, sec. 2710, (d)(7)(B)(ii).

50. Joseph M. Kelly, "American Indian Gaming Law," *New Law Journal*, 26 Nov. 1993, 1672. See also *Lac du Flambeau Indians v. State of Wisconsin*, 770 F Supp 480 (WD Wis 1991).

51. *Indian Gaming Regulatory Act*, sec. 2703, (4).

52. This is, in fact, what happened when the city of Duluth, Minnesota, worked together with the Fond du Lac Chippewa to create a gaming casino in downtown Duluth. The Fond du Luth Casino is clearly not located within the traditional reservation boundaries but on newly defined land. The affirmation of tribal sovereignty in the Cabazon ruling has been manifested

in a number of other interesting trickster legal challenges: the assertion of the right to spearfish and to hunt and gather on ceded lands, as well as the filing of lawsuits to regain long lost territory.

53. The drive toward tribal repossession and independent self-rule has made many Anglos uneasy. As Robert Lance, a member of the Sioux in South Dakota, observes, "For some tribes, the money from gaming means freedom. Maybe the Mille Lacs can live without the white man"; see W. John Moore, "A Winning Hand?" *National Journal*, 17 July 1993, 1800. This possibility has provoked so much anxiety that there are calls to amend the IGRA so that tribes do not have a supposedly "unfair" advantage.

54. Erdrich is not alone in making this kind of conjunction. In an essay tellingly and playfully titled "Latin American Identity and Mixed Temporalities; Or, How to Be Postmodern and Indian at the Same Time," Fernando Calderón cites "the Aymara group WARA, which plays ancestral Indian flutes to the accompaniment of electric guitars" (*boundary 2* 20, no. 3 [1993], 64). Vizenor, who is White Earth Chippewa, is one of the few contemporary Native American writers who adamantly espouses Native American postmodernism; see his introduction and epilogue to *Narrative Chance: Postmodern Discourse on Native American Indian Literatures*, ed. Vizenor (Albuquerque: University of New Mexico Press, 1989). I would argue that Erdrich's postmodernism is not as theoretical or linguistic as Vizenor's. Whereas Vizenor's fiction employs the kind of wild pastiche associated with "classic" 1960s postmodernists such as Thomas Pynchon or Donald Barthelme, Erdrich remains interested in using native storytelling modes in postmodern, postindustrial contexts. Another way to underscore this distinction is to observe that, while Vizenor cites Roland Barthes, Jacques Derrida, Michel Foucault, and other French poststructuralists, Erdrich's sense of postmodernism seems closer to the crisis in historicity that Fredric Jameson discusses as the most significant attribute of postmodernism.

55. Cf. Walter Ong's concept of secondary orality, which is a contemporary revision of traditional oral structures and worldview created by the mass media, in *Orality and Literacy: The Technologizing of the Word* (London: Methuen, 1982).

56. Jean-François Lyotard and Jean-Loup Thébaud, *Just Gaming*, trans. Wlad Godzich (Minneapolis: University of Minnesota Press, 1985), 73–74.

57. Ibid., 100.

58. I should point out that the combination of native traditions and postmodern technologies is not always successful in *The Bingo Palace*. After Gerry's escape, Gerry calls Lipsha for help in fleeing to Canada, but speaks in "the old-time language," Anishinabe, in case the phone line is being tapped. Despite Lipsha's intense concentration on these words, he cannot recall enough of the language to decipher his father's message with any certainty. Humor moderates what might be a moment of despair, though, as Lipsha confesses: "I become confused. My father is either playing Star Wars games at Art's Arcade, or he is holed up at the Fargo library, or he is hiding curled up in the lodge dumpster of the Sons of Norway" — these are "three strange possibilities," Lipsha thinks to himself, as he continues to ponder the message (*BP* 233).

59. Paul Pasquaretta, "On the 'Indianness' of Bingo: Gambling and the Native American Community," *Critical Inquiry* 20 (1993–94): 714.

60. The state of Connecticut vehemently opposed the establishment of a casino on the reservation, but the Pequots sued them in court and won. The Foxwoods Casino opened in February 1992, and even though the casino could offer only class II gaming, it brought in approximately $300 million in revenue for the tribe. When the state of Connecticut faced a severe and ongoing financial crisis, however, Governor Lowell P. Weicker decided to enter into negotiations with the Pequots, giving them the right to run slot machines at the casino in return for a 25 percent cut of the slot revenues, with a guaranteed payment of at least $100 million. In 1994, the Pequots passed along $136 million to the state.

61. Pasquaretta, "On the 'Indianness' of Bingo," 707.

Chapter 3. Toni Morrison and the Desire for a "Genuine Black History Book"

1. Toni Morrison, "Unspeakable Things Unspoken: The Afro-American Presence in American Literature," *Michigan Quarterly Review* 28 (1989): 1–34; Hazel Carby, "The Canon: Civil War and Reconstruction," *Michigan Quarterly Review* 28 (1989): 35–43; Eric Foner, "The Canon and American History," *Michigan Quarterly Review* 28 (1989): 44–49.

2. Foner, "The Canon," 47.

3. Sally Keenan discusses Foner's response in a note to her essay on *Beloved*, arguing that Foner's criticisms stem from his genre confusion (mistaking fiction for history) and his inability to "'read' the modes of resistance, resiliency, and creativity which Morrison delineates"; see "'Four Hundred Years of Silence': Myth, History, and Motherhood in Toni Morrison's *Beloved*," in *Recasting the World: Writing after Colonialism*, ed. Jonathan White (Baltimore: Johns Hopkins University Press,1993), 79 note 12. I read Foner's critical comments somewhat differently—as symptomatic of a larger cultural dilemma regarding what we accept as "History."

4. Foner, "The Canon," 48, 49.

5. See Paul Gray, "Paradise Found," *Time*, 19 Jan. 1998, 63–65.

6. Henry Louis Gates, Jr., review of *Jazz*, by Toni Morrison, in *Toni Morrison: Critical Perspectives Past and Present*, ed. Henry Louis Gates, Jr., and A. K. Appiah (New York: Amistad, 1993), 52.

7. Christine Bold, "An Enclave in the Wilderness," review of *Paradise*, by Toni Morrison, *Times Literary Supplement*, 27 March 1998, 22.

8. Toni Morrison, "Behind the Making of *The Black Book*," *Black World*, Feb. 1974, 88, 89.

9. Quotations from Toni Morrison's novels are cited parenthetically in the text using the following abbreviations: *B* for *Beloved* (New York: Knopf, 1987), *J* for *Jazz* (New York: Knopf, 1992), *P* for *Paradise* (New York: Knopf, 1998).

10. Morrison, "Rediscovering Black History," *New York Times Magazine*, 11 Aug. 1974, 20, 14.

11. Middleton Harris et al., eds., *The Black Book* (New York: Random House, 1974), 82, 96.

12. Toni Morrison, "Behind the Making of *The Black Book*," 89.

13. Harris et al., *Black Book*, 86. This incident is reshaped and retold in Morrison's novels: in *Song of Solomon*, Ruth gives birth to Milkman on the steps of a hospital which refuses to admit her; in *Paradise*, the town of Ruby takes its name from Deacon and Steward's sister, who dies as a result of being denied admission to a hospital.

14. Marilyn Sanders Mobley briefly describes *The Black Book* in her essay on *Beloved*; see "A Different Remembering: Memory, History, and Meaning in *Beloved*," in *Toni Morrison: Critical Perspectives Past and Present*, ed. Henry Louis Gates, Jr., and A. K. Appiah (New York: Amistad, 1993), 356–65. While she sees the significance of this book as bringing Margaret Garner's story to Morrison's attention, I argue that there are other significant points of connection.

15. See *The Black Book*, page 10, for the clipping pertaining to Garner. The fullest account of what happened to Margaret Garner historically is found in Steven Weisenburger's *Modern Medea: A Family Story of Slavery and Child-Murder from the Old South* (New York: Hill and Wang, 1998).

16. Morrison, "Rediscovering Black History," 16.

17. Valerie Smith focuses on such images in the novel, arguing that one of the major purposes of *Beloved* is "to find a way to tell the story of the slave body in pain." Smith's eloquent reading ultimately concludes that the novel can only "circle" this "subject"; paradoxically, however, this circularity points to the novel's greatest strength for Smith: "By representing the inexpressibility of its subject, the novel asserts and reasserts the subjectivity of the former slaves and the depth of their suffering. . . . To the extent that *Beloved* returns the slaves to themselves, the novel humbles contemporary readers before the unknown and finally unknowable horrors the slaves endured"; see " 'Circling the Subject': History and Narrative in *Beloved*," in *Toni Morrison: Critical Perspectives Past and Present*, ed. Henry Louis Gates, Jr., and A. K. Appiah (New York: Amistad, 1993), 348, 354.

18. In a 1989 interview, Morrison talks about the "incredible" details regarding the punishments of slaves she discovered while researching aspects of *Beloved*: "There's a wonderful diary of the Burr family in which he talks about his daily life and says, 'Put the bit on Jenny today.' He says that about 19 times in six months—and he was presumably an enlightened slave owner. . . . There's a description of a woman who had to wear a bell contraption so when she moved they always knew where she was. There were masks slaves wore when they cut cane. They had holes in them, but it was so hot inside that when they took them off, the skin would come off"; see "The Pain of Being Black: An Interview with Toni Morrison," interview by Bonnie Angelo, in *Conversations with Toni Morrison*, ed. Danille Taylor-Guthrie (Jackson: University Press of Mississippi, 1994), 257. Morrison discusses some of these same disciplinary apparatuses of slavery, and how they became recorded as a matter of routine—without any affect attached to them—in the diaries of slaveholders; see the BBC's *Toni Morrison: Profile of*

a Writer, prod. and dir. Alan Benson, ed. Melvyn Bragg, 52 min., London Weekend Television, 1987, videocassette.

19. The ambiguous ethical stance of the novel regarding Sethe's action has troubled some commentators: Carol Iannone, for instance, has criticized Morrison for not "display[ing] a really sure hand in her treatment of the moral dimensions of Sethe's initial act of child murder" ("Toni Morrison's Career," *Commentary*, Dec. 1987, 63). Ashraf Rushdy, however, discusses how the novel creates its own context by which to judge Sethe's story: "by placing such a frame around Sethe's story, Morrison insists on the impossibility of judging an action without reference to the terms of its enactment—the wrongness of assuming a transhistorical ethic outside a historical moment. Morrison is not justifying Sethe's actions; she is writing about them in the only way she knows how—through eyes that accuse and embrace, through a perspective that criticizes while it rejoices"; see "Daughters Signifyin(g) History: The Example of Toni Morrison's *Beloved*," *American Literature* 64 (1993): 577–78.

20. Toni Morrison, "Rootedness: The Ancestor As Foundation," in *Black Women Writers, 1950–1980: A Critical Evaluation*, ed. Mari Evans (New York: Doubleday-Anchor, 1984), 340, 342.

21. Mae Gwendolyn Henderson brilliantly analyzes how Morrison's emphasis on "black motherlines" in *Beloved* creates a historical narrative that disrupts and reconfigures the "Master's" narrative and history; see "Toni Morrison's *Beloved*: Re-Membering the Body as Historical Text," in *Comparative American Identities: Race, Sex, and Nationality in the Modern Text*, ed. Hortense J. Spillers (New York: Routledge, 1991), 62–86.

22. Toni Morrison, "The Site of Memory," in *Inventing the Truth: The Art and Craft of Memoir*, ed. William Zinsser (Boston: Houghton Mifflin, 1987), 110, 111.

23. Morrison's figure of "Sixty Million" refers to the number of black people who died in Africa on their way to the slave ships or during the Middle Passage; see Walter Clemons, "The Ghosts of 'Sixty Million and More,'" *Newsweek*, 28 Sept. 1987, 75. But the astounding figure has been met with disbelief and denial: interviewer Bonnie Angelo writing for *Time*, for instance, asked Morrison if the number was historically proven ("The Pain of Being Black," 257), while Stanley Crouch's infamous review of the novel uses this figure to dismiss *Beloved* as "a blackface holocaust novel" ("Aunt Medea," review of *Beloved*, by Toni Morrison, *New Republic*, 19 Oct. 1987, 40).

24. Most scholars have tended to read the novel as Morrison's successful attempt to repair various gaps in African American history. Along with Henderson, who is mentioned above, two critics of the many who have commented on *Beloved* may serve as examples of the critical trend: Rushdy argues in "Daughters Signifyin(g) History" that "perhaps the greatest achievement of Morrison's novel is that she gives the murdered victim of history voice; she resurrects the unjustly killed and allows that daughter to have renewed historical life by criticizing the sort of history that has hitherto excluded her and her rebellious spirit" (592), while Keenan unites

feminist and postcolonial perspectives to demonstrate how *Beloved* "extends the limits of previous histories and autobiographical writings on slavery through its exploration of the ways subjectivity might be established and inscribed by those who have been denied its possibility" (" 'Four Hundred Years of Silence,' " 47). Caroline Rody's essay, like my argument here, takes a much more problematic view of historical reconstruction in the novel; see "Toni Morrison's *Beloved*: History, 'Rememory,' and a 'Clamor for a Kiss,' " *American Literary History* 7 (1995): 92-119.

25. Morrison has tacitly rejected the term "postmodernism" to describe her work; see "Living Memory: A Meeting with Toni Morrison," interview by Paul Gilroy, in *Small Acts: Thoughts on the Politics of Black Cultures*, by Paul Gilroy (London: Serpent's Tail, 1993), 178-79. But scholars such as Rafael Pérez-Torres and Philip Page have persuasively argued that a postmodern perspective is precisely what is needed to grapple with her fictional world. See Pérez-Torres, "Knitting and Knotting the Narrative Thread—*Beloved* as Postmodern Novel," in *Toni Morrison: Critical and Theoretical Approaches*, ed. Nancy J. Peterson (Baltimore: Johns Hopkins University Press, 1997), 91-109, and Page, *Dangerous Freedom: Fusion and Fragmentation in Toni Morrison's Novels* (Jackson: University Press of Mississippi, 1995).

26. Barbara Christian, " 'Somebody Forgot to Tell Somebody Something': African-American Women's Historical Novels," in *Wild Women in the Whirlwind: Afra-American Culture and the Contemporary Literary Renaissance*, ed. Joanne M. Braxton and Andrée N. McLaughlin (New Brunswick: Rutgers University Press, 1990), 327.

27. This newspaper article perhaps metafictionally signals the limits of even Morrison's own research in fully recovering the "real" story of Margaret Garner. *Beloved* comments directly on the politics of newspaper reports involving African Americans: "A whip of fear broke through the heart chambers as soon as you saw a Negro's face in a paper, since the face was not there because the person had a healthy baby, or outran a street mob. Nor was it there because the person had been killed, or maimed or caught or burned or jailed or whipped or evicted or stomped or raped or cheated, since that could hardly qualify as news in a newspaper. It would have to be something out of the ordinary—something whitepeople would find interesting, truly different, worth a few minutes of teeth sucking if not gasps" (*B* 155-56). This comment prefaces the scene in which Paul D sees the newspaper account of Sethe's "crime." Like other incidents in the novel, it suggests the degree to which so-called "objective reality" is a product of white supremacist ideologies.

28. Walter Benn Michaels, " 'You Who Never Was There': Slavery and the New Historicism, Deconstruction and the Holocaust," *Narrative* 4 (1996): 1-16.

29. Avery Gordon, "Not Only the Footprints But the Water Too and What Is down There," chap. 4 in *Ghostly Matters: Haunting and the Sociological Imagination* (Minneapolis: University of Minnesota Press, 1997), 190.

30. James Phelan concentrates on these last two pages in his essay on *Beloved*, precisely because of their unsettling effects; see "Toward a Rhetorical Reader-Response Criticism: The Difficult, the Stubborn, and the End-

ing of *Beloved*," in *Toni Morrison: Critical and Theoretical Approaches*, ed. Nancy J. Peterson (Baltimore: Johns Hopkins University Press, 1997), 225–44.

31. Most scholars estimate Beloved to be between one and two years old when she is killed; this would be a very long time for a baby to go unnamed.

32. Rody discusses the images of absence and desire in the coda, but draws a much different conclusion from these images than I do: "The past does not exist unless we choose to hear its clamor" ("Toni Morrison's *Beloved*," 113). I would disagree that Morrison's novel reaches such a radically deconstructive or relativist position.

33. Toni Morrison and Gloria Naylor, "A Conversation," in *Conversations with Toni Morrison*, ed. Danille Taylor-Guthrie (Jackson: University Press of Mississippi, 1994), 208. Although Morrison would eventually decide to tell the stories in separate novels, it is clear that strong connections—in terms of theme, image, and purpose—link *Beloved* to *Jazz*. Some of the most significant intratextual connections include "Sth," the voiced syllable that begins *Jazz* and is explained in *Beloved* as one of "the interior sounds a woman makes when she believes she is alone and unobserved at her work" (*B* 172). In addition, the word "trace" and the idea of going "wild" so important to *Jazz* are also first encountered in *Beloved* as undercurrents to the major narrative stream (see *B* 222, 275 for "trace"; *B* 149 on Sethe's wildness). In her 1995 interview with *Belle Lettres*, Morrison even goes so far as to draw strong links between Wild and Beloved, hinting that perhaps Wild *is* Beloved; see "Toni Morrison," interview by Angels Carabi, *Belle Lettres* 10, no. 2 (1995): 43.

34. Morrison and Naylor, "A Conversation," 207.

35. Toni Morrison, Foreword to *The Harlem Book of the Dead*, by James Van Der Zee (photography), Owen Dodson (poetry), and Camille Billops (text) (Dobbs Ferry, N.Y.: Morgan and Morgan, 1978), n.p.

36. Melissa Walker also finds this passage suggestive of Morrison's treatment of history in *Beloved*; see *Down from the Mountaintop: Black Women's Novels in the Wake of the Civil Rights Movement, 1966–1989* (New Haven: Yale University Press, 1991), 38–39. But as this chapter makes clear, we take quite different positions on the relation of private lives and public history in Morrison's work. Walker, it seems to me, overemphasizes "Morrison's rigorous adherence to the historical facts of the African-American experience" (9), especially when she argues that *Beloved* creates "characters whose lives are so intertwined with the exigencies of history that the most private acts and thoughts derive from public policy" (33).

37. Toni Morrison, "Toni Morrison: The Art of Fiction," interview by Elissa Schappell and Claudia Brodsky Lacour, *Paris Review* 128 (1993): 117.

38. See the description of this significant moment in Nathan I. Huggins's *Harlem Renaissance* (New York: Oxford University Press, 1971), 55–56.

39. Gilbert Osofsky emphasizes this fact: "*Prior to World War I*, the neighborhood was already the 'largest colony of colored people, in similar limits, in the world'—and it continued to expand. By 1920 the section of Harlem bordered approximately by One Hundred and Thirtieth Street on the south, One Hundred and Forty-fifth Street on the north and west of Fifth

to Eighth Avenue was predominately Negro—and inhabited by some 73,000 people"; see *Harlem: The Making of a Ghetto* (New York: Harper and Row, 1966), 122–23.

40. In 1969, a landmark exhibit designed to increase public awareness of the history of Harlem opened at the Metropolitan Museum of Art in New York. Titled "Harlem on My Mind," this exhibit sparked controversy and thus huge crowds of people: "During the first week and a half it was open, over seventy-seven thousand visitors saw 'Harlem On My Mind,'" and "every day that the museum was open, long lines of museum-goers of all races stretched down Fifth Avenue"; see Rodger C. Birt, "A Life in American Photography" in *VanDerZee, Photographer, 1886–1983* (New York: Henry Abrams, with the National Portrait Gallery of the Smithsonian Institution, 1993), 64. It also marked the rediscovery of James Van Der Zee, who was living in impoverished conditions when Reginald McGhee, following up on a lead about a photographer who had had a well-known studio in Harlem, located him. Van Der Zee became the single largest contributor to the exhibit, and the showing of his remarkable photographs of Harlem at that exhibit launched a belated integration of his work into the history of photography; see Birt, "A Life in American Photography," 62.

Morrison's novel contributes to this reawakened historical consciousness of Harlem (and indirectly of Van Der Zee), begun by scholars like Osofsky and Huggins, and made popular by exhibits like "Harlem on My Mind." This effort continues in a recent burst of scholarship on Harlem, the Renaissance, and various exhibits of artwork from the period, including a national tour of Jacob Lawrence's *Migration* series in 1995.

41. In "Rootedness: The Ancestor As Foundation," Morrison remarks, "Nice things don't always happen to the totally self-reliant if there is no conscious historical connection" (344)—a comment that anticipates the emphasis of her recent historical novels. A strong connection between claiming one's heritage/history and realizing self-identity for black women is made in Missy Dehn Kubitschek's analysis of contemporary black women's novels, which includes a discussion of Morrison; see *Claiming the Heritage: African-American Women Novelists and History* (Jackson: University Press of Mississippi, 1991).

42. Farah J. Griffin sees *Jazz* as "a portrait of a people in the midst of self-creation, a document of what they created and what they lost along the way"; her chapter on Morrison's novel incisively analyzes "the negative and positive consequences of migration" presented in *Jazz*; see *"Who Set You Flowin'?": The African-American Migration Narrative* (New York: Oxford University Press, 1995), 197.

43. Huggins, *Harlem Renaissance*, 65.

44. Houston A. Baker, Jr., *Workings of the Spirit: The Poetics of Afro-American Women's Writing* (Chicago: University of Chicago Press, 1991), 26, 25, 36.

45. Herman Beavers provides an exceptional reading of southern manhood in Morrison's novels in "The Politics of Space: Southernness and Manhood in the Fictions of Toni Morrison," *Studies in the Literary Imagination* 31, no. 2 (1998): 61–77.

46. In her perceptive essay on the novel, Angelyn Mitchell argues that

"In *Jazz*, Morrison offers a discursive engagement with history in order to contest the erasure and/or misrepresentation of southern Black women within the historical discourse of the hegemonic culture"; see " 'Sth, I Know that Woman': History, Gender, and the South in Toni Morrison's *Jazz*," *Studies in the Literary Imagination* 31, no. 2 (1998): 51–52.

47. Toni Morrison, "Interview with Toni Morrison," interview by Ntozake Shange, *American Rag*, Nov. 1978, 50.

48. Consider the literal wounds the black women, especially mothers, bear in *Beloved*: Sethe learns to identify her mother by the mark she bears under her breast, "a circle and a cross burnt right in the skin" (*B* 61); Sethe is marked by the "tree" schoolteacher's whippings have written on her back; Beloved bears the scar of Sethe's cut; even Nan is distinguished by having one "good arm" and "the stump of the other" (*B* 63).

49. In his essay on *Beloved*, James Berger discusses the Moynihan Report in much greater detail than I do here; see "Ghosts of Liberalism: Morrison's *Beloved* and the Moynihan Report," *PMLA* 111 (1996): 408–20. Although I agree with his argument that *Beloved* critiques the discourse and practices of white liberalism, I would not argue, as he implicitly does, that a central purpose of Morrison's novel is to address the inadequacies of various white-dominant political theories. Morrison has said she thinks of a black audience when she is writing, and such a critique would be old news to her primary audience. Denise Heinze briefly discusses various sociological studies of black families, including Moynihan's, and analyzes the portrayal of black families in all of Morrison's novels in chap. 2 of her book: *The Dilemma of "Double-Consciousness": Toni Morrison's Novels* (Athens: University of Georgia Press, 1993).

50. The reference to Bluebird Records is anachronistic in Morrison's novel: *Jazz* is set in 1926, but Bluebird Records was not founded until 1933 in Chicago. To become overly concerned about this detail, however, would be to miss the larger implications of Morrison's reference.

51. In her *Paris Review* interview, Morrison employs this same terminology while discussing the novel: "It's important not to have a totalizing view. In American literature we [African Americans] have been so totalized — as though there is only one version. We are not one indistinguishable block of people who always behave the same way" ("Toni Morrison: The Art of Fiction," 117).

52. I am aware that my reference to the narrator as a "she" is tenuous. Even though Morrison does not offer any clear indications of the gender of the narrator, I am persuaded by Eusebio Rodrigues's connection of the epigraph from the *Nag Hammadi*, which features a female goddess, to the narrator's identity ("Experiencing *Jazz*," in *Toni Morrison: Critical and Theoretical Approaches*, ed. Nancy J. Peterson [Baltimore: Johns Hopkins University Press, 1997], 260–61), and by the empathy the narrator immediately has for especially black women in the novel. Craig Werner offers a fascinating reading of Morrison's epigraph as invoking the voice of "a visionary African woman"; see *Playing the Changes: From Afro-Modernism to the Jazz Impulse* (Urbana: University of Illinois Press, 1994), 302.

53. Golden Gray is the beautiful, light-skinned baby boy that True Belle

fed Violet stories of while she was growing up. Golden Gray brings the very pregnant Wild to Hunters Hunter's cabin, so he is present at Joe's birth. Morrison's readers are able to put Violet's and Joe's stories together in this way, but we have no indication in the novel that they are aware of this amazing coincidence.

54. Toni Morrison, "Memory, Creation, and Writing," *Thought* 59 (1984): 385.

55. Morrison, "The Site of Memory," 113, 117.

56. Morrison, "Toni Morrison: The Art of Fiction," 116–17.

57. Morrison, perhaps anticipating the difficulties readers would have with these ending paragraphs, offers a direct explanation of the narrative voice: "The voice is the voice of a talking book. . . . This is a love song of a book talking to the reader"; see "Toni Morrison," interview by Angels Carabi, 42.

58. The treatment of history as story in the postmodern novel has often been criticized for sealing off any consideration of the historical real. In his essay on *Beloved*, however, Pérez-Torres suggests that Morrison's postmodernism results not in a flight away from history, but in a complicated return to reference; see "Knitting and Knotting," especially pages 96, 108–9.

59. In fact, Morrison's original idea was to use "War" as the title, but her publisher convinced her to do otherwise; see Toni Morrison, "This Side of Paradise," interview by James Marcus, Jan. 1998, accessed 26 Jan. 1998, ⟨http://www.amazon.com/exec/obidos/ts/feature/7651/103–9598788–9210237⟩.

60. Morrison, "Memory, Creation, and Writing," 389.

61. Kenneth M. Hamilton, *Black Towns and Profit: Promotion and Development in the Trans-Appalachian West, 1877–1915* (Urbana: University of Illinois Press, 1991), 104.

62. Toni Morrison, "Blacks, Modernism, and the American South: An Interview with Toni Morrison," interview by Carolyn Denard, *Studies in the Literary Imagination* 31, no. 2, (1998): 11–12. In addition to her recent research, Morrison would also have come across a mention of Edwin McCabe, who was an important promoter of all-black towns and founder of Langston, in her work on the *Black Book*; see Harris et al., *Black Book*, 51.

63. Norman L. Crockett, *The Black Towns* (Lawrence: Regents Press of Kansas, 1979), 185–86.

64. In her review of the novel, Michelle Cliff connects the ceremony Consolata creates for the Convent women with the Afro-Brazilian ritual *candomble* and interestingly argues that it constitutes a decolonization for the women; see Cliff, "Great Migrations," review of *Paradise*, by Toni Morrison, *Village Voice*, 27 Jan. 1998, 86.

65. Morrison has commented that this idea is so important that she regrets the capitalization of "Paradise" at the end of the novel as the final word: " 'The whole point is to get paradise off its pedestal, as a place for anyone, to open it up for passengers and crew. I want all the readers to put a lower case mark on the *p* ' "; see Bold, "Enclave in the Wilderness," 22.

66. These are the words Morrison uses to describe Sula in "Unspeakable

Things Unspoken," and they echo the words Morrison uses to describe the kind of language that makes literature "Black"; see "Unspeakable Things Unspoken," 25, 11.

67. Toni Morrison, "Nobel Lecture 1993," in *Toni Morrison: Critical and Theoretical Approaches*, ed. Nancy J. Peterson (Baltimore: Johns Hopkins University Press, 1997), 270.

Chapter 4. Remembering Holocaust History

1. *Der khurbn* is a Yiddish term meaning the destruction — an allusion to the first and second destruction of the Temple. *Shoah* is the Hebrew word for catastrophe or destruction. See James E. Young's discussion of the nuances of these terms in *Writing and Rewriting the Holocaust: Narrative and the Consequences of Interpretation* (Bloomington: Indiana University Press, 1988), 85–89.

2. Jean-François Lyotard, *The Postmodern Condition: A Report on Knowledge*, trans. Geoff Bennington and Brian Massumi (Minneapolis: University of Minnesota Press, 1984).

3. See, for example, Lyotard's comments on Auschwitz as that which escapes full articulation — "The silence that surrounds the phrase 'Auschwitz was the extermination camp' is not a state of mind, it is a sign that something remains to be phrased which is not, something which is not determined" — in *The Differend: Phrases in Dispute*, trans. Georges Van Den Abbeele (Minneapolis: University of Minnesota Press, 1988), 56–57.

4. Saul Friedlander, "Trauma, Transference and 'Working through' in Writing the History of the *Shoah*," *History and Memory* 4, no. 1 (1992): 53.

5. Jane Caplan, "Postmodernism, Poststructuralism, and Deconstruction: Notes for Historians," *Central European History* 2 (1989): 278.

6. Friedlander too, while arguing that a "totalizing interpretation [of the Holocaust] is neither possible nor desirable," at the same time views a "deconstructionist approach" to the Holocaust as inadequate because it precludes "any direct reference to some aspects at least of the concrete *reality* that we call the *Shoah*"; see "Trauma," 52.

7. Andreas Huyssen, *Twilight Memories: Marking Time in a Culture of Amnesia* (New York: Routledge, 1995), 1.

8. Ibid., 249.

9. Ibid., 253.

10. For perceptive readings of a wide range of Holocaust museums and memorials, see the groundbreaking work by James E. Young, who has edited an important collection titled *The Art of Memory: Holocaust Memorials in History* (New York: Prestel, 1994) and has developed his own full-length analysis of various memorials in *The Texture of Memory: Holocaust Memorials and Meaning* (New Haven: Yale University Press, 1993). For a detailed comparison of the Holocaust museums in Los Angeles and Washington, D.C., see Edward Norden, "Yes and No to the Holocaust Museums," *Commentary*, Aug. 1993, 23–32, and Vivian M. Patraka, "Spectacles of Suffering: Per-

forming Presence, Absence, and Historical Memory at U.S. Holocaust Museums," in *Performance and Cultural Politics*, ed. Elin Diamond (New York: Routledge, 1996), 89–107.

11. Huyssen, *Twilight Memories*, 259.

12. Quoted in Norden, "Yes and No," 26.

13. Edward T. Linenthal's book contains an important discussion of rejected designs for the museum, as well as reporting the various changes architect James Ingo Freed agreed to make and those he rejected: see *Preserving Memory: The Struggle to Create America's Holocaust Museum* (New York: Viking, 1995), especially pages 75–83 and 99–104.

14. See Zygmunt Bauman's *Modernity and the Holocaust* (Ithaca: Cornell University Press, 1989) for a provocative argument connecting modernism to Nazism.

15. Quoted in Geoffrey H. Hartman, "The Book of the Destruction," in *Probing the Limits of Representation: Nazism and the "Final Solution,"* ed. Saul Friedlander (Cambridge: Harvard University Press, 1982), 326, 333. Dori Laub, eloquently evoking the incommensurability of the Holocaust, writes: "The historical imperative to bear witness could essentially *not be met during the actual occurrence*. The degree to which bearing witness was required, entailed such an outstanding measure of awareness and of comprehension of the event — of its dimensions, consequences, and above all, of its radical *otherness* to all known frames of reference — that it was beyond the limits of human ability (and willingness) to grasp, to transmit, or to imagine. . . . The event could thus unimpededly proceed *as though* there were no witnessing whatsoever, *no witnessing that could decisively impact on it*"; see Shoshana Felman and Dori Laub, *Testimony: Crises of Witnessing in Literature, Psychoanalysis, and History* (New York: Routledge, 1992), 84.

16. I borrow this term from a collection of essays entitled *American Sacred Space*, ed. David Chidester and Edward T. Linenthal (Bloomington: Indiana University Press, 1995).

17. Linenthal, *Preserving Memory*, 224. Cf. Michael Berenbaum's discussion of the failure to bomb Auschwitz in *The World Must Know: The History of the Holocaust as Told in the United States Holocaust Memorial Museum* (Boston: Little, Brown, 1993), 144–45. A comparison of Berenbaum's and Linenthal's discussions of this incident demonstrates that vastly different, yet equally tenable interpretations can be reached using the same evidence.

18. In an essay that incisively examines typical museum practices, Elaine H. Gurian observes, "Unsigned exhibitions reinforce the notion that there is a godlike voice of authority behind the selection of objects"; see "Noodling Around with Exhibition Opportunities," in *Exhibiting Cultures: The Poetics and Politics of Museum Display*, ed. Ivan Karp and Steven D. Lavine (Washington, D.C.: Smithsonian, 1991), 187.

19. The original arrival of these canisters at the museum caused such consternation that one of the staff members contacted the Environmental Protection Agency, while another considered suing the museum for exposing employees to a hazardous substance. Because the canisters had been exposed to air for forty years it was unlikely that they would cause anyone harm; nevertheless, Michael Berenbaum, the project director for the mu-

seum, took them home one night after hours, put them in his garage, and had them tested to make sure there was no hazard; see Linenthal, *Preserving Memory*, 157.

20. Huyssen, *Twilight Memories*, 32–33. Although he does not mention it directly, Huyssen's concept of auratic objects is clearly indebted to Walter Benjamin's work, particularly the essay "The Work of Art in an Age of Mechanical Reproduction"; see Benjamin's *Illuminations: Essays and Reflections*, ed. Hannah Arendt, trans. Harry Zohn (New York: Schocken Books, 1968), 217–51.

21. The *Encyclopedia of the Holocaust* calls the Oneg Shabbat archive (Hebrew for "Sabbath delight") saved in these milk cans "the most important single source for the history of Polish Jewry during the war and the Holocaust"; see Israel Gutman, "Oneg Shabbat," in *Encyclopedia of the Holocaust*, ed. Israel Gutman (New York: Macmillan, 1990), 1087.

22. Richard Appignanesi and Chris Garratt, "Welcome to the Holocaust Theme Park," in *Introducing Postmodernism* (New York: Totem Books, 1995), 122.

23. See Berenbaum, *The World Must Know*, page 147, for the full text of Schulstein's poem.

24. Fredric Jameson, *Postmodernism, or, the Cultural Logic of Late Capitalism* (Durham: Duke University Press, 1991), 7, 8.

25. Patraka, "Spectacles of Suffering," 103.

26. Stephen Greenblatt, "Resonance and Wonder," in *Exhibiting Cultures: The Poetics and Politics of Museum Display*, ed. Ivan Karp and Steven D. Lavine (Washington, D.C.: Smithsonian, 1991), 45.

27. Ibid., 48.

28. Ibid., 44.

29. Linenthal details the controversy that arose among content committee members and museum staff over the planned display of human hair. The separate space was created in the museum to display actual hair, but because of the controversy, the hair remains in a warehouse somewhere outside of Washington, D.C., while the photograph of hair on display at Auschwitz occupies the space; see *Preserving Memory*, 210–16.

30. The red brick chimneys of the crematoria, because of the intensity of the fire used to burn the bodies, would not hold together without steel braces for reinforcement.

31. James Ingo Freed, "The Holocaust Memorial Museum," *Partisan Review* 61 (1994): 448, 450, 452.

32. Young, *Writing and Rewriting the Holocaust*, 15–16.

33. Ken Johnson takes a much more critical view of the abstract art in the museum; see "Art and Memory," *Art in America*, Nov. 1993, 92–95.

34. The museum includes two other commissioned works of abstract art: Richard Serra's *Gravity*, a large vertical slab of unpolished steel that intentionally hinders traffic flow at one end of the Hall of Witness, and Joel Shapiro's *Loss and Regeneration*, a two-piece sculpture that is placed outside the museum in Eisenhower Plaza.

35. Linenthal, *Preserving Memory*, 253.

36. This phrase echoes an observation from Dori Laub, who writes in one

of his chapters in *Testimony,* "I recognize three separate, distinct levels of witnessing in relation to the Holocaust experience: the level of being a witness to oneself within the experience; the level of being a witness to the testimonies of others; and the level of being a witness to the process of witnessing itself"; see Felman and Laub, *Testimony,* 75.

37. Freed, "Holocaust Memorial Museum," 456.

38. Quoted in Linenthal, *Preserving Memory,* 30–31.

39. Quoted in Linenthal, *Preserving Memory,* 142, 143.

40. See Jeshajahu Weinberg and Rina Elieli, *The Holocaust Museum in Washington* (New York: Rizzoli, 1995), 197.

41. The 445,000 estimate comes from Yisrael Gutman in *The Jews of Warsaw, 1939–1943: Ghetto, Underground, Revolt,* trans. Ina Friedman (Bloomington: Indiana University Press, 1982), 63. But some of the Nazis' own records, as cited by Ulrich Keller, suggest even more than 500,000 Jews could have occupied the ghetto in 1941; see the introduction to *The Warsaw Ghetto in Photographs: 206 Views Made in 1941,* ed. Keller (New York: Dover, 1984), vii. Jews in the Warsaw Ghetto were dying in large numbers before the major deportation actions: from January 1941 until the July 1942 liquidation action, approximately 80,000 Jews died from starvation, disease (typhus, in particular), and slave labor, according to Gutman (*Jews of Warsaw,* 62–65). Assuming 350,000 Jews were left in the ghetto when the July 1942 forced deportations began, Gutman estimates that 265,000 of them were transported to Treblinka and killed. Philip Friedman offers a higher estimate, citing SS officer Jürgen Stroop's official report, which stated that 310,322 Jews were deported to Treblinka from the Warsaw Ghetto during August, September, and October 1942; see Friedman's *Roads to Extinction: Essays on the Holocaust* (New York: Conference on Jewish Social Studies/ Jewish Publication Society of America, 1980), 229. The circumstances of genocide mean that population and depopulation figures of Jews under the Nazi extermination policy are always approximations.

42. Klepfisz was part of a group of fighters who had their escape route cut off. He stepped in front of a machine gun to allow his comrades to escape. One of them, Marek Edelman, survived not only the Uprising but the rest of the war. Klepfisz is often included in historical accounts or memoirs of the Uprising: see Ber Mark's *Uprising in the Warsaw Ghetto,* trans. Gershon Freidlin, rev. ed. (New York: Schocken, 1975), which mentions Michał Klepfisz's heroism briefly in the chronological account of the Uprising and in the historical documents section; Tzvetan Todorov's *Facing the Extreme: Moral Life in the Concentration Camps,* trans. Arthur Denner and Abigail Pollak (New York: Henry Holt, 1996) cites Klepfisz's heroism as part of a discussion of what constitutes heroism and saintliness under the conditions of the Holocaust; Vladka Meed, who knew Michał, recalls his bravery and generosity at various points in her memoir, *On Both Sides of the Wall: Memoirs from the Warsaw Ghetto,* trans. Steven Meed (New York: Holocaust Library, 1979), and includes a photograph of him on page 137; Reuben Ainsztein's *The Warsaw Ghetto Revolt* (New York: Holocaust Library, 1979) credits Michał's ability to procure arms on the Aryan side of Warsaw. Michał Klepfisz was posthumously awarded the Silver Cross of Virtuti Militari, the highest

ranking Polish military medal, by the Polish government in exile on February 18, 1944; his medal is on display at the U.S. Holocaust Memorial Museum in Washington, D.C.

43. Rich's chapter on Klepfisz in *What Is Found There: Notebooks on Poetry and Politics* (New York: Norton, 1993), 128–44, is a slightly revised version of the introduction Rich wrote for the Eighth Mountain Press edition of Klepfisz's selected poems. Rich and Klepfisz, both Jewish lesbian-feminists, became acquainted through their work on the periodicals *Conditions* and *Bridges*. In addition, they were members of a group in the 1980s called *di vilde chayes*, a Jewish lesbian group.

44. Adrienne Rich, *What Is Found There*, 131, 141.

45. All subsequent references to Klepfisz's essays and poems will be cited parenthetically in the text, using the following abbreviations: *DI* for *Dreams of an Insomniac: Jewish Feminist Essays, Speeches, and Diatribes* (Portland: Eighth Mountain Press, 1990); *FW* for *A Few Words in the Mother Tongue: Poems Selected and New (1971–1990)* (Portland: Eighth Mountain Press, 1990).

46. There is, in fact, an oblique connection between Klepfisz's argument here and the museum: in a subsequent essay on Holocaust memory and Jewish identity, Klepfisz includes a note that refers to a 1990 *New York Times Magazine* article on the controversies surrounding the development of the museum; see *DI* 211 note 19.

47. Klepfisz adds a note that when she revisited Poland in 1988, she was surprised to see that "the gas station was gone. A huge memorial of white and black marble walls now marks the place from which half a million Jews left for Treblinka" (*DI* 112 note 7). See Konstanty Gebert's "The Dialectics of Memory in Poland: Holocaust Memorials in Warsaw," in *The Art of Memory: Holocaust Memorials in History*, ed. James E. Young (New York: Prestel, 1994), 121–29, for a discussion of recent memorial building in Warsaw.

48. Klepfisz also visited the oldest Jewish cemetery in Poland: Bródno, located in a suburb of Warsaw called Praga. This cemetery was destroyed in the 1960s during a wave of anti-Semitic violence; when Klepfisz was in Poland in 1983 it was illegal to visit the spot. See Marian Fuks, et al., *Polish Jewry: History and Culture*, trans. Bogna Piotrowska and Lech Petrowicz (Warsaw: Interpress Publishers, 1982), 179, 189, 194–196, for photographs showing the neglect of Jewish cemeteries in Poland.

49. Klepfisz's mother had a gravestone erected for Michał in the Jewish cemetery in Warsaw in 1966, but the spot where his friend Marek Edelman buried him in the ghetto is not marked.

50. The bitter tone of this poem may bring to mind Sylvia Plath's "Daddy," but with a crucial difference: for Plath the Holocaust is a powerful metaphor, while for Klepfisz it is a haunting personal history. See Young's *Writing and Rewriting the Holocaust*, 117–33, for a compelling discussion of Plath's use of Holocaust imagery.

51. Selections from *periods of stress* (1975; distributed by Out & Out Books) are included in *A Few Words in the Mother Tongue* (39–104).

52. Adrienne Rich, *What Is Found There*, 137.

53. *Keeper of Accounts*, originally published by Persephone Press in 1982, is reprinted in its entirety in *A Few Words in the Mother Tongue* (105–210).

54. Rich, "Compulsory Heterosexuality and Lesbian Existence," in *Blood, Bread, and Poetry: Selected Prose, 1979–1985* (New York: Norton, 1986), 23–75.

55. Felman and Laub, *Testimony*, xvii–xviii.

56. On her personal struggles to find the financial support that would allow her to write full time, see Klepfisz's acknowledgments page in the original edition of *Keeper of Accounts* (Watertown, Mass.: Persephone Press, 1982) and the essay "The Distances Between Us: Feminism, Consciousness, and the Girls at the Office" (*DI* 15–49).

57. See in particular the essay "Secular Jewish Identity: *Yidishkayt* in America" (*DI* 143–66).

58. This quotation comes from "Notes of an Immigrant Daughter: Atlanta," which appears in the important anthology *Nice Jewish Girls: A Lesbian Anthology*, ed. Evelyn Torton Beck, rev. ed. (Boston: Beacon, 1989).

59. Elza Frydrych, like Klepfisz, was a child survivor, but unlike Irena, she was orphaned. Having been left in a Polish household and told by her parents not to admit to being a Jew and not to go with anyone other than them, Elza refused to admit who she was when friends of her parents came to reclaim her at the end of the war. The Polish "protectors" who were caring for her had to be bribed to release her. Elza, who appeared to be adjusting to life as a survivor in America, committed suicide just before her twenty-sixth birthday. See *DI* 87, 167, as well as Klepfisz's poem "*Bashert*" (*FW* 183–200).

60. Susan Stanford Friedman, "Craving Stories: Narrative and Lyric in Contemporary Theory and Women's Long Poems," in *Feminist Measures: Soundings in Poetry and Theory*, ed. Lynn Keller and Cristanne Miller (Ann Arbor: University of Michigan Press, 1994), 34.

61. Klepfisz has commented on the woman-centeredness of the three long poems that comprise the final section of *Keeper of Accounts*: "all the figures in the last section of *Keeper of Accounts*, 'Inhospitable Soil,' are women who struggled to survive in Europe, women who struggle to survive here. Without realizing it, I was beginning to think from a Jewish feminist perspective, helping to make visible a woman's link in the chain of Jewish history" (*DI* 170).

62. Cathy Caruth, *Unclaimed Experience: Trauma, Narrative, and History* (Baltimore: Johns Hopkins University Press, 1996), 18.

63. Caruth, *Unclaimed Experience*, 11.

64. Lucy S. Dawidowicz, *The Holocaust and the Historians* (Cambridge: Harvard University Press, 1981), 14.

65. Klepfisz has translated texts from Yiddish women writers into English and has written her own bilingual poems. She has been influenced by the work of Chicana feminist Gloria Anzaldúa in this endeavor. Their mutual regard, in fact, is readily apparent in their separate volumes. In Anzaldúa's *Borderlands / La Frontera: The New Mestiza* (San Francisco: Spinsters-Aunt Lute, 1987), the poem "Poets have strange eating habits" (140–41) is dedicated to Klepfisz, and Anzaldúa names Klepfisz as one of her supporters in the acknowledgments section. Klepfisz names Anzaldúa in the acknowledgments sections of both her volumes of poems and essays, and she also cites

Anzaldúa's influence on her bilingual poetry in various essays (see *DI* 49, 162, 171). See also Jane Hedley, "Nepantilist Poetics: Narrative and Cultural Identity in the Mixed-Language Writings of Irena Klepfisz and Gloria Anzaldúa," *Narrative* 4 (1996): 36–54.

66. The final poem in *A Few Words in the Mother Tongue*, "East Jerusalem, 1987: *Bet Shalom* (House of Peace)" (*FW* 237–40), expresses Klepfisz's concern that parallels between the Jewish diaspora in WWII and the contemporary Palestinian situation were being ignored. Her awareness of the risks she takes in making such Holocaust analogies is clear in the essay "*Yom Hashoah, Yom Yerushalayim*: A Meditation" (*DI* 115–40).

67. Rich, *What Is Found There*, 132.

68. This issue is also of concern to Holocaust scholar James E. Young, who has written in *Writing and Rewriting the Holocaust*: "Unfortunately, the unassimilable images of the wretched dead and survivors have become for many in America not only the sum of European Jewish civilization but also the sum of knowledge about the Holocaust and its survivors. Too often the point of departure for the 'popular study' of the Holocaust begins and ends with these images alone, the unmitigated horror at the end of Jewish history in continental Europe, not the conditions of history, politics, culture, and mind — or the rich history of European Jewry — that preceded it" (163).

69. Pierre Nora, "Between Memory and History: *Les Lieux de Mémoire*," *Representations* 26 (1989): 9, 24.

Chapter 5. Joy Kogawa and the Peculiar "Logic" of Internment

1. In recent years, museum exhibits have helped to invigorate collective historical memory of Japanese immigration, internment, and resettlement in both countries. *A Dream of Riches* is the text for an exhibition that documented the first one-hundred years of Japanese experience in Canada; see Japanese Canadian Centennial Project Committee, *A Dream of Riches: The Japanese Canadians, 1877–1977* (Vancouver: Japanese Canadian Centennial Project Committee, 1978). The Japanese American National Museum in Los Angeles has organized important exhibitions of internment art; see David Yoo's "Captivating Memories: Museology, Concentration Camps, and Japanese American History," *American Quarterly* 48 (1996): 680–99, for a review of a 1995 exhibition provocatively entitled "American Concentration Camps." *The View from Within: Japanese American Art from the Internment Camps, 1942–1945*, ed. Karen M. Higa (Los Angeles: Japanese American National Museum, 1992) is the catalog for an important exhibition of internment art originally organized by the Japanese American National Museum. See also Kristine C. Kuramitsu's excellent essay on internment art: "Internment and Identity in Japanese American Art," *American Quarterly* 47 (1995): 619–58.

2. Ansel Adams, *Born Free and Equal: Photographs of the Loyal Japanese-Americans at Manzanar Relocation Center, Inyo County, California* (New York: U.S. Camera, 1944).

3. John Armor and Peter Wright, *Manzanar* (New York: Times Books-Random House, 1988), xviii. Armor and Wright have collected Adams's photographs with their own commentary about life at Manzanar. They also include a lengthy essay by John Hersey (who wrote about the horror of Hiroshima for the *New Yorker* in 1946) that is critical of the internment period.

4. Judith Fryer Davidov compares Adams's and Lange's photographs of Manzanar to argue that Lange poignantly captures the devastating indignities and injustices of internment in her images, but Adams falls back on the natural beauty of the terrain and the pristine mountains in the background, thus evading the politics of the camps; see " 'The Color of My Skin, the Shape of My Eyes': Photographs of the Japanese-American Internment by Dorothea Lange, Ansel Adams, and Toyo Miyatake," *Yale Journal of Criticism* 9 (1996): 223–44.

5. See Stan Yogi's essay on Sansei internment poetry for a more detailed analysis of this problem: "Yearning for the Past: The Dynamics of Memory in Sansei Internment Poetry," in *Memory and Cultural Politics: New Approaches to American Ethnic Literatures*, ed. Amritjit Singh, Joseph T. Skerrett, Jr., and Robert E. Hogan (Boston: Northeastern University Press, 1996), 245–65.

6. Janice D. Tanaka, *When You're Smiling*, 60 min., Visual Communications, Los Angeles, 1999, videocassette.

7. Rea Tajiri, *History and Memory (for Akiko and Takeshige)*, 33 min., Electronic Arts Intermix, New York, 1991, videocassette. I want to thank Holly Mickelson for bringing this film to my attention.

8. Miné Okubo, *Citizen 13660* (Seattle: University of Washington Press, 1983); John Okada, *No-No Boy* (Seattle: University of Washington Press, 1986); Monica Sone, *Nisei Daughter* (Seattle: University of Washington Press, 1979); Jeanne Wakatsuki Houston and James D. Houston, *Farewell to Manzanar* (Boston: Houghton Mifflin, 1973). The popularity of David Guterson's novel *Snow Falling on Cedars* (New York: Harcourt Brace, 1994) might seem to be an exception to my argument here; however, Guterson's novel frames the story of internment with an interracial romance and courtroom drama, and thus seems to suggest that internment by itself is not a story that can spark the interest of American readers.

9. Joy Kogawa, *Obasan* (Toronto: Lester and Orphen Dennys, 1981; New York: Anchor-Doubleday, 1994). All quotations from *Obasan* are taken from the Anchor-Doubleday reprint edition, and will be cited parenthetically in the text.

10. Ann Gomer Sunahara, *The Politics of Racism: The Uprooting of Japanese Canadians During the Second World War* (Toronto: Lorimer, 1981). Kitagawa's letters had not yet been published when Kogawa and Sunahara wrote their books. They were published for the first time in 1985; see Muriel Kitagawa, *This Is My Own: Letters to Wes and Other Writings on Japanese Canadians, 1941–1948*, ed. Roy Miki (Vancouver: Talonbooks, 1985).

11. The case in America may be somewhat similar: in October 1981 Peter Irons surprisingly discovered Justice Department files from the 1940s which indicated that crucial information had been suppressed in the Supreme

Court cases that challenged the curfew and exclusion orders. Armed with this information, Irons was able to use a little-known judicial remedy called *coram nobis* to have the Korematsu and Hirabayashi convictions (discussed below) vacated in 1984 and 1987 respectively.

12. See Roger Daniels's *Concentration Camps: North America*, rev. ed. (Malabar, Fla.: Krieger, 1989), 208–9, for the full text of Executive Order 9066 and PC 1486.

13. Sunahara, *The Politics of Racism*, 47.

14. See the section of photographs that follows chap. 4 in Sunahara's *The Politics of Racism* for reproductions of the notices affecting "male enemy aliens" and "all persons of Japanese racial origin."

15. In the United States, 120,000 people of Japanese ancestry were interned; approximately 65 percent of them were American born and thus citizens. In Canada, 12,000 people of Japanese ancestry were placed in camps, while an additional 8,000 were forced to leave the British Columbia coast and moved to places on the prairies or in some cases farther east to Toronto and Montreal; of the 21,000 people forced to leave the British Columbia coast, approximately 15 percent were naturalized citizens and 60 percent were Canadian-born citizens.

16. See Geoffrey S. Smith's "Racial Nativism and Origins of Japanese American Relocation," in *Japanese Americans: From Relocation to Redress*, ed. Roger Daniels, Sandra C. Taylor, and Harry H. L. Kitano (Salt Lake City: University of Utah Press, 1986), 79–87, for more on the pernicious effects of nativist discourse.

17. Armor and Wright, *Manzanar*, 81–82.

18. Ken Adachi reports a particularly poignant example of such injustice involving Sergeant George Yasuzo Shoji, who despite being a veteran of World War I, was not allowed to keep his Fraser Valley farm: "Shoji had bought 19 acres of land in the Fraser Valley village of Wonnock in 1931 under the soldiers' Settlement Act and then cleared and cultivated nine acres. In 1943, his land, a two-storied house, four chicken houses, an electric incubator and 2,500 fowls were sold, without his consent, for $1,492.59. After deductions for taxes and commissions, Shoji received a cheque for $39.32 which he promptly declined, claiming a loss of $4,725.02"; see Adachi, *The Enemy that Never Was: A History of the Japanese Canadians* (Toronto: McClelland and Stewart, 1976), 324.

19. Although people of Japanese ancestry under wartime measures in the United States and Canada were never subjected to the terrors of the death camps as Jews under Nazi control were, because the breach in democratic principles in both countries was so extreme and because racism was such an important factor in the wartime hysteria that led to internment, commentators then and now could not help but draw comparisons between internment and Nazism. In February 1941, even before the bombing of Pearl Harbor, the infamous anti-Asian alderman from Vancouver, Halford Wilson, seemed to invite such a direct comparison by proposing that Asians be segregated into "ghettos," as the Jews were in Nazi Germany; see Adachi, *The Enemy That Never Was*, 187. Henry Forbes Angus, who worked for the Department of External Affairs during World War II and was a

staunch defender of the rights of Japanese Canadians, protested Canadian policy in a letter to Prime Minister Mackenzie King, arguing that the dispossession of Canadian citizens could be regarded "as comparable to the Nazi Nuremberg laws dispossessing Jews in Germany" (Sunahara, *The Politics of Racism*, 106; see also 33 and 41). Michi Weglyn cites evidence that shows the analogy between Nazism and internment was part of the debates about internment in the 1940s and reports the startling fact that Nazis cited the U.S. Supreme Court rulings justifying internment as part of their defense at the Nuremberg Trials; see Weglyn, *Years of Infamy: The Untold Story of America's Concentration Camps* (New York: Morrow, 1976), 67, 75, 291 note 14. It is important to keep in mind when making such analogies, however, that the experience of Japanese Americans and Canadians in the camps, while traumatic, was not equivalent to the horrors of the Nazi death camps and systematic genocide. Perhaps the most important point to note is that internment became such a cataclysmic experience that some commentators alluded to Nazism and the Holocaust in order to find a way to register and articulate the trauma.

Roger Daniels makes a different kind of analogy; he argues that the United States' treatment of Indians makes a better comparison than Nazism in understanding the treatment of Japanese Americans during the Second World War; see *Concentration Camps*, especially page 105. His argument is compelling in several respects: certainly the reservation system was a significant model for how to set up internment camps, which were, like many reservations, established in isolated locations on barren land. Also, Lt. General DeWitt, in charge of troops on the West Coast and an advocate of internment, was the son of an army doctor who served in various forts during the Indian wars in the nineteenth century, and Dillon Myer, the director of the War Relocation Authority, which administered internment, became Commissioner of Indian Affairs in the 1950s.

20. In both countries, a distinction was made between "relocation centers" (the euphemism in the United States) or "detention camps" (the Canadian term) and "internment camps" for "disloyal" "Japanese," criminals, and prisoners of war. The ten "relocation centers" in the United States were located at Tule Lake and Manzanar in California; Heart Mountain in Wyoming; Rohwer and Jerome in Arkansas; Minidoka in Idaho; Granada (Amache) in Colorado; Topaz in Utah; and Poston and Gila River in Arizona. Canada had five detention camps, located in former mining towns that had become ghost towns: Slocan, Greenwood, New Denver, Sandon, and Kaslo — all located in the British Columbia interior. Unlike the American camps, the Canadian camps were not surrounded by barbed wire, nor were armed guards omnipresent. Despite the difference in terminology and circumstances, however, I would argue that forced confinement — whether in "relocation centers" or in "detention camps" — made them all internment camps.

Although Canada and the United States had agreed to set similar policies regarding their "Japanese" populations, Canadian internment was more grievous in certain respects: the forced dispossession cited above is one instance, in addition to the cruel separation of families in the initial stages of internment, the belated enfranchisement of Japanese Canadian citizens, and the mandatory dispersal of Japanese Canadians east of the Rocky Mountains when internment ended.

21. The Supreme Court opinions in each case can be found as follows: *Hirabayashi v. United States*, 320 US 81 (1943); *Korematsu v. United States*, 323 US 214 (1944); *Ex parte Endo*, 323 US 284 (1944). There was another noted internment case that I do not have the space to discuss here involving Minoru Yasui, a University of Oregon Law School graduate and a former U.S. soldier, who was working for the Japanese Consulate in Chicago when Pearl Harbor was bombed. He resigned his position the day after the bombing and returned to Oregon to enlist as a U.S. soldier but was refused. He later deliberately defied the curfew order by walking into a police station late at night, and used the appeals to his conviction as a means of protesting and testing the orders. For a more detailed treatment of *Yasui v. United States*, see 320 US 115 (1943) and Peter Irons's *Justice Delayed: The Record of the Japanese American Internment Cases* (Middletown, Conn.: Wesleyan University Press, 1989).

22. The Supreme Court limited its review of the Hirabayashi conviction to the constitutionality of the curfew orders. Some judicial scholars have argued that following the doctrine of judicial self-restraint in this case allowed the justices to ignore the larger problem of internment; see Howard Ball, "Judicial Parsimony and Military Necessity Disinterred: A Reexamination of the Japanese Exclusion Cases, 1943–44," in *Japanese Americans: From Relocation to Redress*, ed. Roger Daniels, Sandra C. Taylor, and Harry H. L. Kitano (Salt Lake City: University of Utah Press, 1986), 176–85.

23. Ball, "Judicial Parsimony," 178.

24. Irons, *Justice Delayed*, 63, 69.

25. See the essays collected in *The Mass Internment of Japanese Americans and the Quest for Legal Redress*, ed. Charles McClain (New York: Garland, 1994) for a useful analysis of the circumstances surrounding these unfortunate rulings. The courts in Canada were similarly inefficacious in putting a halt to the unjust dispossession order; see Sunahara, *The Politics of Racism*, 109, and Adachi, *The Enemy That Never Was*, 307–34.

26. Roger Daniels cites an official government report detailing the problem of resettlement for Japanese Americans: "Those who attempted to cross into the interior states ran into all kinds of trouble. Some were turned back by armed posses at the border of Nevada; others were clapped into jail and held overnight by panicky local peace officers; nearly all had difficulty in buying gasoline; many were greeted by 'No Japs Wanted' signs on the main streets of interior communities; and a few were threatened, or felt that they were threatened, with possibilities of mob violence"; see *Concentration Camps*, 84.

27. Ball, "Judicial Parsimony," 183–84.

28. The quotation comes from DeWitt's Final Report of 1943, which attempted to explain the rationale behind and necessity for exclusion and internment; see Irons, *Justice Delayed*, 95. Supreme Court Justice Murphy

cited this line in his scathing analysis of DeWitt's report, which was part of his dissenting opinion for *Korematsu v. United States*; see Irons, *Justice Delayed*, 90–96 for the full opinion.

29. Although Japanese Americans (understandably) did not volunteer for the armed forces in the numbers officials would have liked, the U.S. 442 Regiment was made up of mostly Nisei. This regiment, known for its bravery and sacrifice, sustained high casualty rates while fighting in Italy and France, and became the most decorated unit of the war.

30. Daniels, *Concentration Camps*, 113.

31. Ibid., 114. See also Weglyn, *Years of Infamy*, especially chap. 8, for a more detailed discussion of the questionnaire debacle.

32. Weglyn, *Years of Infamy*, 229.

33. Weglyn reports that 5,461 Nisei from Tule Lake (approximately 70%) renounced their citizenship, in stark contrast to 128 renunciants (total) from the nine other camps; see *Years of Infamy*, 247.

34. Ibid., 254, 263.

35. Sunahara, *The Politics of Racism*, 123.

36. See the Commission's final report: Commission on Wartime Relocation and Internment of Civilians, *Personal Justice Denied* (Washington, D.C.: GPO, 1983). Despite the Commission's thorough investigation, internment apologists continue to debate its conclusions: one of these is Karl R. Bendetsen, who, as an army colonel during World War II, helped to come up with the plan to circumvent the Constitution and intern Japanese American citizens. Another is Lillian Baker, associated with the internment-denial group, Americans for Historical Accuracy. The title of Baker's 1988 book indicates her view: *Dishonoring America: The Collective Guilt of American Japanese* (Medford, Ore.: Webb Research Group, 1988). See also the "facts" she presents in *American and Japanese Relocation in World War II: Fact, Fiction and Fallacy*, which includes an introduction written by Bendetsen (Medford, Ore.: Webb Research Group, 1989).

37. Local protests are led by a World War II veteran named W. W. Hastings, who insists that Japanese Americans "were never interned" and has even rejected commonly accepted information about Manzanar's purpose, exclaiming, "A concentration camp? That is the biggest lie that ever was." See Carl Nolte, "Lonesome Monument to a National Heartache," *San Francisco Chronicle*, 13 April 1997, sec. Z1.

38. Sau-ling Wong, *Reading Asian American Literature: From Necessity to Extravagance* (Princeton: Princeton University Press, 1993), 128.

39. Hilda L. Thomas reviewed Sunahara's book and Kogawa's novel together for *Canadian Literature* in 1983 and voiced a clear preference for the novel's presentation of history over Sunahara's study; see "A Time to Remember," review of *The Politics of Racism*, by Ann Gomer Sunahara, and *Obasan*, by Joy Kogawa, *Canadian Literature* 96 (1983): 103–5. Although I do not share Thomas's critical view of Sunahara's book, I do agree with her claim that novels like *Obasan* can offer important sites for remembering history. For a detailed comparison of *Obasan* to "historical rhetoric" and "documentary writing," see Marilyn Russell Rose's "Politics into Art: Ko-

gawa's *Obasan* and the Rhetoric of Fiction," *Mosaic* 21, nos. 2–3 (1988): 215–26.

40. Erika Gottlieb, "The Riddle of Concentric Worlds in *Obasan,*" *Canadian Literature* 109 (1986): 34.

41. Gayle K. Fujita, "'To Attend the Sound of Stone': The Sensibility of Silence in *Obasan,*" *MELUS* 12, no. 3 (1985): 33.

42. Gottlieb's "Riddle of Concentric Worlds" convincingly discusses these aspects of the novel.

43. Cathy Caruth, *Unclaimed Experience: Trauma, Narrative, and History* (Baltimore: Johns Hopkins University Press, 1996), 4.

44. The authors of the memo enumerate ten arguments against orders in council PC 7355–57, which made it possible to exile Japanese Canadian citizens and to coerce Japanese nationals into "requesting" to leave Canada. A major theme running throughout the ten separate points is that civilized countries do not practice such actions. Adachi reports that the Cooperative Committee on Japanese Canadians (CCJC) began as a small group of Toronto citizens who originally worked to make resettlement easier for the internees and then became best known for their efforts to oppose deportment. In late 1945, the CCJC "distributed 75,000 copies of a pamphlet entitled *From Citizens to Refugees—It's Happening Here,*" and Adachi credits these efforts of the CCJC with making Prime Minister Mackenzie King aware of the growing unpopularity of the deportation policies; see *The Enemy That Never Was,* 291, 309, 310.

45. A. Lynne Magnusson's Lacanian reading illuminates this dimension of the novel; see "Language and Longing in Joy Kogawa's *Obasan,*" *Canadian Literature* 116 (1988): 58–66. I share Magnusson's interest in the oblique and indirect methods or poetics of *Obasan*; however, while she uses psychoanalysis to explain this aspect, I find a new historicist explanation more useful.

46. King-Kok Cheung, *Articulate Silences: Hisaye Yamamoto, Maxine Hong Kingston, Joy Kogawa* (Ithaca: Cornell University Press, 1993).

47. The loss of her own family's house is a wound that has never healed for Kogawa, who commented in a 1984 interview: "I still think that the people who have my parents['] house have stolen property"; see Fujita, "'To Attend the Sound of Stone,'" 41 note 3.

48. Cheung offers an important discussion of the destructive and positive aspects of silence in the novel; see *Articulate Silences,* especially pages 146–51.

49. Naomi, in fact, becomes incensed at Aunt Emily's calls to remember the past precisely at the moment when the hard years of sugar beet farming come to mind. Naomi recognizes that Aunt Emily can have no real understanding of what those years were like, despite her historical research. See Kogawa, *Obasan,* 232–33.

50. Gurleen Grewal reads Morrison's *Beloved* and Kogawa's *Obasan* together to explore issues relating to the preservation and recovery of memory; see "Memory and the Matrix of History: The Poetics of Loss and Recovery in Joy Kogawa's *Obasan* and Toni Morrison's *Beloved,*" in *Memory*

and Cultural Politics: New Approaches to American Ethnic Literatures, ed. Amrit-jit Singh, Joseph T. Skerrett, Jr., and Robert E. Hogan (Boston: Northeastern University Press, 1996), 140–74.

51. There is perhaps another motivation at work here as well: by saving these objects of Stephen's childhood, Obasan preserves a moment in time when she and Stephen were in constant connection, as opposed to the distance the adult Stephen maintains between them.

52. Caruth, *Unclaimed Experience*, 18.

53. Donald C. Goellnicht, "Minority History as Metafiction: Joy Kogawa's *Obasan*," *Tulsa Studies in Women's Literature* 8 (1989): 291.

54. Arnold Davidson, *Writing Against the Silence: Joy Kogawa's* Obasan (Toronto: ECW, 1993), 19.

55. Rachelle Kanefsky, "Debunking a Postmodern Conception of History: A Defence of Humanist Values in the Novels of Joy Kogawa," *Canadian Literature* 148 (1996): 14. Goellnicht's and Kanefsky's essays on *Obasan* have valuable moments of insight. Goellnicht adeptly reads the novel's deconstruction of euphemisms and official language. Kanesfsky does an important service in reminding readers, through reference to the Holocaust, what is at stake in the postmodern-humanist debates on history. But both essays conflate poststructuralism and postmodernism, which leads to their contention that postmodernism theorizes the loss of all historical referentiality. A tension between postmodern and humanist approaches to the novel can be found in many other critical essays: see, for instance, Manina Jones, "The Avenues of Speech and Silence: Telling Difference in Joy Kogawa's *Obasan*," in *Theory Between the Disciplines: Authority/Vision/Politics*, ed. Martin Kreiswirth and Mark A. Cheetham (Ann Arbor: University of Michigan Press, 1990), 213–29, which advances an interesting deconstructive reading of the novel, while Rose's "Politics into Art," offers an important humanist reading.

56. Caruth, *Unclaimed Experience*, 18, 24.

57. Quoted in Cheung, *Articulate Silences*, 138.

58. David Palumbo-Liu, "The Politics of Memory: Remembering History in Alice Walker and Joy Kogawa," in *Memory and Cultural Politics: New Approaches to American Ethnic Literatures*, ed. Amritjit Singh, Joseph T. Skerrett, Jr., and Robert E. Hogan (Boston: Northeastern University Press, 1996), 218, 224.

59. Davidson cites the *1991 Canada's Who's Who* entry for Kogawa, which credits her work as being "instrumental in influencing the Candn. Govt.'s 1988 settlement with Japanese-Canadians for their loss of liberty and property in Canada during World War II"; see Davidson, *Writing Against the Silence*, 14. Kogawa's second novel, a sequel to *Obasan* titled *Itsuka* (Toronto: Viking Canada, 1992; New York: Anchor-Doubleday, 1994), ends with the "acknowledgment of injustices" the government made as part of this agreement. Japanese Canadians who survived internment received $21,000 (Canadian) each as compensation. In the United States, Congress approved a redress bill in August 1988, which included a national apology and awarded $20,000 (U.S.) to each survivor of the internment camps. Although President Ronald Reagan signed the bill on August 10, 1988,

appropriations to cover the payments were not made by Congress until 1989 and Japanese American internees did not begin to receive their payments until October 1990. See Leslie T. Hatamiya's *Righting a Wrong: Japanese Americans and the Passage of the Civil Liberties Act of 1988* (Stanford: Stanford University Press, 1993) for a detailed account of the redress and reparations movement in the United States.

Epilogue: History and Healing

1. Linda Hogan, *Solar Storms* (New York: Scribner, 1995). All subsequent references to the novel will be cited parenthetically in the text.

2. Janice Mirikitani, *We, the Dangerous: New and Selected Poems* (Berkeley: Celestial Arts, 1995). While the poems I cite from Mirikitani were previously published in various collections, they appear in slightly revised form in *We, the Dangerous*, and so all quotations are taken from this volume and are cited parenthetically in the text.

3. "In 1864" is included in Luci Tapahonso's collection *Sáanii Dahataal: The Women Are Singing* (Tucson: University of Arizona Press, 1993), 7–10.

4. Gloria Anzaldúa, *Borderlands / La Frontera: The New Mestiza* (San Francisco: Spinsters-Aunt Lute, 1987). All quotations are taken from this volume and will be cited parenthetically in the text.

5. Kate Adams, "Northamerican Silences: History, Identity and Witness in the Poetry of Gloria Anzaldúa, Cherríe Moraga, and Leslie Marmon Silko," in *Listening to Silences: New Essays in Feminist Criticism*, ed. Elaine Hedges and Shelley Fisher Fishkin (New York: Oxford University Press, 1994), 134.

6. Norma Alarcón provides a marvelous reading of the postnationalist dimensions and doubly deconstructive strategies of *Borderlands / La Frontera*; see "Anzaldúa's *Frontera*: Inscribing Gynetics," in *Displacement, Diaspora, and Geographies of Identity*, ed. Smadar Lavie and Ted Swedenburg (Durham: Duke University Press, 1996), 41–53.

Bibliography

Adachi, Ken. *The Enemy that Never Was: A History of the Japanese Canadians.* Toronto: McClelland and Stewart, 1976.

Adams, Ansel. *Born Free and Equal: Photographs of the Loyal Japanese-Americans at Manzanar Relocation Center, Inyo County, California.* New York: U.S. Camera, 1944.

Adams, Kate. "Northamerican Silences: History, Identity and Witness in the Poetry of Gloria Anzaldúa, Cherríe Moraga, and Leslie Marmon Silko." In *Listening to Silences: New Essays in Feminist Criticism,* ed. Elaine Hedges and Shelley Fisher Fishkin, 130–45. New York: Oxford University Press, 1994.

Ainsztein, Reuben. *The Warsaw Ghetto Revolt.* New York: Holocaust Library, 1979.

Alarcón, Norma. "Anzaldúa's *Frontera*: Inscribing Gynetics." In *Displacement, Diaspora, and Geographies of Identity,* ed. Smadar Lavie and Ted Swedenburg, 41–53. Durham: Duke University Press, 1996.

Anzaldúa, Gloria. *Borderlands / La Frontera: The New Mestiza.* San Francisco: Spinsters-Aunt Lute, 1987.

Appignanesi, Richard, and Chris Garratt. "Welcome to the Holocaust Theme Park." In *Introducing Postmodernism,* 122–25. New York: Totem Books, 1995.

Armor, John, and Peter Wright. *Manzanar.* New York: Times Books-Random House, 1988.

Baker, Houston A., Jr. *Workings of the Spirit: The Poetics of Afro-American Women's Writing.* Chicago: University of Chicago Press, 1991.

Baker, Lillian. *American and Japanese Relocation in World War II: Fact, Fiction, and Fallacy.* Medford, Ore.: Webb Research Group, 1989.

———. *Dishonoring America: The Collective Guilt of American Japanese.* Medford, Ore.: Webb Research Group, 1988.

Ball, Howard. "Judicial Parsimony and Military Necessity Disinterred: A Reexamination of the Japanese Exclusion Cases, 1943–44." In *Japanese Americans: From Relocation to Redress,* ed. Roger Daniels, Sandra C. Taylor, and Harry H. L. Kitano, 176–85. Salt Lake City: University of Utah Press, 1986.

Barnouw, Victor. *Wisconsin Chippewa Myths and Tales.* Madison: University of Wisconsin Press, 1977.

Barthes, Roland. "Historical Discourse." In *Introduction to Structuralism*, ed. Michael Lane, 145–55. New York: Basic Books, 1970.

Bauman, Zygmunt. *Modernity and the Holocaust.* Ithaca: Cornell University Press, 1989.

Beavers, Herman. "The Politics of Space: Southernness and Manhood in the Fictions of Toni Morrison." *Studies in the Literary Imagination* 31, no. 2 (1998): 61–77.

Beck, Evelyn Torton, ed. *Nice Jewish Girls: A Lesbian Anthology.* Rev. ed. Boston: Beacon, 1989.

Benjamin, Walter. *Illuminations: Essays and Reflections.* Ed. Hannah Arendt. Trans. Harry Zohn. New York: Schocken Books, 1968.

Berenbaum, Michael. *The World Must Know: The History of the Holocaust as Told in the United States Holocaust Memorial Museum.* Boston: Little, Brown, 1993.

Berenson, Edward. "The Use and Abuse of History." *American Quarterly* 48 (1996): 507–15.

Berger, James. "Ghosts of Liberalism: Morrison's *Beloved* and the Moynihan Report." *PMLA* 111 (1996): 408–20.

Birt, Rodger C. "A Life in American Photography." In *VanDerZee, Photographer, 1886–1983*, 26–73. New York: Henry Abrams, with the National Portrait Gallery of the Smithsonian, 1993.

Black Elk and John G. Neihardt. *Black Elk Speaks.* 1932. Rpt. Lincoln: University of Nebraska Press, 1979.

Blaeser, Kimberly M. "The New 'Frontier' of Native American Literature: Dis-Arming History with Tribal Humor." In *Native Perspectives on Literature and History*, ed. Alan R. Velie, 37–50. Norman: University of Oklahoma Press, 1994.

Bold, Christine. "An Enclave in the Wilderness." Review of *Paradise*, by Toni Morrison. *Times Literary Supplement*, 27 March 1998, 22.

Brooks, Drex. *Sweet Medicine: Sites of Indian Massacres, Battlefields, and Treaties.* Albuquerque: University of New Mexico Press, 1995.

Bruckner, D. J. R. Review of *Love Medicine*, by Louise Erdrich. *New York Times*, 20 Dec. 1984, C21.

Calderón, Fernando. "Latin American Identity and Mixed Temporalities; Or, How to Be Postmodern and Indian at the Same Time." *boundary 2* 20, no. 3 (1993): 55–64.

Camp, Gregory S. "Working Out Their Own Salvation: The Allotment of Land in Severalty and the Turtle Mountain Chippewa Band, 1870–1920." *American Indian Culture and Research Journal* 14, no. 2 (1990): 19–38.

Caplan, Jane. "Postmodernism, Poststructuralism, and Deconstruction: Notes for Historians." *Central European History* 2 (1989): 260–78.

Carby, Hazel. "The Canon: Civil War and Reconstruction." *Michigan Quarterly Review* 28 (1989): 35–43.

Caruth, Cathy. "Introduction: The Insistence of Reference." In *Critical Encounters: Reference and Responsibility in Deconstructive Writing*, ed. Caruth and Deborah Esch, 1–8. New Brunswick: Rutgers University Press, 1995.
———. *Unclaimed Experience: Trauma, Narrative, and History.* Baltimore: Johns Hopkins University Press, 1996.
Castillo, Susan Pérez. "Postmodernism, Native American Literature, and the Real: The Silko-Erdrich Controversy." *Massachusetts Review* 32 (1991): 285–94.
Cheung, King-Kok. *Articulate Silences: Hisaye Yamamoto, Maxine Hong Kingston, Joy Kogawa.* Ithaca: Cornell University Press, 1993.
Chidester, David, and Edward T. Linenthal, eds. *American Sacred Space.* Bloomington: Indiana University Press, 1995.
Christian, Barbara. " 'Somebody Forgot to Tell Somebody Something': African-American Women's Historical Novels." In *Wild Women in the Whirlwind: Afra-American Culture and the Contemporary Literary Renaissance*, ed. Joanne M. Braxton and Andrée N. McLaughlin, 326–41. New Brunswick: Rutgers University Press, 1990.
Cixous, Hélène. "The Laugh of the Medusa." Trans. Keith Cohen and Paula Cohen. *Signs* 1 (1976): 875–93.
Clemons, Walter. "The Ghosts of 'Sixty Million and More.' " *Newsweek*, 28 Sept. 1987, 75.
Cliff, Michelle. "Great Migrations. " Review of *Paradise*, by Toni Morrison. *Village Voice*, 27 Jan. 1998, 85–86.
Commission on Wartime Relocation and Internment of Civilians. *Personal Justice Denied.* Washington, D.C.: GPO, 1983.
Cowart, David. *History and the Contemporary Novel.* Carbondale: Southern Illinois University Press, 1989.
Crockett, Norman L. *The Black Towns.* Lawrence: Regents Press of Kansas, 1979.
Crouch, Stanley. "Aunt Medea." Review of *Beloved*, by Toni Morrison. *New Republic*, 19 Oct. 1987, 38–43.
Culin, Stewart. *Games of Chance.* Vol. 1 of *Games of the North American Indians.* 1907. Rpt. Lincoln: University of Nebraska Press, 1992.
Daniels, Roger. *Concentration Camps: North America.* Rev. ed. Malabar, Fla.: Krieger, 1989.
Davidov, Judith Fryer. " 'The Color of My Skin, the Shape of My Eyes': Photographs of the Japanese-American Internment by Dorothea Lange, Ansel Adams, and Toyo Miyatake." *Yale Journal of Criticism* 9 (1996): 223–44.
Davidson, Arnold. *Writing Against the Silence: Joy Kogawa's Obasan.* Toronto: ECW, 1993.
Dawidowicz, Lucy S. *The Holocaust and the Historians.* Cambridge: Harvard University Press, 1981.
DeMallie, Raymond, J. *The Sixth Grandfather: Black Elk's Teachings Given to John G. Neihardt.* Lincoln: University of Nebraska Press, 1984.
Derrida, Jacques. *Of Grammatology.* Trans. Gayatri C. Spivak. Baltimore: Johns Hopkins University Press, 1976.
Edmunds, R. David. "Native Americans, New Voices: American Indian History, 1895–1995." *American Historical Review* 100 (1995): 717–40.

Elkins, Stanley M. *Slavery: A Problem in American Institutional Life.* Chicago: University of Chicago Press, 1959.

Erdrich, Louise. *The Beet Queen.* New York: Henry Holt, 1986.

———. *The Bingo Palace.* New York: Henry Holt, 1994.

———. *Jacklight.* New York: Henry Holt, 1984.

———. *Love Medicine.* 1984. Rev. ed. New York: Harper, 1993.

———. *Tracks.* New York: Henry Holt, 1988.

Erdrich, Louise, and Michael Dorris. "An Interview with Louise Erdrich and Michael Dorris." Interview by Hertha Wong. In *Conversations with Louise Erdrich and Michael Dorris*, ed. Allan Chavkin and Nancy Fehl Chavkin, 30–53. Jackson: University Press of Mississippi, 1994. First published in *North Dakota Quarterly* 55, no. 1 (1987): 196–218.

———. "Louise Erdrich and Michael Dorris." Interview by Bill Moyers. In *Conversations with Louise Erdrich and Michael Dorris*, ed. Allan Chavkin and Nancy Fehl Chavkin, 138–50. Jackson: University Press of Mississippi, 1994. First published in *A World of Ideas*, by Bill Moyers (New York: Doubleday, 1989), 460–69.

———. "Who Owns the Land?" *New York Times Magazine*, 4 Sept. 1988, 32–36+.

Felman, Shoshana, and Dori Laub. *Testimony: Crises of Witnessing in Literature, Psychoanalysis, and History.* New York: Routledge, 1992.

Foner, Eric. "The Canon and American History." *Michigan Quarterly Review* 28 (1989): 44–49.

Forché, Carolyn. Introduction to *Against Forgetting: Twentieth-Century Poetry of Witness*, ed. Forché. New York: Norton, 1993.

Freed, James Ingo. "The Holocaust Memorial Museum." *Partisan Review* 61 (1994): 448–56.

Friedlander, Saul. "Trauma, Transference and 'Working through' in Writing the History of the *Shoah.*" *History and Memory* 4, no. 1 (1992): 39–59.

Friedman, Philip. *Roads to Extinction: Essays on the Holocaust.* New York: Conference on Jewish Social Studies/Jewish Publication Society of America, 1980.

Friedman, Susan Stanford. "Craving Stories: Narrative and Lyric in Contemporary Theory and Women's Long Poems." In *Feminist Measures: Soundings in Poetry and Theory*, ed. Lynn Keller and Cristanne Miller, 15–42. Ann Arbor: University of Michigan Press, 1994.

———. "Identity Politics, Syncretism, Catholicism, and Anishinabe Religion in Louise Erdrich's *Tracks.*" *Religion and Literature* 26, no. 1 (1994): 107–33.

Fujita, Gayle K. " 'To Attend the Sound of Stone': The Sensibility of Silence in *Obasan.*" *MELUS* 12, no. 3 (1985): 33–42.

Fuks, Marian, Zygmunt Hoffman, Maurycy Horn, and Jerzy Tomaszewski. *Polish Jewry: History and Culture.* Trans. Bogna Piotrowska and Lech Petrowicz. Warsaw: Interpress Publishers, 1982.

Gates, Henry Louis, Jr. Review of *Jazz*, by Toni Morrison. In *Toni Morrison: Critical Perspectives Past and Present*, ed. Henry Louis Gates, Jr., and A. K. Appiah, 52–55. New York: Amistad, 1993.

————. *The Signifying Monkey: A Theory of African-American Literary Criticism.* New York: Oxford University Press, 1988.

Gebert, Konstanty. "The Dialectics of Memory in Poland: Holocaust Memorials in Warsaw." In *The Art of Memory: Holocaust Memorials in History,* ed. James E. Young, 121–29. New York: Prestel, 1994.

Gleason, William. " 'Her Laugh an Ace': The Function of Humor in Louise Erdrich's *Love Medicine." American Indian Culture and Research Journal* 11, no. 3 (1987): 51–73.

Goellnicht, Donald C. "Minority History as Metafiction: Joy Kogawa's *Obasan." Tulsa Studies in Women's Literature* 8 (1989): 287–306.

Gottlieb, Erika. "The Riddle of Concentric Worlds in *Obasan." Canadian Literature* 109 (1986): 34–53.

Gordon, Avery F. *Ghostly Matters: Haunting and the Sociological Imagination.* Minneapolis: University of Minnesota Press, 1997.

Gray, Paul. "Paradise Found." *Time,* 19 Jan. 1998, 63–68.

Greenblatt, Stephen. "Resonance and Wonder." In *Exhibiting Cultures: The Poetics and Politics of Museum Display,* ed. Ivan Karp and Steven D. Lavine, 42–56. Washington, D.C.: Smithsonian, 1991.

Grewal, Gurleen. "Memory and the Matrix of History: The Poetics of Loss and Recovery in Joy Kogawa's *Obasan* and Toni Morrison's *Beloved.*" In *Memory and Cultural Politics: New Approaches to American Ethnic Literatures,* ed. Amritjit Singh, Joseph T. Skerrett, Jr., and Robert E. Hogan, 140–74. Boston: Northeastern University Press, 1996.

Griffin, Farah J. *"Who Set You Flowin'?": The African-American Migration Narrative.* New York: Oxford University Press, 1995.

Gurian, Elaine Heumann. "Noodling Around with Exhibition Opportunities." In *Exhibiting Cultures: The Poetics and Politics of Museum Display,* ed. Ivan Karp and Steven D. Lavine, 176–90. Washington, D.C.: Smithsonian, 1991.

Gutman, Israel. "Oneg Shabbat." In *Encyclopedia of the Holocaust,* ed. Israel Gutman. 4 vols. New York: Macmillan, 1990.

Gutman, Yisrael. *The Jews of Warsaw, 1939–1943: Ghetto, Underground, Revolt.* Trans. Ina Friedman. Bloomington: Indiana University Press, 1982.

Hamilton, Kenneth M. *Black Towns and Profit: Promotion and Development in the Trans-Appalachian West, 1877–1915.* Urbana: University of Illinois Press, 1991.

Harris, Middleton, et al., eds. *The Black Book.* New York: Random House, 1974.

Hartman, Geoffrey H. "The Book of the Destruction." In *Probing the Limits of Representation: Nazism and the "Final Solution,"* ed. Saul Friedlander, 318–34. Cambridge: Harvard University Press, 1982.

Hatamiya, Leslie T. *Righting a Wrong: Japanese Americans and the Passage of the Civil Liberties Act of 1988.* Stanford: Stanford University Press, 1993.

Hedley, Jane. "Nepantilist Poetics: Narrative and Cultural Identity in the Mixed-Language Writings of Irena Klepfisz and Gloria Anzaldúa." *Narrative* 4 (1996): 36–54.

Heinze, Denise. *The Dilemma of "Double-Consciousness": Toni Morrison's Novels.* Athens: University of Georgia Press, 1993.

Henderson, Mae Gwendolyn. "Toni Morrison's *Beloved*: Re-Membering the Body as Historical Text." In *Comparative American Identities: Race, Sex, and Nationality in the Modern Text*, ed. Hortense J. Spillers, 62–86. New York: Routledge, 1991.

Higa, Karin M., ed. *The View from Within: Japanese American Art from the Internment Camps, 1942–1945*. Los Angeles: Japanese American National Museum, 1992.

Hogan, Linda. *Solar Storms*. New York: Scribner, 1995.

hooks, bell. *Black Looks: Race and Representation*. Boston: South End Press, 1992.

Hornung, Rick. *One Nation Under the Gun*. New York: Pantheon, 1991.

Houston, Jeanne Wakatsuki, and James D. Houston. *Farewell to Manzanar*. Boston: Houghton Mifflin, 1973.

Huggins, Nathan I. *Harlem Renaissance*. New York: Oxford University Press, 1971.

Hutcheon, Linda. *The Politics of Postmodernism*. New York: Routledge, 1989.

Huyssen, Andreas. *Twilight Memories: Marking Time in a Culture of Amnesia*. New York: Routledge, 1995.

Iannone, Carol. "Toni Morrison's Career." *Commentary*, Dec. 1987, 59–63.

Irons, Peter. *Justice Delayed: The Record of the Japanese American Internment Cases*. Middletown, Conn.: Wesleyan University Press, 1989.

Jameson, Fredric. *The Political Unconscious: Narrative as a Socially Symbolic Act*. Ithaca: Cornell University Press, 1981.

———. *Postmodernism, or, the Cultural Logic of Late Capitalism*. Durham: Duke University Press, 1991.

Japanese Canadian Centennial Project Committee. *A Dream of Riches: The Japanese Canadians, 1877–1977*. Vancouver: Japanese Canadian Centennial Project Committee, 1978.

Johnson, Ken. "Art and Memory." *Art in America*, Nov. 1993, 90–99.

Jones, Manina. "The Avenues of Speech and Silence: Telling Difference in Joy Kogawa's *Obasan*." In *Theory Between the Disciplines: Authority/Vision/Politics*, ed. Martin Kreiswirth and Mark A. Cheetham, 213–29. Ann Arbor: University of Michigan Press, 1990.

Kanefsky, Rachelle. "Debunking a Postmodern Conception of History: A Defence of Humanist Values in the Novels of Joy Kogawa." *Canadian Literature* 148 (1996): 11–36.

Keenan, Sally. " 'Four Hundred Years of Silence': Myth, History, and Motherhood in Toni Morrison's *Beloved*." In *Recasting the World: Writing after Colonialism*, ed. Jonathan White, 45–81. Baltimore: Johns Hopkins University Press, 1993.

Keller, Ulrich. Introduction to *The Warsaw Ghetto in Photographs: 206 Views Made in 1941*, ed. Keller. New York: Dover, 1984.

Kelly, Joseph M. "American Indian Gaming Law." *New Law Journal*, 26 Nov. 1993, 1672–73.

Kingston, Maxine Hong. *China Men*. New York: Knopf, 1980.

———. "Eccentric Memories: A Conversation with Maxine Hong Kingston." Interview by Paula Rabinowitz. *Michigan Quarterly Review* 26 (1987): 177–87.

——. "Talk with Mrs. Kingston." Interview by Timothy Pfaff. *New York Times Book Review*, 15 June 1980, 1, 25–27.

——. *The Woman Warrior*. New York: Knopf, 1976.

Kitagawa, Muriel. *This Is My Own: Letters to Wes and Other Writings on Japanese Canadians, 1941–1948*. Ed. Roy Miki. Vancouver: Talonbooks, 1985.

Klein, Laura F., and Lillian A. Ackerman, eds. *Women and Power in Native North America*. Norman: University of Oklahoma Press, 1995.

Klepfisz, Irena. *Dreams of an Insomniac: Jewish Feminist Essays, Speeches, and Diatribes*. Portland: Eighth Mountain Press, 1990.

——. *A Few Words in the Mother Tongue: Poems Selected and New (1971–1990)*. Portland: Eighth Mountain Press, 1990.

——. *Keeper of Accounts*. Watertown, Mass.: Persephone Press, 1982.

Kogawa, Joy. *Itsuka*. Toronto: Viking Canada, 1992; New York: Anchor-Doubleday, 1994.

——. *Obasan*. Toronto: Lester and Orphen Dennys, 1981; New York: Anchor-Doubleday, 1994.

Kohn, Richard H. "History and the Culture Wars: The Case of the Smithsonian Institution's *Enola Gay* Exhibition." *Journal of American History* 82 (Dec. 1995): 1036–63.

Krupat, Arnold. *Ethnocriticism: Ethnography, History, Literature*. Berkeley: University of California Press, 1992.

Kubitschek, Missy Dehn. *Claiming the Heritage: African-American Women Novelists and History*. Jackson: University Press of Mississippi, 1991.

Kuramitsu, Kristine C. "Internment and Identity in Japanese American Art." *American Quarterly* 47 (1995): 619–58.

Limerick, Patricia Nelson. "Haunted America." In *Sweet Medicine: Sites of Indian Massacres, Battlefields, and Treaties*, by Drex Brooks, 119–63. Albuquerque: University of New Mexico Press, 1995.

Lincoln, Kenneth. *Indi'n Humor: Bicultural Play in Native America*. New York: Oxford University Press, 1993.

Linenthal, Edward T. *Preserving Memory: The Struggle to Create America's Holocaust Museum*. New York: Viking, 1995.

——. "Struggling with History and Memory." *Journal of American History* 82 (Dec. 1995): 1094–1101.

Linenthal, Edward T., and Tom Engelhardt, eds. *History Wars: The Enola Gay and Other Battles for the American Past*. New York: Metropolitan Books-Henry Holt, 1996.

Lowenthal, David. *The Past Is a Foreign Country*. Cambridge: Cambridge University Press, 1985.

Lyman, Christopher. *The Vanishing Race and Other Illusions: Photographs of Indians by Edward S. Curtis*. Washington, D.C.: Smithsonian, 1982.

Lyotard, Jean-François. *The Differend: Phrases in Dispute*. Trans. Georges Van Den Abbeele. Minneapolis: University of Minnesota Press, 1988.

——. *The Postmodern Condition: A Report on Knowledge*. Trans. Geoff Bennington and Brian Massumi. Minneapolis: University of Minnesota Press, 1984.

Lyotard, Jean-François, and Jean-Loup Thébaud. *Just Gaming*. Trans. Wlad Godzich. Minneapolis: University of Minnesota Press, 1985.

Magnusson, A. Lynne. "Language and Longing in Joy Kogawa's *Obasan.*" *Canadian Literature* 116 (1988): 58–66.

Maristuen-Rodakowski, Julie. "The Turtle Mountain Reservation in North Dakota: Its History as Depicted in Louise Erdrich's *Love Medicine* and *The Beet Queen.*" *American Indian Culture and Research Journal* 12, no. 3 (1988): 33–48.

Mark, Ber. *Uprising in the Warsaw Ghetto*. Trans. Gershon Freidlin. Rev. ed. New York: Schocken, 1975.

Martin, Calvin, ed. *The American Indian and the Problem of History*. New York: Oxford University Press, 1987.

Mathes, Valerie Sherer. "American Indian Women and the Catholic Church." *North Dakota History* 47, no. 4 (1980): 20–25.

McClain, Charles, ed. *The Mass Internment of Japanese Americans and the Quest for Legal Redress*. New York: Garland, 1994.

Meed, Vladka. *On Both Sides of the Wall: Memoirs from the Warsaw Ghetto*. Trans. Steven Meed. New York: Holocaust Library, 1979.

Michaels, Walter Benn. " 'You Who Never Was There': Slavery and the New Historicism, Deconstruction and the Holocaust." *Narrative* 4 (1996): 1–16.

Mirikitani, Janice. *We, the Dangerous: New and Selected Poems*. Berkeley: Celestial Arts, 1995.

Mitchell, Angelyn. " 'Sth, I Know that Woman': History, Gender, and the South in Toni Morrison's *Jazz.*" *Studies in the Literary Imagination* 31, no. 2 (1998): 49–60.

Mobley, Marilyn Sanders. "A Different Remembering: Memory, History, and Meaning in *Beloved.*" In *Toni Morrison: Critical Perspectives Past and Present*, ed. Henry Louis Gates, Jr., and A. K. Appiah, 356–65. New York: Amistad, 1993.

Moore, W. John. "A Winning Hand?" *National Journal*, 17 July 1993, 1796–1800.

Moraga, Cherríe, and Gloria Anzaldúa, eds. *This Bridge Called My Back: Writings by Radical Women of Color*. 2nd ed. New York: Kitchen Table Press, 1983.

[Morrison, Toni] Chloe Ardelia Wofford. "Virginia Woolf's and William Faulkner's Treatment of the Alienated." Master's thesis, Cornell University, 1955.

Morrison, Toni. "Behind the Making of *The Black Book.*" *Black World*, Feb. 1974, 86–90.

———. *Beloved*. New York: Knopf, 1987.

———. "Blacks, Modernism, and the American South: An Interview with Toni Morrison." Interview by Carolyn Denard. *Studies in the Literary Imagination* 31, no. 2 (1998): 1–16.

———. Foreword to *The Harlem Book of the Dead*, by James Van Der Zee (photography), Owen Dodson (poetry), and Camille Billops (text). Dobbs Ferry, N.Y.: Morgan and Morgan, 1978.

———. "Interview with Toni Morrison." Interview by Ntozake Shange. *American Rag*, Nov. 1978, 48–52.

———. *Jazz*. New York: Knopf, 1992.

———. "Living Memory: A Meeting with Toni Morrison." Interview by Paul Gilroy. In *Small Acts: Thoughts on the Politics of Black Cultures*, by Paul Gilroy, 175–82. London: Serpent's Tail, 1993.

———. "Memory, Creation, and Writing." *Thought* 59 (1984): 385–90.

———. "Nobel Lecture 1993." In *Toni Morrison: Critical and Theoretical Approaches*, ed. Nancy J. Peterson, 267–73. Baltimore: Johns Hopkins University Press, 1997.

———. "The Pain of Being Black: An Interview with Toni Morrison." Interview by Bonnie Angelo. In *Conversations with Toni Morrison*, ed. Danille Taylor-Guthrie, 255–61. Jackson: University Press of Mississippi, 1994. First published in *Time*, 22 May 1989, 120–23.

———. *Paradise*. New York: Knopf, 1998.

———. "Rediscovering Black History." *New York Times Magazine*, 11 Aug. 1974, 14–24.

———. "Rootedness: The Ancestor As Foundation." In *Black Women Writers, 1950–1980: A Critical Evaluation*, ed. Mari Evans, 339–45. New York: Doubleday-Anchor, 1984.

———. "The Site of Memory." In *Inventing the Truth: The Art and Craft of Memoir*, ed. William Zinsser, 101–24. Boston: Houghton Mifflin, 1987.

———. "This Side of Paradise." Interview by James Marcus. Jan. 1998; accessed 26 Jan. 1998, ⟨http://www.amazon.com/exec/obidos/ts/feature/7651/103-9598788-9210237⟩.

———. "Toni Morrison." Interview by Angels Carabi. *Belle Lettres* 10, no. 2 (1995): 40–43.

———. "Toni Morrison: The Art of Fiction." Interview by Elissa Schappell and Claudia Brodsky Lacour. *Paris Review* 128 (1993): 83–125.

———. "Unspeakable Things Unspoken: The Afro-American Presence in American Literature." *Michigan Quarterly Review* 28 (1989): 1–34.

Morrison, Toni, and Gloria Naylor. "A Conversation." In *Conversations with Toni Morrison*, ed. Danille Taylor-Guthrie, 188–217. Jackson: University Press of Mississippi, 1994. First published in the *Southern Review* 21 (1985): 567–93.

Moynihan, Daniel Patrick. *The Negro Family: The Case for National Action*. 1965. Reprinted in *The Moynihan Report and the Politics of Controversy*, ed. Lee Rainwater and William L. Yancey, 39–124. Cambridge: MIT Press, 1967.

Munslow, Alan. *Deconstructing History*. London: Routledge, 1997.

Murray, Stanley N. "The Turtle Mountain Chippewa, 1882–1905." *North Dakota History* 51, no. 1 (1984): 14–37.

Nabokov, Peter, ed. *Native American Testimony: A Chronicle of Indian-White Relations from Prophecy to the Present, 1492–1992*. New York: Viking-Penguin, 1991.

National Standards for United States History: Exploring the American Experience. Los Angeles: National Center for History in the Schools/UCLA, 1994.

Nietzsche, Friedrich. *The Use and Abuse of History*. Trans. Adrian Collins. Indianapolis: Bobbs-Merrill / Library of Liberal Arts, 1957. Originally published as *Vom Nutzen und Nachteil der Historie für das Leben* (1874).

Nolte, Carl. "Lonesome Monument to a National Heartache." *San Francisco Chronicle*, 13 April 1997, sec. Z1.

Nora, Pierre. "Between Memory and History: *Les Lieux de Mémoire*." *Representations* 26 (1989): 7–25.

Norden, Edward. "Yes and No to the Holocaust Museums." *Commentary*, Aug. 1993, 23–32.

Okada, John. *No-No Boy*. Tokyo and Rutland, Vt.: C. E. Tuttle Co., 1957; Seattle: University of Washington Press, 1986.

Okubo, Miné. *Citizen 13660*. New York: Columbia University Press, 1946; Seattle: University of Washington Press, 1983.

Olster, Stacey. *Reminiscence and Re-Creation in Contemporary American Fiction*. Cambridge: Cambridge University Press, 1989.

Ong, Walter. *Orality and Literacy: The Technologizing of the Word*. London: Methuen, 1982.

Osofsky, Gilbert. *Harlem: The Making of a Ghetto*. New York: Harper and Row, 1966.

Page, Philip. *Dangerous Freedom: Fusion and Fragmentation in Toni Morrison's Novels*. Jackson: University Press of Mississippi, 1995.

Palumbo-Liu, David. "The Ethnic as 'Post-': Reading *Reading the Literatures of Asian America*." *American Literary History* 7 (1995): 161–68.

———. Introduction to *The Ethnic Canon: Histories, Institutions, and Interventions*, ed. Palumbo-Liu. Minneapolis: University of Minnesota Press, 1995.

———. "The Politics of Memory: Remembering History in Alice Walker and Joy Kogawa." In *Memory and Cultural Politics: New Approaches to American Ethnic Literatures*, ed. Amritjit Singh, Joseph T. Skerrett, Jr., and Robert E. Hogan, 211–26. Boston: Northeastern University Press, 1996.

Pasquaretta, Paul. "On the 'Indianness' of Bingo: Gambling and the Native American Community." *Critical Inquiry* 20 (1993–94): 694–714.

Patraka, Vivian M. "Spectacles of Suffering: Performing Presence, Absence, and Historical Memory at U.S. Holocaust Museums." In *Performance and Cultural Politics*, ed. Elin Diamond, 89–107. New York: Routledge, 1996.

Pérez-Torres, Rafael. "Knitting and Knotting the Narrative Thread — *Beloved* as Postmodern Novel." In *Toni Morrison: Critical and Theoretical Approaches*, ed. Nancy J. Peterson, 91–109. Baltimore: Johns Hopkins University Press, 1997.

———. *Movements in Chicano Poetry: Against Myths, Against Margins*. Cambridge: Cambridge University Press, 1995.

Phelan, James. "Toward a Rhetorical Reader-Response Criticism: The Difficult, the Stubborn, and the Ending of *Beloved*." In *Toni Morrison: Critical and Theoretical Approaches*, ed. Nancy J. Peterson, 225–44. Baltimore: Johns Hopkins University Press, 1997.

Philip, Marlene Nourbese. *She Tries Her Tongue, Her Silence Softly Breaks*. Charlottetown, Can.: Ragweed Press, 1989.

Price, David W. *History Made, History Imagined: Contemporary Literature, Poiesis, and the Past*. Urbana: University of Illinois Press, 1999.

Purdy, John. "Against All Odds: Games of Chance in the Novels of Louise

Erdrich." In *The Chippewa Landscape of Louise Erdrich*, ed. Allan Chavkin, 8–35. Tuscaloosa: University of Alabama Press, 1999.

Radin, Paul. *The Trickster: A Study in American Indian Mythology.* London: Routledge and Kegan Paul, 1956.

Rainwater, Catherine. *Dreams of Fiery Stars: The Transformations of Native American Fiction.* Philadelphia: University of Pennsylvania Press, 1999.

——. "Reading between Worlds: Narrativity in the Fiction of Louise Erdrich." *American Literature* 62 (1990): 405–22.

Rich, Adrienne. *Blood, Bread, and Poetry: Selected Prose, 1979–1985.* New York: Norton, 1986.

——. *The Fact of a Doorframe: Poems Selected and New, 1950–1984.* New York: Norton, 1984.

——. *What Is Found There: Notebooks on Poetry and Politics.* New York: Norton, 1993.

Rodrigues, Eusebio. "Experiencing *Jazz.*" In *Toni Morrison: Critical and Theoretical Approaches,* ed. Nancy J. Peterson, 245–66. Baltimore: Johns Hopkins University Press, 1997.

Rody, Caroline. "Toni Morrison's *Beloved*: History, 'Rememory,' and a 'Clamor for a Kiss.'" *American Literary History* 7 (1995): 92–119.

Rose, Marilyn Russell. "Politics into Art: Kogawa's *Obasan* and the Rhetoric of Fiction." *Mosaic* 21, nos. 2–3 (1988): 215–26.

Rushdy, Ashraf. "Daughters Signifyin(g) History: The Example of Toni Morrison's *Beloved.*" *American Literature* 64 (1993): 567–97.

Saldívar-Hull, Sonia. "Feminism on the Border: From Gender Politics to Geopolitics." In *Criticism in the Borderlands: Studies in Chicano Literature, Culture, and Ideology,* ed. Héctor Calderón and José David Saldívar, 203–20. Durham: Duke University Press, 1991.

Schneider, Mary Jane. *North Dakota Indians.* Dubuque: Kendall-Hunt, 1986.

Shoemaker, Nancy, ed. *Negotiators of Change: Historical Perspectives on Native American Women.* New York: Routledge, 1995.

Silberman, Robert. "Opening the Text: *Love Medicine* and the Return of the Native American Woman." In *Narrative Chance: Postmodern Discourse on Native American Indian Literatures,* ed. Gerald Vizenor, 101–20. Albuquerque: University of New Mexico Press, 1989.

Silko, Leslie Marmon. "Here's an Odd Artifact for the Fairy-Tale Shelf." Review of *The Beet Queen,* by Louise Erdrich. *Impact/Albuquerque Journal,* 17 Oct. 1986, 10–11. Reprinted in *Studies in American Indian Literatures,* n.s., 10, no. 4 (1986): 177–84.

Smith, Geoffrey S. "Racial Nativism and Origins of Japanese American Relocation." In *Japanese Americans: From Relocation to Redress,* ed. Roger Daniels, Sandra C. Taylor, and Harry H. L. Kitano, 79–87. Salt Lake City: University of Utah Press, 1986.

Smith, Valerie. "'Circling the Subject': History and Narrative in *Beloved.*" In *Toni Morrison: Critical Perspectives Past and Present,* ed. Henry Louis Gates, Jr., and A. K. Appiah, 342–55. New York: Amistad, 1993.

Sone, Monica. *Nisei Daughter.* Boston, Little, Brown 1953; Seattle: University of Washington Press, 1979.

Stead, Deborah. "Unlocking the Tale." *New York Times Book Review*, 2 Oct. 1988, 41.

Stripes, James D. "The Problem(s) of (Anishinaabe) History in the Fiction of Louise Erdrich: Voices and Contexts." *Wicazo Sa Review* 7, no. 2 (1991): 26–33.

Sunahara, Ann Gomer. *The Politics of Racism: The Uprooting of Japanese Canadians During the Second World War.* Toronto: Lorimer, 1981.

Tajiri, Rea. *History and Memory (for Akiko and Takeshige).* 33 min. Electronic Arts Intermix, New York, 1991. Videocassette.

Tanaka, Janice D. *When You're Smiling.* 60 min. Visual Communications, Los Angeles, 1999. Videocassette.

Tapahonso, Luci. *Sáanii Dahataal: The Women Are Singing.* Tucson: University of Arizona Press, 1993.

Thomas, Hilda L. "A Time to Remember." Review of *The Politics of Racism*, by Ann Gomer Sunahara, and *Obasan*, by Joy Kogawa. *Canadian Literature* 96 (1983): 103–5.

Todorov, Tzvetan. *Facing the Extreme: Moral Life in the Concentration Camps.* Trans. Arthur Denner and Abigail Pollak. New York: Henry Holt, 1996.

Toni Morrison: Profile of a Writer. Produced and directed by Alan Benson. Ed. Melvyn Bragg. 52 min. London Weekend Television, 1987. Videocassette.

Van Der Zee, James (photography), Owen Dodson (poetry), and Camille Billops (text). *The Harlem Book of the Dead.* Dobbs Ferry, N.Y.: Morgan and Morgan, 1978.

Vidal-Naquet, Pierre. *Assassins of Memory: Essays on the Denial of the Holocaust.* New York: Columbia University Press, 1992.

Vizenor, Gerald. "Casino Coups." In *Manifest Manners: Postindian Warriors of Survivance,* by Gerald Vizenor, 138–48. Hanover, N.H.: Wesleyan University Press-University Press of New England, 1994.

———. *Crossbloods: Bone Courts, Bingo, and Other Reports.* Minneapolis: University of Minnesota Press, 1990.

———. *The Heirs of Columbus.* Hanover, N.H.: Wesleyan University Press-University Press of New England, 1991.

———. *The People Named the Chippewa: Narrative Histories.* Minneapolis: University of Minnesota Press, 1984.

———. "A Postmodern Introduction." In *Narrative Chance: Postmodern Discourse on Native American Indian Literatures,* ed. Gerald Vizenor, 3–16. Albuquerque: University of New Mexico Press, 1989.

———, editor and interpreter. *Summer in the Spring: Anishinaabe Lyric Poems and Stories.* Rev. ed. Norman: University of Oklahoma Press, 1993.

———. "Trickster Discourse." In *Narrative Chance: Postmodern Discourse on Native American Indian Literatures,* ed. Vizenor, 187–211. Albuquerque: University of New Mexico Press, 1989.

Waldman, Carl. *Atlas of the North American Indian.* New York: Facts on File Publications, 1985.

Walker, Melissa. *Down from the Mountaintop: Black Women's Novels in the Wake of the Civil Rights Movement, 1966–1989.* New Haven: Yale University Press, 1991.

Wallace, Mike. *Mickey Mouse History and Other Essays on American Memory.* Philadelphia: Temple University Press, 1996.

Walsh, Dennis M., and Ann Braley. "The Indianness of Louise Erdrich's *The Beet Queen*: Latency As Presence." *American Indian and Culture Research Journal* 18, no. 3 (1994): 1–17.

Washburn, Wilcomb E., ed. *History of Indian-White Relations.* Vol. 4 of *Handbook of North American Indians.* Ed. William C. Sturtevant. Washington, D.C.: Smithsonian, 1988.

Weglyn, Michi. *Years of Infamy: The Untold Story of America's Concentration Camps.* New York: Morrow, 1976.

Weil, Simone. *The Need for Roots: Prelude to a Declaration of Duties Toward Mankind.* New York: G. P. Putman's Sons, 1952.

Weinberg, Jeshajahu, and Rina Elieli. *The Holocaust Museum in Washington.* New York: Rizzoli, 1995.

Weisenburger, Steven. *Modern Medea: A Family Story of Slavery and Child-Murder from the Old South.* New York: Hill and Wang, 1998.

Werner, Craig H. *Playing the Changes: From Afro-Modernism to the Jazz Impulse.* Urbana: University of Illinois Press, 1994.

Wesseling, Elisabeth. *Writing History as a Prophet: Postmodernist Innovations of the Historical Novel.* Amsterdam: John Benjamins Publishing, 1991.

White, Hayden. "Getting Out of History." *Diacritics* 12, no. 3 (1982): 2–13.

———. *Metahistory: The Historical Imagination in Nineteenth Century Europe.* Baltimore: Johns Hopkins University Press, 1973.

———. *Tropics of Discourse: Essays in Cultural Criticism.* Baltimore: Johns Hopkins University Press, 1978.

Wong, Hertha. "Adoptive Mothers and Thrown-Away Children in the Novels of Louise Erdrich." In *Narrating Mothers: Theorizing Maternal Subjectivities,* ed. Brenda O. Daly and Maureen T. Reddy, 174–92. Knoxville: University of Tennessee Press, 1991.

Wong, Sau-ling. *Reading Asian American Literature: From Necessity to Extravagance.* Princeton: Princeton University Press, 1993.

Yogi, Stan. "Yearning for the Past: The Dynamics of Memory in Sansei Internment Poetry." In *Memory and Cultural Politics: New Approaches to American Ethnic Literatures,* ed. Amritjit Singh, Joseph T. Skerrett, Jr., and Robert E. Hogan, 245–65. Boston: Northeastern University Press, 1996.

Yoo, David. "Captivating Memories: Museology, Concentration Camps, and Japanese American History." *American Quarterly* 48 (1996): 680–99.

Young, James E., ed. *The Art of Memory: Holocaust Memorials in History.* New York: Prestel, 1994.

———. "The Art of Memory: Holocaust Memorials in History." In *The Art of Memory: Holocaust Memorials in History,* ed. Young, 19–38. New York: Prestel, 1994.

———. *The Texture of Memory: Holocaust Memorials and Meaning.* New Haven: Yale University Press, 1993.

———. *Writing and Rewriting the Holocaust: Narrative and the Consequences of Interpretation.* Bloomington: Indiana University Press, 1988.

Zamora, Lois Parkinson. *The Usable Past: The Imagination of History in Recent Fiction of the Americas.* Cambridge: Cambridge University Press, 1997.

Index

Acknowledgments

I have benefited enormously from conversations with friends and colleagues over the years as I worked on *Against Amnesia*. I am grateful for the intellectual rapport I have enjoyed with current and former colleagues in English at Purdue University, including Richard Dienst, John Duvall, Wendy Flory, Geraldine Friedman, Vincent Leitch, Monica Macaulay, Patrick O'Donnell, and Siobhan Somerville. As heads of the Department of English during my work on this book, Thomas Adler and Margaret Moan Rowe were instrumental in lending their support to the project and for funding my travel to several conferences, where I benefited from presenting my work while it was in progress. My colleagues in interdisciplinary programs at Purdue, including Berenice Carroll, Susan Curtis, and Donald Parman, willingly shared their expertise and offered encouragement. My students, both undergraduates and graduates, also contributed to this project by bringing a range of questions and perspectives to our study of the literary texts discussed in the book. Most notably, I am grateful to the School of Liberal Arts Dean's Office at Purdue University for supporting my research with two faculty incentive grants.

I could not have begun this work without the long-time mentoring and support of Susan Stanford Friedman and Nellie McKay, nor would it have been completed without the helpful interest of Alan Chavkin, Emory Elliott, Alan Nadel, Miles Orvell, Donald Pease, Catherine Rainwater, Hertha Wong, Lois Parkinson Zamora, and others at crucial moments. I am deeply thankful, as always, and in ways too numerous to describe here, to Aparajita Sagar and Marcia

Stephenson, who read and reread the manuscript, sharing their wisdom, asking the necessary questions, and offering sisterhood in the most profound sense.

Drex Brooks was especially generous in allowing me to reprint his photograph of the Mystic Massacre Site. Donna Van Der Zee graciously granted me permission to use the image from *The Harlem Book of the Dead.* The National Archives and Records Administration made available the photograph of Manzanar by Dorothea Lange included in Chapter 5. In addition, I received valuable assistance from several individuals in obtaining permission to reprint the other photographs included in the book: Camille Billops of the Hatch-Billops Collection, Lindsay Harris of the United States Holocaust Memorial Museum, Anna Mogyorosy of Norman McGrath Studios, and Marilyn Rader of AP/Wide World Photos.

Portions of this study have appeared in slightly different or earlier versions: part of Chapter 2 was originally published in *PMLA*, and another section of that same chapter appeared in *The Chippewa Landscape of Louise Erdrich*, edited by Alan Chavkin (University of Alabama Press). Part of Chapter 3 was included in *Toni Morrison: Critical and Theoretical Approaches*, a collection which I edited (Johns Hopkins University Press). A special thanks goes to the various editors and reviewers of these venues, who helped to refine and strengthen the original articles. For granting me permission to include material that was previously copyrighted, I wish to express my appreciation to the Modern Language Association, the University of Alabama Press, and Johns Hopkins University Press.

An extraordinary kind of gratitude goes to Dennis Drews, and to Will, Sam, and Lulu, for understanding the countless times when a stack of books or a computer screen commanded all my attention, and for listening to the stories of wounded histories as I reckoned with them.